Three Plays

BOOKS BY THORNTON WILDER

Novels

The Cabala

The Bridge of San Luis Rey

The Woman of Andros

Heaven's My Destination

The Ides of March

The Eighth Day

Theophilus North

Collections of Short Plays

The Angel That Troubled the Waters

The Long Christmas Dinner & Other Plays in One Act

Plays

Our Town

The Merchant of Yonkers

The Skin of Our Teeth

The Matchmaker

The Alcestiad

Essays

American Characteristics & Other Essays

The Journals of Thornton Wilder, 1939–1961

Three Plays

Our Town

The Skin of Our Teeth

The Matchmaker

HARPER**PERENNIAL** ● MODERN**CLASSICS**

NEW YORK ● LONDON ● TORONTO ● SYDNEY

A hardcover edition of this book was published in 1957 by Harper & Row, Publishers, Inc. It is here reprinted by arrangement with the Estate of Thornton Wilder.

Caution: Professionals and amateurs are hereby warned that OUR TOWN, THE SKIN OF OUR TEETH, and THE MATCHMAKER, being fully protected under the copyright laws of the United States of America, the United Kingdom, Canada, and all other countries of the Copyright Union, is subject to a royalty. All rights, including, but not limited to, professional, amateur, motion picture, recitation, lecturing, public reading, radio broadcasting, television, video, or sound taping, all other forms of mechanical or electronic reproduction, such as information storage and retrieval systems and photocopying, and the rights of translation into foreign languages are strictly reserved. All inquiries concerning all rights (other than amateur) should be addressed to the author's agent Robert A. Freedman Dramatic Agency, Inc., 1501 Broadway, Suite 2310, New York, NY 10036, without whose permission in writing no performance of the play must be made. All inquiries concerning the amateur acting rights should be addressed to Samuel French, Inc., 45 West 25th Street, New York, NY 10010. No amateur performance of the play may be given without obtaining in advance the written permission of Samuel French, Inc., and paying the requisite royalty fee.

First Perennial Library edition published 1985.
First Perennial Classics edition published 1998.
Reissued in Harper Perennial Modern Classics 2006.

The Library of Congress has catalogued the previous edition as follows:

Wilder, Thornton, 1897–1975.
    Three Plays / Thornton Wilder.
      p. cm
  ISBN 0-06-092985-5
  Contents: Our town—The skin of our teeth—The matchmaker.
  1. Historical drama, American. I. Title
  PS3545.I345A6 1998
  812'.52–dc21   98-34803

ISBN: 978-0-06-051264-4 (reissue)
ISBN-10: 0-06-051264-4 (reissue)

10 11 RRD 10 9 8 7 6

Contents

Foreword

—∿—

The Puzzle of America

In 1937, Gertrude Stein wrote to her friend Thornton Wilder: "[Y]ou are a puzzle to me and if I could solve that puzzle I could solve the puzzle of America."

Thornton Wilder a puzzle? Didn't he write the simplest and most lovable of plays? Solving him solves the puzzle of America? That's a pretty tall order. What even is the puzzle of America? And more puzzling, why would Gertrude Stein put Wilder at the heart of this puzzle? Where to start?

I ask myself *What would Thornton do?* He was a scholar, a teacher. I pull down the *OED* and look up "puzzle." No surprise definitions. "State of being puzzled or bewildered . . . perplexity how to act or decide. Enigma. To cause [anyone] to be at a loss what to do or where to turn; to embarrass with difficulties—to exercise one's self with difficult problems. Origin of word obscure."

Granted, life is a difficult problem, but the very idea of a puzzle is un-American. American is can-do; can-do can't abide the puzzle. Don't tell me I can't find the easy way into any problem. *Nuclear Physics for Dummies.* CliffsNotes. Play the piano in Six Easy Lessons. America exists to solve problems. America *is* the solution to the problem, the unqualified answer, the bright light on the alien darkness. Perhaps the theme of how we live with the puzzle of the unknown is the great subject in American literature, whether it be Hawthorne and the mysterious *House of the Seven Gables* or Melville's messianic pursuit of the white whale. And who is Gatsby? For Henry James, isn't the darkness of men's motives the difference between America and Europe? And isn't the perception of that darkness the very basis of experience? A no-nonsense self-made American millionaire like Henry Ford could say that in life, experience counts the most.

But in this vast country of ours, where do we go for experience? How do we trust experience? Herman Melville sailed to the South Seas. Samuel Clemens steamed up and down the Mississippi, reinventing himself as Mark Twain. If America is the place where you reinvent yourself, that means you create a new mask for yourself. How do we see through the mask? What is truth? How do we find the truth and experience at the same time? Is this Gertrude Stein's puzzle? Under all that sunny generosity of Wilder's, who's really there? What's under that mask? Is there a mask?

Theater is the place of masks. Do the three plays in this volume provide any answer to the puzzle? *The Matchmaker*? No puzzle there. Thornton transformed the work of Johann Nestroy, a minor Austrian nineteenth-century playwright, into a major delight. It became *Hello, Dolly!* and made him a fortune without his "having to lift a finger," as he said. No puzzle there.

Our Town. The day after 9/11, the actress Joanne Woodward woke up and realized she had to produce *Our Town*. Why? It's a play of verities, a play of reassurance, and people need that now. A year later, her Westport Country Playhouse production played on Broadway to packed houses. Sure, Paul Newman was the stage manager and who wouldn't want Paul Newman being the stage manager of all our lives?

The Skin of Our Teeth is a history of mankind from the Ice Age down to our age fending off every disaster from the onset of the glaciers to the evil of Cain. It opened in 1942 and showed man can survive anything. The philosophers of the world will even show up to see us through. Life is clear and wondrous. No puzzle. Pure America. Yet Bertolt Brecht would choose this as the first American play to be produced at East Germany's Berliner Ensemble.

What kind of puzzle is Gertrude Stein talking about? Is Thornton Wilder the mystery man of the American playwrights, remembered for the three plays in this volume, all written between the years 1936 and 1942? We carry images of the doomed, damned O'Neill who wrote dozens of plays. We think of the psychic anguish of Tennessee Williams who wrote dozens of plays. Their plays seem ripped out of their guts in some terribly private way. But Wilder's . . .

A few years ago, the U.S. Post office issued stamps honoring dead American playwrights. I kept sheets of them, my version of baseball trading cards. I'd put Eugene O'Neill on a letter to a friend in trouble. I'd stick Tennessee Williams onto the Con Edison bill in honor of the lights of the world that were turned off for Blanche DuBois when her young husband died. Then there was the Thornton Wilder stamp bearing the benign face of the balding man who might be an insurance executive or a school principal or a Kiwanis club member. Does he simply belong on the same soothing shelf with George M. Cohan? John Philip Sousa. Norman Rockwell. Irving Berlin. White bread. General Motors. Protestant. Apple pie. Soothing. I never knew who to send a letter to with the Thornton Wilder stamp. My sweet old great aunts in New Hampshire who liked being soothed had long since died.

Wilder wrote in an introduction to a translation of a play called *Jacob's Dream* by Richard Beer-Hofmann: "Soothing stories have been plentiful in all ages. . . . To survive, a story must arouse wonder, wonder in both the senses in which we now employ the word: astonishment at the extent of man's capability of good and evil, and speculation as to the sources of that capability."

What are some of Wilder's sources?

I read his early pre-theater novels for clues. He published his first one in 1926, *The Cabala*. He set it in Rome, where he had spent time, and dedicated it to his friends at the American Academy in Rome 1920–21. (During his time in Rome, he saw and was very taken with the first production of Pirandello's *Six Characters in Search of an Author*.) The novel's plot: A young man, much like Wilder, goes to Rome where he's taken up by a mysterious clique of powerful people called the Cabala. The Cabala has some puzzling secret that the young man tries to uncover. What is the darkness that binds this strange covey of cardinals, spinsters, contessas together? What do these old people want from the young man? Sex? No, the novel is amazingly sexless. "I who know nothing about such things" says the young narrator, regarding matters of the flesh. You read on in this charming tale waiting for Wilder to reveal the secret of the Cabala. Miss Grier, an American spinster, finally breaks its secret. Hold onto your hat: "The gods of antiquity did not die with the arrival of Christianity. Naturally when they began to lose worshipers they began to lose some of their divine attributes. They even found themselves able to die if they wanted to. But when one of them died his godhead was passed onto someone else. . . . I sometimes think that you are the new god Mercury."

The gods currently assembled in Rome pursued the young scholar because they recognized he just might be Mercury! The young man, the young Thornton, is not that amazed by this possibility, for "Mercury is not only the messenger of the gods; he is the conductor of the dead as well. If in the least part his powers had fallen to me I should be able to invoke spirits." And he invokes the poet Virgil, who promptly appears advising him: "Nothing is eternal save Heaven. . . . Seek out some city that is young. The secret is to make a city, not rest in it." A ship carries the young scholar/Thornton "eagerly toward the new world and the last and greatest of all cities."

But the young Thornton aka Mercury did not make a city out of New York or even the United States. Instead he imagined Peru, and true to his role as Mercury attended to the deaths of five people in the collapse of *The Bridge of San Luis Rey*. This second book, published in 1927, made a tremendous success, won a Pulitzer for the thirty-year-old author. He had a reputation. I think of *Our Town* when I read its last lines: "There is a land of the living and a land of the dead and the bridge is love, the only survival, the only meaning."

What's next? He had written some forty three-minute plays from the time he was a teenager until he was thirty. "I had discovered a literary form that satisfied my passion for compression." In 1928, the newly famous author published sixteen of these plays under the title *The Angel That Troubled the Waters*. They're all vaguely religious but he says, "religious in that dilute fashion that is a believer's concession to a contemporary standard of good manners." A very Protestant, sanitized American religion. They're arty, a young man's work. But he knows this. "How different the practice of writing would be if one did not permit oneself to be pretentious. Some hands have no choice: they would rather fail with an oratorio than succeed with a ballad." They don't have a stage life. They don't have a voice. But they might have a use.

What does Mercury do next? A young man who just might be a god has only one place to go and that's ancient Greece. His third novel, *The Woman of Andros,* published in 1930, involves a middle-aged courtesan who appears with an entourage on a small Greek island. Wilder reveals something of himself in speaking through her: "I am alone. Why have I never seen that before? I am alone."

And alone Thornton was, in spite of his barrage of fame-found friends. He'd write in *The Woman of Andros*: "How does one live? What does one do first?" What does a young successful god do after publishing his third novel? He lectures up and down and across the width and breadth of America. He takes a post at the University of Chicago. He's criticized for not writing about America. No writing for the young god about the Great Depression that paralyzed America. No, he was reading about Asian theater, Chinese theater, reading what wise French playwrights like Paul Claudel had to say about Japanese Noh theater that took place in some space between life and afterlife. Was he inspired to find out about Asian theater because of his childhood in Shanghai and Hong Kong?

In 1931 he published a collection of one-act plays under the title of *The Long Christmas Dinner.* The title play is still brilliantly stageworthy, as are *Pullman Car Hiawatha* and *The Happy Journey to Trenton and Camden.* He's liberated by the device of the Stage Manager ". . . who as in the Chinese Theatre hovers about the action, picking his teeth, handing the actors their properties, and commenting dryly to the audience," he would write a few years later to Stein.

What a break from the naturalistic theater that ruled at this time. Claudel would write about "the idea of the chorus in Noh drama . . . [that] takes a word from the lips of the actor and weaves it into a tapestry of images and sayings. It adapts thought to speech." Wilder must have sat up and said, *This is what I've been looking for,* the compression he'd been seeking in 1928. The plays in this book would be the tool box for his later work.

In 1935, perhaps to answer his critics who said he was an aesthete uninterested in the problems of America, he wrote his first American novel: *Heaven's My Destination.* It's imperative reading if you want to know about Wilder. He tells a tale of a young innocent who wants to be a saint and simply fix this rotten world. It's charming, funny, wise, satiric—but you have to ask what is its target of satire? Is it about the impossibility of being a saint in America? Or are the sinners the object of satire? You can see why it wasn't initially successful. The saintly hero, George Marvin Brush, can exasperate the reader as much as he does the sinners he meets on his journey through America selling textbooks. You see where Wilder's homespun reputation begins. George says, "You know what I think is the greatest thing in the world? It's when a man, I mean an American, sits down to Sunday dinner with his wife and six children around him." You know George Brush means it. Does Wilder? He can't, can he? Is this a satire or not? Aren't these platitudes? Wilder would write in his last novel, *Theophilus North:* "If we shrink from platitudes, platitudes will shrink from us." In an interview with *Time* magazine, Wilder said, "Literature is the orchestration of platitudes." The unlikely homespun identity begins to collect. It would appear that life held no puzzles for Wilder.

And one day his life changes—another god appears on the scene.

Gertrude Stein descended on Chicago at the end of 1934, flush with her first commercial success, *The Autobiography of Alice B. Toklas*. The legendary ex-pat had embarked on a triumphal lecture tour across America. Sudden American acclaim enchanted her after decades of living in France. She comes to Chicago to lecture and meets Wilder; he is bowled over by her. No, not love—she traveled with her eponymous life companion, Alice B. Toklas. Wilder lends her his apartment. They begin conversations that she records in her book *The Geographical History of America; or the Relation of Human Nature to the Human Mind*. He vows to get her work published and known in America, promising in effect to be her Mercury delivering her words to the American people—which he does. They form their own cabala. They talk of large-scale success and the effects of fame. Fame is a puzzle—a conundrum. If a democracy makes all men equal, how does an American deal with success, which only makes you unique? He thinks of a more public life and stops writing novels and starts writing full-length plays. What does she give him? He writes her: "Yes, I'm crazy about America. And you did that to me. . . . My country 'tis of thee. I always knew I loved it, but I never knew I loved it like this. . . . I was born into the best country in the world, Gertrude told me so."

Stein the goddess—Juno herself!—has given the young Mercury the supreme gift: a home, a country which can feed him. This expatriate from Baltimore who found her true life in Paris had the ironic victory. She made America not just acceptable to Thornton, but necessary; she connected him to the country he'd been running away from in forays to ancient Rome and Greece. Thornton loses that nettling, unsure take on America that troubled *Heaven's My Destination*, a view in which you couldn't tell whether or not he meant it to be satirical.

Now he embraces America wholeheartedly, without irony, without satire, with love.

What will the fruit of his discovery of America be? Critics said he couldn't handle the Depression? Maybe they were right. He'd therefore go back to an earlier time in America, back to that time before "the First World War—which started Americans moving about all over the country and changing their residences on a whim—[when] every man, woman and child believed he or she lived in the best town in the best state in the best country in the world. This conviction filled them with a certain strength." This is from his 1967 novel, *The Eighth Day*.

In a letter dated 1937, he writes to Stein: "I can no longer conceal from you that I'm writing the most beautiful little play you can imagine. Every morning brings an hour's increment to it, and that's all, but I've finished two acts already. It's a little play with all the big subjects in it; and it's a big play with all the little things of life lovingly impressed into it. . . . This play is an immersion, immersion into a New Hampshire town. It's called *Our Town* and its third act is based on your ideas, as on great pillars, and whether you know it or not, until further notice, you're in a deep-knit collaboration already."

It would seem that Stein had shown the man Thornton how to free himself from the scholar Thornton and trust his own voice. He writes to Stein and Alice: "Everything I write is influenced by Gertrude's style . . ." and in 1937 ". . . I'm a slow digester. How many of Gertrude's ideas have taken a whole year to flower in me; but when they come, they come to stay and they grow and cover whole hillside and reproduce their kind."

And this hillside is in Grover's Corners, if not a city, at least a place he's finally invented. The voice of *Our Town* is different. It sounds like America, straight-shooting, plain-spoken, no irony. In those years of travel around America, he'd been listening.

But was Thornton's scholarly past of no value? I think of this passage from *The Woman of Andros*:

> Once upon a time there was a hero who had done a great service to Zeus. When he came to die and was wandering in the grey marshes of Hell, he called to Zeus reminding him of that service and asking a service in return: he asked to return to earth for one day. Zeus was greatly troubled and said that it was not in his power to grant this, since even he could not bring above ground the dead who had descended to his brother's kingdom. But Zeus was so moved by the memory of the past that he went to the palace of his brother and clasping his knees asked him to accord him this favor. And the King of the Dead could not grant this thing without involving the return to life in some difficult and painful condition. But the hero gladly accepted whatever difficult and painfull condition was involved, and the King of the Dead was greatly troubled, saying that even he who was King of the Dead permitted him to return not only to the earth but to the past, and to live over again that day in all the twenty-two thousand days of his lifetime that had been least eventful; but that it must be with a mind divided into two persons—the participant and the onlooker: the participant who does the deeds and says the words of so many years before, and the onlooker who foresees the end. So the hero returned to the sunlight and to a certain day in his fifteenth year . . . as he awoke in his boyhood's

room pain filled his heart—not only because it had
started beating again, but because he saw the walls
of his home and knew that in a moment he would
see his parents who lay long since in the earth of
that country. He descended into the courtyard. His
mother lifted her eyes from the loom and greeted
him and went on with her work. His father passed
through the court unseeing, for on that day his mind
had been full of care. Suddenly the hero saw that the
living too are dead and that we can only be said to
be alive in those moments when our hearts are con-
scious of our treasure; for our hearts are not strong
enough to love every moment. And not an hour had
gone by before the hero who was both watching life
and living it called on Zeus to release him from so
terrible a dream. The gods heard him, but before he
left he fell upon the ground and kissed the soil of the
world that is too dear to be realized.

Wilder transmogrified the ornate, dated event of this
passage into the exhilarating third act of *Our Town* with such
economy and beauty that it is this *coup de theatre* that helps
sweep the play out of the commonplace into the realm of the
eternal. "To survive, a story must arouse wonder."

At the same time as he was writing *Our Town,* he was also
writing *The Merchant of Yonkers.* It did not succeed. Nearly
twenty years later, he would rewrite it minimally and retitle
it as *The Matchmaker* and have his friend, Ruth Gordon, star
in it. It was a triumph. Thornton's contribution to Nestroy's
nineteenth-century farce was more than changing the original setting from Austria to the upper reaches of New York
City. Wilder made the play his by the brilliant comic inven-
tion of Mrs. Dolly Gallagher Levi. I've even come to believe

that Dolly Gallagher Levi herself could be based on the very canny Gertrude Stein. Thornton once wrote her regarding the marriage of two mutual friends, "I shall never doubt that you had a hand in that wedding."

Listen to Stein's voice in a 1936 letter to Thornton: "It is funny about money. . . . The thing no animal can do is count, and the thing no animal can know is money and so long as the earth turns around there will be men on it and they will count and they will count money . . . I hope Detroit is a success, I love to be a success . . . I like that, oh how I do like that, and you do not mention it but I guess you have sent (the) mss to Random House by now . . ."

He had modeled *Our Town* structurally on Stein's *Making of Americans.* Is it wildly out of line to suggest that he could take on her voice?

Wilder was nothing if not susceptible to the powerful personality. He once described his life as "a series of infatuations for admired writers." He could report in his 1936 journal that "I bought a *cahier* and started a 'talk without myself' . . . in the manner of Henry James." An interesting phrase. "A talk without myself" but in the style of someone else. Thornton could confess to Stein in 1936 that he ". . . had lunch with [the playwright] Jean Giraudoux last Friday. One of the few authors on the planet who could stir up any hero worship in me."

But when an author did stir up hero worship in Thornton it became an obsession, as happened with the publication in 1939 of James Joyce's *Finnegans Wake.* And what a betrayal this was. Gertrude Stein saw herself as the very embodiment of twentieth-century literature and then along came 1922 and the scandalous publication of *Ulysses.* James Joyce became Stein's *bête noir.* James Mellow reports in his book *Charmed Circle: Gertrude Stein & Company* that "Gertrude clearly viewed Joyce as her principal rival as a literary innovator, and she was fond of quoting Picasso's remark: "Yes, Braque and James Joyce, they are the incomprehensibles whom anybody can understand." John Malcolm Brinnin writes in his study of Stein called *The Third Rose*: "Her wish to dissociate herself from all connection to Joyce was based . . . upon her conviction that it was a writer's business to stick to English. Joyce, she felt, had not resisted temptations she well understood but had indulged in the fabrication of a language of his own." Thornton was Stein's trusted friend. He must have known his new devotion to Joyce would wound her. Why did he do it? Had her spell become suffocating? Is this how he escaped? By flirting with the enemy, by lecturing on that impenetrable opus, *Finnegans Wake*. He wrote about it, pored over it, until finally it succeeded in becoming a mask out of which he could produce the ebullient *The Skin of Our Teeth*.

After the play's Broadway opening in 1942, and a third Pulitzer, he could take hat in hand and write to Stein: "I have a new enthusiasm in my life; it is the figure of Simóne Bolívar. I read the thousands of letters by him and laugh all the time at the contemplation of such gifts, and I hope I get just that mixture that you and he have of complete despair and complete hope, and now I see where Freud and Joyce got it wrong and have returned from my infidelities to your dear knees and shall go no more a-whoring."

But he wasn't telling Stein the truth. The obsession didn't end. He would write in 1950, four years after Stein's death, that "*Finnegans Wake* addicts are a curious [bunch] of cats."

Between 1950 and 1975, Wilder exchanged enough letters on the subject of his passionate addiction to *Finnegans Wake* with Adaline Glasheen, one of those cats, to fill a 732-page volume (published in Ireland in 2001 by the University College Dublin Press).

But just think of what had happened in that extraordinary six-year period between 1936 and 1942, with the world on the brink of war and then tumbling into it. The enthusiastic young god Mercury aka Thornton Wilder produced the three plays in this volume that guarantee his reputation for generations to come. One was an adaptation and two, as he proclaimed loudly, were written from behind the masks of Stein and Joyce, with a little Pirandello thrown in. Is that why it's hard to get a handle on the literally mercurial Thornton Wilder? He could only find his true voice by announcing that he had taken on the voice of others. He diminished his reputation by giving too much credit to Stein and Joyce for inspiring two of these plays.

Can we really believe him when he graciously wrote in his famous Preface to these three plays that "I am not an innovator but a rediscoverer of forgotten goods . . ."?

He honored his enthusiasms in the most public of voices. Is this part of his Calvinist upbringing? "Don't think you're so special." I can imagine that being something his righteous father would say. Is this what makes it so difficult to get a handle on Thornton Wilder—the credit he gave to others? But maybe he wanted it that way. One of Mercury's greatest attributes is his cloak of invisibility.

Is that part of the answer to the puzzle of America? In this enormous country where you can be anything you want, where do we go for experience? The literal fact of a journey doesn't guarantee any results. Not every painter who went to Tahiti came back a Gaugin. Not every writer who goes off to sea comes back a Melville or a Eugene O'Neill. Not everyone who goes down the Mississippi or on the road or off to war comes back a Twain or a Kerouac or a Hemingway. And not everyone who goes to the library comes back a Thornton Wilder. But hadn't James Joyce pointed the way of the mask to Wilder when he took on the mask of Homer to write *Ulysses?*

It's fitting that in the genealogy of Mount Olympus, the great grandson of Mercury is none other than Ulysses. I think of Thornton sailing from influence to influence as if each author were an island, sailing from the isle of Pirandello to the isle of Claudel to the isles of Virgil and Stein and Joyce and who knows who else. But in six splendid years he found a remarkable home. He found the isle of Thornton Wilder. He managed to flourish there for six remarkable years.

After *The Skin of Our Teeth*, he returned to writing novels set either in ancient Rome or early-twentieth-century America. He left unfinished one series of one-act plays on the seven ages of man and another on the deadly sins. In the 1930s, he had worked on a play based on the legend of Alcestis, a wife so loving she consented to die in her husband's place. It was finally performed in Edinburgh in 1955. It went on to sucess on the continent, but never found and audience in America. A play about America, *The Emporium*, remained unfinished and unfocused at the time of his death.

Somehow Wilder was never able to get the masks to fit as perfectly again as they do in these three plays—or to find new masks to replace the old.

Is that a fault? No, the taking on, the absorption of new identities, the loss of old identities seems to me to be definitively American. Come to America and start all over again. Lose yourself. Find yourself. Reinvention is the essence of America. Isn't this part of deciphering the puzzle not just of Wilder, but of America itself?

Was the playwright with whom he shared initials any different? Young Thomas Lanier Williams, a repressed shy factory worker/poet, fled St. Louis for New Orleans, where he became the flamboyantly gifted Tennessee Williams, liberated by the aesthetic aegis of the poet Hart Crane.

I have to confess Wilder was never a puzzle for me. When I was a boy, I looked up to see what was in the papers on the day I was born, which was February 5, 1938. All the reviews in the paper on that day were raves for *Our Town*, a play that had opened the night before. I read it immediately. I've always felt a kinship with *Our Town*. We started life on the same day. (Look, when you're a kid and want to be a playwright, you look for omens, signs everywhere to tell you you're on the right track. Luckily, in my canon, anything can be a good sign.) I can still remember in my teens the shock of reading *The Skin of Our Teeth*, whose third act I thought was the smartest thing I had ever read in my life. When I was in my early twenties I was so moved by the simplicity of *The Happy Journey to Trenton and Camden* that I took on the mask of Wilder and wrote my version of his play called *The Happy Journey from 58th Street and 8th Avenue to 59th Street and 9th Avenue*. That mask of Wilder's showed me a way to deal with life on an emotional level I had never dared before. That play became a Yale one-act called *Something I'll Tell You Tuesday*, which then became a one-act called *To Wally Pantoni We Leave a Credenza* that was done at the Edward Albee/Barr/Wilder Workshop in 1965 and then grew into a full-length play called *Lake Hollywood* in 1998. Thirty-seven years had elapsed after that reading of Wilder, and his mask, as far as this play was concerned, hadn't left me.

I can still remember the thrill of seeing the great Ruth Gordon as Dolly Gallagher Levi in Tyrone Guthrie's splendidly rejuvenating production of *The Matchmaker* in 1955. She talked right out to the audience. She talked to me. There was no fourth wall. But we were in a theater. I had never experienced that impact in a straight play. You mean you could do it not only in musicals but also in a play? You could get that close to an audience? That revelation of the essential joyous intimate nature of theater has stayed with me to this day. I can't forget the emotional wallop packed by Gregory Mosher's 1988 Lincoln Center production of *Our Town* with Spalding Gray as the Stage Manager.

Wilder was never a puzzle to me. I sailed to the isle of Wilder and found life. I sailed to other islands like Joe Orton and Chekhov. Wilder taught me you had to do that. If you love something, it is a categorical imperative commanding you to absorb what it is you love and make it yours.

The mask doesn't diminish the writer. Writers need all the energies they can get. Is Thornton Wilder such a mystery because he is who his plays say he is?

Gertrude Stein concludes her portrait of Thornton in her *Geographical History* this way:

He has no fears
at most he has no tears.
For them very likely he is made of them.

Was Thornton Wilder a puzzle to Stein because at heart he was no puzzle? He truly believed in those verities, those platitudes. He wrote as if he were writing about life and birth and love and death on the very day before those thoughts became platitudes.

The ink is still wet on these three plays because he wrote them with power and love and craft and genius. He saw with clear eyes his America—a world in which he could write as he did in *Our Town*, "Oh, earth, you're too wonderful for anyone to ever realize you" and know he means it. Is it that unselfconscious wisdom, that unabashed absence of ridicule, that plainspoken passionate innocence, and the ultimate irony: the seeming absence of mask, the very thing that made him a puzzle to Stein? Yes. Wilder is what he appears to be, what he dares to be. And that's why he's still the most American of American playwrights.

A puzzle?

These plays are a gift.

—JOHN GUARE

Preface

—ɯ—

By Thornton Wilder

Toward the end of the twenties I began to lose pleasure in going to the theatre. I ceased to believe in the stories I saw presented there. When I did go it was to admire some secondary aspect of the play, the work of a great actor or director or designer. Yet at the same time the conviction was growing in me that the theatre was the greatest of all the arts. I felt that something had gone wrong with it in my time and that it was fulfilling only a small part of its potentialities. I was filled with admiration for presentations of classical works by Max Reinhardt and Louis Jouvet and the Old Vic, as I was by the best plays of my own time, like *Desire Under the Elms* and *The Front Page;* but it was with a grudging appreciation, for I didn't believe a word of them. I was like a schoolmaster grading a paper; to each of these offerings I gave an A+, but the condition of mind of one grading a paper is not that of one being overwhelmed by an artistic creation. The response we make when we "believe" a work of the imagination is that of saying: "This is the way things are. I have always known it without being fully aware that I knew it. Now in the presence of this play or novel or poem (or picture or piece of music) I know that I know it." It is this form of knowledge which Plato called "recollection." We have all murdered, in thought; and been murdered. We have all seen the ridiculous in estimable persons and in ourselves. We have all known terror as well as enchantment. Imaginative literature has nothing to say to those who do not recognize—who cannot be *reminded*—of such conditions. Of all the arts the theatre is best endowed to awaken this recollection within us—to believe is to say "yes"; but in the theatres of my time I did not feel myself prompted to any such grateful and self-forgetting acquiescence.

This dissatisfaction worried me. I was not ready to condemn myself as blasé and overfastidious, for I knew that I was still capable of belief. I believed every word of *Ulysses* and of Proust and of *The Magic Mountain,* as I did of hundreds of plays when I read them. It was on the stage that imaginative narration became false. Finally, my dissatisfaction passed into resentment. I began to feel that the theatre was not only inadequate, it was evasive; it did not wish to draw upon its deeper potentialities. I found the word for it: it aimed to be *soothing.* The tragic had no heat; the comic had no bite; the social criticism failed to indict us with responsibility. I began to search for the point where the theatre had run off the track, where it had chosen—and been permitted—to become a minor art and an inconsequential diversion.

The trouble began in the nineteenth century and was connected with the rise of the middle classes—they wanted their theatre soothing. There's nothing wrong with the middle classes in themselves. We know that now. The United States and Scandinavia and Germany are middle-class countries, so completely so that they have lost the very memory of their once despised and ludicrous inferiority (they had been inferior not only to the aristocracy but, in human dignity, to the peasantry).

When a middle class is new, however, there is much that is wrong with it. When it is emerging from under the shadow of an aristocracy, from the myth and prestige of those well-born Higher-ups, it is alternately insecure and aggressively complacent. It must find its justification and reassurance in making money and displaying it. To this day, members of the middle classes in England, France, and Italy feel themselves to be a little ridiculous and humiliated. The prestige of aristocracies is based upon a dreary untruth that moral superiority and the qualifications for leadership are transmittable through the chromosomes, and the secondary lie, that the environment afforded by privilege and leisure tends to nurture the flowers of the spirit. An aristocracy, defending and fostering its lie, extracts from the arts only such elements as can further its interests, the aroma and not the sap, the grace and not the trenchancy. Equally harmful to culture is the newly arrived middle class. In the English-speaking world the middle classes came into power early in the nineteenth century and gained control over the theatre. They were pious, law-abiding, and industrious. They were assured of eternal life in the next world and, in this, they were squarely seated on Property and the privileges that accompany it. They were attended by devoted servants who knew their place. They were benevolent within certain limits, but chose to ignore wide tracts of injustice and stupidity in the world about them; and they shrank from contemplating those elements within themselves that were ridiculous, shallow, and harmful. They distrusted the passions and tried to deny them. Their questions about the nature of life seemed to be sufficiently answered by the demonstration of financial status and by conformity to some clearly established rules of decorum. These were precarious positions; abysses yawned on either side. The air was loud with questions that must not be asked. These audiences fashioned a theatre which could not disturb them. They thronged to melodrama (which deals with tragic possibilities in such a way that you know from the beginning that all will end happily) and to sentimental drama (which accords a total license to the supposition that the wish is father to the thought) and to comedies in which the characters were so represented that they always resembled someone else and not oneself. Between the plays that Sheridan wrote in his twenties and the first works of Wilde and Shaw there was no play of even moderate interest written in the English language. (Unless you happen to admire and except Shelley's *The Cenci*.) These audiences, however, also thronged to Shakespeare. How did they shield themselves against his probing? How did they smother the theatre—and with such effect that it smothers us still? The box set was already there, the curtain, the proscenium, but not taken "seriously"—it was a convenience in view of the weather in northern countries. They took it seriously and emphasized and enhanced everything that thus removed, cut off, and boxed the action; they increasingly shut the play up into a museum showcase.

Let us examine why the box-set stage stifles the life in drama and why and how it militates against belief.

Every action which has ever taken place—every thought, every emotion—has taken place only once, at one moment in time and place. "I love you," "I rejoice," "I suffer," have been said and felt many billions of times, and never twice the same. Every person who has ever lived has lived an unbroken succession of unique occasions. Yet the more one is aware of this individuality in experience (innumerable! innumerable!) the more one becomes attentive to what these disparate moments have in common, to repetitive patterns. As an artist (or listener or beholder) which "truth" do you prefer—that of the isolated occasion, or that which includes and resumes the innumerable? Which truth is more worth telling? Every age differs in this. Is the Venus de Milo "one woman"? Is the play *Macbeth* the story of "one destiny"? The theatre is admirably fitted to tell both truths. It has one foot planted firmly in the particular, since each actor before us (even when he wears a mask!) is indubitably a living, breathing "one"; yet it tends and strains to exhibit a general truth since its relation to a specific "realistic" truth is confused and undermined by the fact that it is an accumulation of untruths, pretenses and fiction. The novel is preeminently the vehicle of the unique occasion, the theatre of the generalized one. It is through the theatre's power to raise the exhibited individual action into the realm of idea and type and universal that it is able to evoke our belief. But power is precisely what those nineteenth-century audiences did not—dared not—confront. They tamed it and drew its teeth; squeezed it into that removed showcase. They loaded the stage with specific objects, because every concrete object on the stage fixes and narrows the action to one moment in time and place. (Have you ever noticed that in the plays of Shakespeare no one—except occasionally a ruler—ever sits down? There were not even chairs on the English or Spanish stages in the time of Elizabeth I.) So it was by a jugglery with time that the middle classes devitalized the theatre. When you emphasize *place* in the theatre, you drag down and limit and harness time to it. You thrust the action back into past time, whereas it is precisely the glory of the stage that it is always "now" there. Under such production methods the characters are all dead before the action starts. You don't have to pay deeply from your heart's participation. No great age in the theatre ever attempted to capture the audiences' belief through this kind of specification and localization. I became dissatisfied with the theatre because I was unable to lend credence to such childish attempts to be "real."

I began writing one-act plays that tried to capture not verisimilitude but reality. In *The Happy Journey to Trenton and Camden* four kitchen chairs represent an automobile and a family travels seventy miles in twenty minutes. Ninety years go by in *The Long Christmas Dinner.* In *Pullman Car Hiawatha* some more plain chairs serve as berths and we hear the very vital statistics of the towns and fields that passengers are traversing; we hear their thoughts; we even hear the planets over their heads. In Chinese drama a character, by straddling a stick, conveys to us that he is on horseback. In almost every No play of the Japanese an actor makes a tour of the stage and we know that he is making a long journey. Think of the ubiquity that Shakespeare's stage afforded for the battle scenes at the close of *Julius Caesar* and *Antony and Cleopatra.* As we see them today what a cutting and hacking of the text takes place—what condescension, what contempt for his dramaturgy.

Our Town is not offered as a picture of life in a New Hampshire village; or as a speculation about the conditions of life after death (that element I merely took from Dante's *Purgatory*). It is an attempt to find a value above all price for the smallest events in our daily life. I have made the claim as preposterous as possible, for I have set the village against the largest dimensions of time and place. The recurrent words in this play (few have noticed it) are "hundreds," "thousands," and "millions."

Emily's joys and griefs, her algebra lessons and her birthday presents—what are they when we consider all the billions of girls who have lived, who are living, and who will live? Each individual's assertion to an absolute reality can only be inner, very inner. And here the method of staging finds its justification—in the first two acts there are at least a few chairs and tables; but when she revisits the earth and the kitchen to which she descended on her twelfth birthday, the very chairs and table are gone. Our claim, our hope, our despair are in the mind—not in things, not in "scenery." Molière said that for the theatre all he needed was a platform and a passion or two. The climax of this play needs only five square feet of boarding and the passion to know what life means to us.

The Matchmaker is an only slightly modified version of *The Merchant of Yonkers,* which I wrote in the year after I had written *Our Town.* One way to shake off the nonsense of the nineteenth-century staging is to make fun of it. This play parodies the stock-company plays that I used to see at Ye Liberty Theatre, Oakland, California, when I was a boy. I have already read small theses in German comparing it with the great Austrian original on which it is based. The scholars are very bewildered. There is most of the plot (except that our friend Dolly Levi is not in Nestroy's play); there are some of the tags; but it's all "about" quite different matters. My play is about the aspirations of the young (and not only of the young) for a fuller, freer participation in life. Imagine an Austrian pharmacist going to the shelf to draw from a bottle which he knows to contain a stinging corrosive liquid, guaranteed to remove warts and wens; and imagine his surprise when he discovers that it has been filled overnight with very American birch-bark beer.

The Skin of Our Teeth begins, also, by making fun of old-fashioned play writing; but the audience soon perceives that he is seeing "two times at once." The Antrobus family is living both in prehistoric times and in a New Jersey commuters' suburb today. Again, the events of our homely daily life—this time the family life—are depicted against the vast dimensions of time and place. It was written on the eve of our entrance into the war and under strong emotion and I think it mostly comes alive under conditions of crisis. It has been often charged with being a bookish fantasia about history, full of rather bloodless schoolmasterish jokes. But to have seen it in Germany soon after the war, in the shattered churches and beer halls that were serving as theatres, with audiences whose price of admission meant the loss of a meal and for whom it was of absorbing interest that there was a "recipe for grass soup that did not cause the diarrhea," was an experience that was not so cool. I am very proud that this year it has received a first and overwhelming reception in Warsaw. The play is deeply indebted to James Joyce's *Finnegans Wake*. I should be very happy if, in the future, some author should feel similarly indebted to any work of mine. Literature has always more resembled a torch race than a furious dispute among heirs.

The theatre has lagged behind the other arts in finding the "new ways" to express how men and women think and feel in our time. I am not one of the new dramatists we are looking for. I wish I were. I hope I have played a part in preparing the way for them. I am not an innovator but a rediscoverer of forgotten goods and I hope a remover of obtrusive bric-a-brac. And as I view the work of my contemporaries I seem to feel that I am exceptional in one thing—I give (don't I?) the impression of having enormously enjoyed it.

Our Town
A Play in Three Acts

The first performance of this play took place at the McCarter Theatre, Princeton, New Jersey, on January 22, 1938. The first New York performance was at the Henry Miller Theater, February 4, 1938. It was produced and directed by Jed Harris. The technical director was Raymond Sovey; the costumes were designed by Madame Hélène Pons. The role of the Stage Manager was played by Frank Craven. The Gibbs family were played by Jay Fassett, Evelyn Varden, John Craven and Marilyn Erskine; the Webb family by Thomas Ross, Helen Carew, Martha Scott (as Emily) and Charles Wiley, Jr.; Mrs. Soames was played by Doro Merande; Simon Stimson by Philip Coolidge.

CHARACTERS (in the order of their appearance)

STAGE MANAGER
DR. GIBBS
JOE CROWELL
HOWIE NEWSOME
MRS. GIBBS
MRS. WEBB
GEORGE GIBBS
REBECCA GIBBS
WALLY WEBB
EMILY WEBB
PROFESSOR WILLARD
MR. WEBB
WOMAN IN THE BALCONY
MAN IN THE AUDITORIUM
LADY IN THE BOX
SIMON STIMSON
MRS. SOAMES
CONSTABLE WARREN
SI CROWELL
THREE BASEBALL PLAYERS
SAM CRAIG
JOE STODDARD

The entire play takes place in Grover's Corners,
New Hampshire.

—m—

Act I

No curtain.

   No scenery.

   The audience, arriving, sees an empty stage in half-light.

   Presently the STAGE MANAGER, *hat on and pipe in mouth, enters and begins placing a table and three chairs downstage left, and a table and three chairs downstage right.*

   He also places a low bench at the corner of what will be the Webb house, left.

   "Left" and "right" are from the point of view of the actor facing the audience. "Up" is toward the back wall.

   As the house lights go down he has finished setting the stage and leaning against the right proscenium pillar watches the late arrivals in the audience.

   When the auditorium is in complete darkness he speaks:

   STAGE MANAGER:

This play is called "Our Town." It was written by Thornton Wilder; produced and directed by A. . . . (or: produced by A. . . .; directed by B. . . .). In it you will see Miss C. . . .; Miss D. . . .;

Miss E. . . .; and Mr. F. . . .; Mr. G. . . .; Mr. H. . . .; and many others. The name of the town is Grover's Corners, New Hampshire—just across the Massachusetts line: latitude 42 degrees 40 minutes; longitude 70 degrees 37 minutes. The First Act shows a day in our town. The day is May 7, 1901. The time is just before dawn.

A rooster crows.

The sky is beginning to show some streaks of light over in the East there, behind our mount'in.

The morning star always gets wonderful bright the minute before it has to go,—doesn't it?

He stares at it for a moment, then goes upstage.

Well, I'd better show you how our town lies. Up here—

That is: parallel with the back wall.

is Main Street. Way back there is the railway station; tracks go that way. Polish Town's across the tracks, and some Canuck families.

Toward the left.

Over there is the Congregational Church; across the street's the Presbyterian.

Methodist and Unitarian are over there.

Baptist is down in the holla' by the river.

Catholic Church is over beyond the tracks.

Here's the Town Hall and Post Office combined; jail's in the basement.

Bryan once made a speech from these very steps here.

Along here's a row of stores. Hitching posts and horse blocks in front of them. First automobile's going to come along in about five years—belonged to Banker Cartwright, our richest citizen . . . lives in the big white house up on the hill.

Here's the grocery store and here's Mr. Morgan's drugstore. Most everybody in town manages to look into those two stores once a day.

Public School's over yonder. High School's still farther over. Quarter of nine mornings, noontimes, and three o'clock afternoons, the hull town can hear the yelling and screaming from those schoolyards.

He approaches the table and chairs downstage right.

This is our doctor's house,—Doc Gibbs'. This is the back door.

Two arched trellises, covered with vines and flowers, are pushed out, one by each proscenium pillar.

There's some scenery for those who think they have to have scenery.

This is Mrs. Gibbs' garden. Corn . . . peas . . . beans . . . hollyhocks . . . heliotrope . . . and a lot of burdock.

Crosses the stage.

In those days our newspaper come out twice a week—the Grover's Corners *Sentinel*—and this is Editor Webb's house.

And this is Mrs. Webb's garden.

Just like Mrs. Gibbs', only it's got a lot of sunflowers, too.

He looks upward, center stage.

Right here . . . 's a big butternut tree.

He returns to his place by the right proscenium pillar and looks at the audience for a minute.

Nice town, y'know what I mean?

Nobody very remarkable ever come out of it, s'far as we know.

The earliest tombstones in the cemetery up there on the mountain say 1670–1680—they're Grovers and Cartwrights and Gibbses and Herseys—same names as are around here now.

Well, as I said: it's about dawn.

The only lights on in town are in a cottage over by the tracks where a Polish mother's just had twins. And in the Joe Crowell house, where Joe Junior's getting up so as to deliver the paper. And in the depot, where Shorty Hawkins is gettin' ready to flag the 5:45 for Boston.

A train whistle is heard. The STAGE MANAGER *takes out his watch and nods.*

Naturally, out in the country—all around—there've been lights on for some time, what with milkin's and so on. But town people sleep late.

So—another day's begun.

There's Doc Gibbs comin' down Main Street now, comin' back from that baby case. And here's his wife comin' downstairs to get breakfast.

MRS. GIBBS, *a plump, pleasant woman in the middle thirties, comes "downstairs" right. She pulls up an imaginary window shade in her kitchen and starts to make a fire in her stove.*

Doc Gibbs died in 1930. The new hospital's named after him.

Mrs. Gibbs died first—long time ago, in fact. She went out to visit her daughter, Rebecca, who married an insurance man in Canton, Ohio, and died there—pneumonia—but her body was brought back here. She's up in the cemetery there now—in with a whole mess of Gibbses and Herseys—she was Julia Hersey 'fore she married Doc Gibbs in the Congregational Church over there.

In our town we like to know the facts about everybody.

There's Mrs. Webb, coming downstairs to get her breakfast, too.

—That's Doc Gibbs. Got that call at half past one this morning.

And there comes Joe Crowell, Jr., delivering Mr. Webb's *Sentinel.*

DR. GIBBS *has been coming along Main Street from the left. At the point where he would turn to approach his house, he stops, sets down his—imaginary—black bag, takes off his hat, and rubs his face with fatigue, using an enormous handkerchief.*

MRS. WEBB, *a thin, serious, crisp woman, has entered her kitchen, left, tying on an apron. She goes through the motions of putting wood into a stove, lighting it, and preparing breakfast.*

Suddenly, JOE CROWELL, JR., *eleven, starts down Main Street from the right, hurling imaginary newspapers into doorways.*

JOE CROWELL, JR.:

Morning, Doc Gibbs.

DR. GIBBS:

Morning, Joe.

JOE CROWELL, JR.:

Somebody been sick, Doc?

DR. GIBBS:

No. Just some twins born over in Polish Town.

JOE CROWELL, JR.:

Do you want your paper now?

DR. GIBBS:

Yes, I'll take it.—Anything serious goin' on in the world since Wednesday?

JOE CROWELL, JR.:

Yessir. My schoolteacher, Miss Foster, 's getting married to a fella over in Concord.

DR. GIBBS:

I declare.—How do you boys feel about that?

JOE CROWELL, JR.:

Well, of course, it's none of my business—but I think if a person starts out to be a teacher, she ought to stay one.

DR. GIBBS:

How's your knee, Joe?

JOE CROWELL, JR.:

Fine, Doc, I never think about it at all. Only like you said, it always tells me when it's going to rain.

DR. GIBBS:

What's it telling you today? Goin' to rain?

JOE CROWELL, JR.:

No, sir.

DR. GIBBS:

Sure?

JOE CROWELL, JR.:

Yessir.

DR. GIBBS:

Knee ever make a mistake?

JOE CROWELL, JR.:

No, sir.

JOE *goes off.* DR. GIBBS *stands reading his paper.*

STAGE MANAGER:

Want to tell you something about that boy Joe Crowell there. Joe was awful bright—graduated from high school here, head of his class. So he got a scholarship to Massachusetts Tech. Graduated head of his class there, too. It was all wrote up in the Boston paper at the time. Goin' to be a great engineer, Joe was. But the war broke out and he died in France.—All that education for nothing.

HOWIE NEWSOME:

Off left.

Giddap, Bessie! What's the matter with you today?

STAGE MANAGER:

Here comes Howie Newsome, deliverin' the milk.

HOWIE NEWSOME, *about thirty, in overalls, comes along Main Street from the left, walking beside an invisible horse and wagon and carrying an imaginary rack with milk bottles. The sound of clinking milk bottles is heard. He leaves some bottles at Mrs. Webb's trellis, then, crossing the stage to Mrs. Gibbs', he stops center to talk to Dr. Gibbs.*

HOWIE NEWSOME:

Morning, Doc.

DR. GIBBS:

Morning, Howie.

HOWIE NEWSOME:

Somebody sick?

DR. GIBBS:

Pair of twins over to Mrs. Goruslawski's.

HOWIE NEWSOME:

Twins, eh? This town's gettin' bigger every year.

DR. GIBBS:

Goin' to rain, Howie?

HOWIE NEWSOME:

No, no. Fine day—that'll burn through. Come on, Bessie.

DR. GIBBS:

Hello Bessie.

He strokes the horse, which has remained up center.

How old is she, Howie?

HOWIE NEWSOME:

Going on seventeen. Bessie's all mixed up about the route ever since the Lockharts stopped takin' their quart of milk every day. She wants to leave 'em a quart just the same—keeps scolding me the hull trip.

He reaches Mrs. Gibbs' back door. She is waiting for him.

MRS. GIBBS:

Good morning, Howie.

HOWIE NEWSOME:

Morning, Mrs. Gibbs. Doc's just comin' down the street.

MRS. GIBBS:

Is he? Seems like you're late today.

HOWIE NEWSOME:

Yes. Somep'n went wrong with the separator. Don't know what 'twas.

He passes Dr. Gibbs up center.

Doc!

DR. GIBBS:

Howie!

MRS. GIBBS:

Calling upstairs.

Children! Children! Time to get up.

HOWIE NEWSOME:

Come on, Bessie!

He goes off right.

MRS. GIBBS:

George! Rebecca!

DR. GIBBS *arrives at his back door and passes through the trellis into his house.*

MRS. GIBBS:

Everything all right, Frank?

DR. GIBBS:

Yes. I declare—easy as kittens.

MRS. GIBBS:

Bacon'll be ready in a minute. Set down and drink your coffee. You can catch a couple hours' sleep this morning, can't you?

DR. GIBBS:

Hm! . . . Mrs. Wentworth's coming at eleven. Guess I know what it's about, too. Her stummick ain't what it ought to be.

MRS. GIBBS:

All told, you won't get more'n three hours' sleep. Frank Gibbs, I don't know what's goin' to become of you. I do wish I could get you to go away someplace and take a rest. I think it would do you good.

MRS. WEBB:

Emilceee! Time to get up! Wally! Seven o'clock!

MRS. GIBBS:

I declare, you got to speak to George. Seems like something's come over him lately. He's no help to me at all. I can't even get him to cut me some wood.

DR. GIBBS:

Washing and drying his hands at the sink. MRS. GIBBS *is busy at the stove.*

Is he sassy to you?

MRS. GIBBS:

No. He just whines! All he thinks about is that baseball— George! Rebecca! You'll be late for school.

DR. GIBBS:

M-m-m . . .

MRS. GIBBS:

George!

DR. GIBBS:

George, look sharp!

GEORGE'S VOICE:

Yes, Pa!

DR. GIBBS:

As he goes off the stage.

Don't you hear your mother calling you? I guess I'll go upstairs and get forty winks.

MRS. WEBB:

Walleee! Emileee! You'll be late for school! Walleee! You wash yourself good or I'll come up and do it myself.

REBECCA GIBBS' VOICE:

Ma! What dress shall I wear?

MRS. GIBBS:

Don't make a noise. Your father's been out all night and needs his sleep. I washed and ironed the blue gingham for you special.

REBECCA:

Ma, I hate that dress.

MRS. GIBBS:

Oh, hush-up-with-you.

REBECCA:

Every day I go to school dressed like a sick turkey.

MRS. GIBBS:

Now, Rebecca, you always look *very* nice.

REBECCA:

Mama, George's throwing soap at me.

MRS. GIBBS:

I'll come and slap the both of you,—that's what I'll do.

A factory whistle sounds.

The CHILDREN *dash in and take their places at the tables. Right,* GEORGE, *about sixteen, and* REBECCA, *eleven. Left,* EMILY *and* WALLY, *same ages. They carry strapped school-books.*

STAGE MANAGER:

We've got a factory in our town too—hear it? Makes blankets. Cartwrights own it and it brung 'em a fortune.

MRS. WEBB:

Children! Now I won't have it. Breakfast is just as good as any other meal and I won't have you gobbling like wolves. It'll stunt your growth,—that's a fact. Put away your book, Wally.

WALLY:

Aw, Ma! By ten o'clock I got to know all about Canada.

MRS. WEBB:

You know the rule's well as I do—no books at table. As for me, I'd rather have my children healthy than bright.

EMILY:

I'm both, Mama: you know I am. I'm the brightest girl in school for my age. I have a wonderful memory.

MRS. WEBB:

Eat your breakfast.

WALLY:

I'm bright, too, when I'm looking at my stamp collection.

MRS. GIBBS:

I'll speak to your father about it when he's rested. Seems to me twenty-five cents a week's enough for a boy your age. I declare I don't know how you spend it all.

GEORGE:

Aw, Ma,—I gotta lotta things to buy.

MRS. GIBBS:

Strawberry phosphates—that's what you spend it on.

GEORGE:

I don't see how Rebecca comes to have so much money. She has more'n a dollar.

REBECCA:

Spoon in mouth, dreamily.

I've been saving it up gradual.

MRS. GIBBS:

Well, dear, I think it's a good thing to spend some every now and then.

REBECCA:

Mama, do you know what I love most in the world—do you?— Money.

MRS. GIBBS:

Eat your breakfast.

THE CHILDREN:

Mama, there's first bell.—I gotta hurry.—I don't want any more.—I gotta hurry.

The CHILDREN *rise, seize their books and dash out through the trellises. They meet, down center, and chattering, walk to Main Street, then turn left.*

The STAGE MANAGER *goes off, unobtrusively, right.*

MRS. WEBB:

Walk fast, but you don't have to run. Wally, pull up your pants at the knee. Stand up straight, Emily.

MRS. GIBBS:

Tell Miss Foster I send her my best congratulations—can you remember that?

REBECCA:

Yes, Ma.

MRS. GIBBS:

You look real nice, Rebecca. Pick up your feet.

ALL:

Good-by.

MRS. GIBBS *fills her apron with food for the chickens and comes down to the footlights.*

MRS. GIBBS:

Here, chick, chick, chick.

No, go away, you. Go away.

Here, chick, chick, chick.

What's the matter with *you?* Fight, fight, fight,—that's all you do.

Hm . . . *you* don't belong to me. Where'd you come from?

She shakes her apron.

Oh, don't be so scared. Nobody's going to hurt you.

MRS. WEBB *is sitting on the bench by her trellis, stringing beans.*

Good morning, Myrtle. How's your cold?

MRS. WEBB:

Well, I still get that tickling feeling in my throat. I told Charles I didn't know as I'd go to choir practice tonight. Wouldn't be any use.

MRS. GIBBS:

Have you tried singing over your voice?

MRS. WEBB:

Yes, but somehow I can't do that and stay on the key. While I'm resting myself I thought I'd string some of these beans.

MRS. GIBBS:

Rolling up her sleeves as she crosses the stage for a chat.

Let me help you. Beans have been good this year.

MRS. WEBB:

I've decided to put up forty quarts if it kills me. The children say they hate 'em, but I notice they're able to get 'em down all winter.

Pause. Brief sound of chickens cackling.

MRS. GIBBS:

Now, Myrtle. I've got to tell you something, because if I don't tell somebody I'll burst.

MRS. WEBB:

Why, Julia Gibbs!

MRS. GIBBS:

Here, give me some more of those beans. Myrtle, did one of those secondhand-furniture men from Boston come to see you last Friday?

MRS. WEBB:

No-o.

MRS. GIBBS:

Well, he called on me. First I thought he was a patient wantin' to see Dr. Gibbs. 'N he wormed his way into my parlor, and, Myrtle Webb, he offered me three hundred and fifty dollars for Grandmother Wentworth's highboy, as I'm sitting here!

MRS. WEBB:

Why, Julia Gibbs!

MRS. GIBBS:

He did! That old thing! Why, it was so big I didn't know where to put it and I almost give it to Cousin Hester Wilcox.

MRS. WEBB:

Well, you're going to take it, aren't you?

MRS. GIBBS:

I don't know.

MRS. WEBB:

You don't know—three hundred and fifty dollars! What's come over you?

MRS. GIBBS:

Well, if I could get the Doctor to take the money and go away someplace on a real trip, I'd sell it like that.—Y'know, Myrtle, it's been the dream of my life to see Paris, France.—Oh, I don't know. It sounds crazy, I suppose, but for years I've been promising myself that if we ever had the chance—

MRS. WEBB:

How does the Doctor feel about it?

MRS. GIBBS:

Well, I did beat about the bush a little and said that if I got a legacy—that's the way I put it—I'd make him take me somewhere.

MRS. WEBB:

M-m-m . . . What did he say?

MRS. GIBBS:

You know how he is. I haven't heard a serious word out of him since I've known him. No, he said, it might make him discontented with Grover's Corners to go traipsin' about Europe; better let well enough alone, he says. Every two years he makes a trip to the battlefields of the Civil War and that's enough treat for anybody, he says.

MRS. WEBB:

Well, Mr. Webb just *admires* the way Dr. Gibbs knows everything about the Civil War. Mr. Webb's a good mind to give up Napoleon and move over to the Civil War, only Dr. Gibbs being one of the greatest experts in the country just makes him despair.

MRS. GIBBS:

It's a fact! Dr. Gibbs is never so happy as when he's at Antietam or Gettysburg. The times I've walked over those hills, Myrtle, stopping at every bush and pacing it all out, like we were going to buy it.

MRS. WEBB:

Well, if that secondhand man's really serious about buyin' it, Julia, you sell it. And then you'll get to see Paris, all right. Just keep droppin' hints from time to time—that's how I got to see the Atlantic Ocean, y'know.

MRS. GIBBS:

Oh, I'm sorry I mentioned it. Only it seems to me that once in your life before you die you ought to see a country where they don't talk in English and don't even want to.

The STAGE MANAGER *enters briskly from the right. He tips his hat to the ladies, who nod their heads.*

STAGE MANAGER:

Thank you, ladies. Thank you very much.

MRS. GIBBS *and* MRS. WEBB *gather up their things, return into their homes and disappear.*

Now we're going to skip a few hours.

But first we want a little more information about the town, kind of a scientific account, you might say.

So I've asked Professor Willard of our State University to sketch in a few details of our past history here.

Is Professor Willard here?

PROFESSOR WILLARD, *a rural savant, pince-nez on a wide satin ribbon, enters from the right with some notes in his hand.*

May I introduce Professor Willard of our State University.

A few brief notes, thank you, Professor,—unfortunately our time is limited.

PROFESSOR WILLARD:

Grover's Corners . . . let me see . . . Grover's Corners lies on the old Pleistocene granite of the Appalachian range. I may say it's some of the oldest land in the world. We're very proud of that. A shelf of Devonian basalt crosses it with vestiges of Mesozoic shale, and some sandstone outcroppings; but that's all more recent: two hundred, three hundred million years old.

Some highly interesting fossils have been found . . . I may say: unique fossils . . . two miles out of town, in Silas Peckham's cow pasture. They can be seen at the museum in our University at any time—that is, at any reasonable time. Shall I read some of Professor Gruber's notes on the meteorological situation—mean precipitation, et cetera?

STAGE MANAGER:

Afraid we won't have time for that, Professor. We might have a few words on the history of man here.

PROFESSOR WILLARD:

Yes . . . anthropological data: Early Amerindian stock. Cotahatchee tribes . . . no evidence before the tenth century of this era . . . hm . . . now entirely disappeared . . . possible traces in three families. Migration toward the end of the seventeenth century of English brachiocephalic blue-eyed stock . . . for the most part. Since then some Slav and Mediterranean—

STAGE MANAGER:

And the population, Professor Willard?

PROFESSOR WILLARD:

Within the town limits: 2,640.

STAGE MANAGER:

Just a moment, Professor.

He whispers into the professor's ear.

PROFESSOR WILLARD:

Oh, yes, indeed?—The population, *at the moment,* is 2,642. The Postal District brings in 507 more, making a total of 3,149.—Mortality and birth rates: constant.—By MacPherson's gauge: 6.032.

STAGE MANAGER:

Thank you very much, Professor. We're all very much obliged to you, I'm sure.

PROFESSOR WILLARD:

Not at all, sir; not at all.

STAGE MANAGER:

This way, Professor, and thank you again.

Exit PROFESSOR WILLARD.

Now the political and social report: Editor Webb.—Oh, Mr. Webb?

MRS. WEBB *appears at her back door.*

MRS. WEBB:

He'll be here in a minute. . . . He just cut his hand while he was eatin' an apple.

STAGE MANAGER:

Thank you, Mrs. Webb.

MRS. WEBB:

Charles! Everybody's waitin'.

Exit MRS. WEBB.

STAGE MANAGER:

Mr. Webb is Publisher and Editor of the Grover's Corners *Sentinel.* That's our local paper, y'know.

MR. WEBB *enters from his house, pulling on his coat. His finger is bound in a handkerchief.*

MR. WEBB:

Well . . . I don't have to tell you that we're run here by a Board of Selectmen.—All males vote at the age of twenty-one. Women vote indirect. We're lower middle class: sprinkling of professional men . . . ten per cent illiterate laborers. Politically, we're eighty-six per cent Republicans; six per cent Democrats; four per cent Socialists; rest, indifferent.

Religiously, we're eighty-five per cent Protestants; twelve per cent Catholics; rest, indifferent.

STAGE MANAGER:

Have you any comments, Mr. Webb?

MR. WEBB:

Very ordinary town, if you ask me. Little better behaved than most. Probably a lot duller.

But our young people here seem to like it well enough. Ninety per cent of 'em graduating from high school settle down right here to live—even when they've been away to college.

STAGE MANAGER:

Now, is there anyone in the audience who would like to ask Editor Webb anything about the town?

WOMAN IN THE BALCONY:

Is there much drinking in Grover's Corners?

MR. WEBB:

Well, ma'am, I wouldn't know what you'd call *much*. Satiddy nights the farmhands meet down in Ellery Greenough's stable and holler some. We've got one or two town drunks, but they're always having remorses every time an evangelist comes to town. No, ma'am, I'd say likker ain't a regular thing in the home here, except in the medicine chest. Right good for snake bite, y'know—always was.

BELLIGERENT MAN AT BACK OF AUDITORIUM:

Is there no one in town aware of—

STAGE MANAGER:

Come forward, will you, where we can all hear you—What were you saying?

BELLIGERENT MAN:

Is there no one in town aware of social injustice and industrial inequality?

MR. WEBB:

Oh, yes, everybody is—somethin' terrible. Seems like they spend most of their time talking about who's rich and who's poor.

BELLIGERENT MAN:

Then why don't they do something about it?

He withdraws without waiting for an answer.

MR. WEBB:

Well, I dunno. . . . I guess we're all hunting like everybody else for a way the diligent and sensible can rise to the top and the lazy and quarrelsome can sink to the bottom. But it ain't easy to find. Meanwhile, we do all we can to help those that

can't help themselves and those that can we leave alone.—
Are there any other questions?

LADY IN A BOX:

Oh, Mr. Webb? Mr. Webb, is there any culture or love of
beauty in Grover's Corners?

MR. WEBB:

Well, ma'am, there ain't much—not in the sense you mean.
Come to think of it, there's some girls that play the piano at
High School Commencement; but they ain't happy about it.
No, ma'am, there isn't much culture; but maybe this is the
place to tell you that we've got a lot of pleasures of a kind here:
we like the sun comin' up over the mountain in the morning,
and we all notice a good deal about the birds. We pay a lot of
attention to them. And we watch the change of the seasons;
yes, everybody knows about them. But those other things—
you're right, ma'am,—there ain't much.—*Robinson Crusoe* and
the Bible; and Handel's "Largo," we all know that; and
Whistler's "Mother"—those are just about as far as we go.

LADY IN A BOX:

So I thought. Thank you, Mr. Webb.

STAGE MANAGER:

Thank you, Mr. Webb.

MR. WEBB *retires.*

Now, we'll go back to the town. It's early afternoon. All 2,642
have had their dinners and all the dishes have been washed.

MR. WEBB, *having removed his coat, returns and starts
pushing a lawn mower to and fro beside his house.*

There's an early-afternoon calm in our town: a buzzin' and a hummin' from the school buildings; only a few buggies on Main Street—the horses dozing at the hitching posts; you all remember what it's like. Doc Gibbs is in his office, tapping people and making them say "ah." Mr. Webb's cuttin' his lawn over there; one man in ten thinks it's a privilege to push his own lawn mower.

No, sir. It's later than I thought. There are the children coming home from school already.

Shrill girls' voices are heard, off left. EMILY *comes along Main Street, carrying some books. There are some signs that she is imagining herself to be a lady of startling elegance.*

EMILY:

I *can't*, Lois. I've got to go home and help my mother. I *promised*.

MR. WEBB:

Emily, walk simply. Who do you think you are today?

EMILY:

Papa, you're terrible. One minute you tell me to stand up straight and the next minute you call me names. I just don't listen to you.

She gives him an abrupt kiss.

MR. WEBB:

Golly, I never got a kiss from such a great lady before.

He goes out of sight. EMILY *leans over and picks some flowers by the gate of her house.*

GEORGE GIBBS *comes careening down Main Street. He is*
throwing a ball up to dizzying heights, and waiting to catch
it again. This sometimes requires his taking six steps
backward. He bumps into an OLD LADY *invisible to us.*

GEORGE:

Excuse me, Mrs. Forrest.

STAGE MANAGER:

As Mrs. Forrest.

Go out and play in the fields, young man. You got no business playing baseball on Main Street.

GEORGE:

Awfully sorry, Mrs. Forrest.—Hello, Emily.

EMILY:

H'lo.

GEORGE:

You made a fine speech in class.

EMILY:

Well . . . I was really ready to make a speech about the Monroe
Doctrine, but at the last minute Miss Corcoran made me talk
about the Louisiana Purchase instead. I worked an awful long
time on both of them.

GEORGE:

Gee, it's funny, Emily. From my window up there I can just
see your head nights when you're doing your homework over
in your room.

EMILY:

Why, can you?

GEORGE:

You certainly do stick to it, Emily. I don't see how you can sit still that long. I guess you like school.

EMILY:

Well, I always feel it's something you have to go through.

GEORGE:

Yeah.

EMILY:

I don't mind it really. It passes the time.

GEORGE:

Yeah.—Emily, what do you think? We might work out a kinda telegraph from your window to mine; and once in a while you could give me a kinda hint or two about one of those algebra problems. I don't mean the answers, Emily, of course not . . . just some little hint . . .

EMILY:

Oh, I think *hints* are allowed.—So—ah—if you get stuck, George, you whistle to me; and I'll give you some hints.

GEORGE:

Emily, you're just naturally bright, I guess.

EMILY:

I figure that it's just the way a person's born.

GEORGE:

Yeah. But, you see, I want to be a farmer, and my Uncle Luke says whenever I'm ready I can come over and work on his farm and if I'm any good I can just gradually have it.

EMILY:

You mean the house and everything?

Enter MRS. WEBB *with a large bowl and sits on the bench by her trellis.*

GEORGE:

Yeah. Well, thanks . . . I better be getting out to the baseball field. Thanks for the talk, Emily.—Good afternoon, Mrs. Webb.

MRS. WEBB:

Good afternoon, George.

GEORGE:

So long, Emily.

EMILY:

So long, George.

MRS. WEBB:

Emily, come and help me string these beans for the winter. George Gibbs let himself have a real conversation, didn't he? Why, he's growing up. How old would George be?

EMILY:

I don't know.

MRS. WEBB:

Let's see. He must be almost sixteen.

EMILY:

Mama, I made a speech in class today and I was very good.

MRS. WEBB:

You must recite it to your father at supper. What was it about?

EMILY:

The Louisiana Purchase. It was like silk off a spool. I'm going to make speeches all my life.—Mama, are these big enough?

MRS. WEBB:

Try and get them a little bigger if you can.

EMILY:

Mama, will you answer me a question, serious?

MRS. WEBB:

Seriously, dear—not serious.

EMILY:

Seriously,—will you?

MRS. WEBB:

Of course, I will.

EMILY:

Mama, am I good looking?

MRS. WEBB:

Yes, of course you are. All my children have got good features; I'd be ashamed if they hadn't.

EMILY:

Oh, Mama, that's not what I mean. What I mean is: am I *pretty*?

MRS. WEBB:

I've already told you, yes. Now that's enough of that. You have a nice young pretty face. I never heard of such foolishness.

EMILY:

Oh, Mama, you never tell us the truth about anything.

MRS. WEBB:

I *am* telling you the truth.

EMILY:

Mama, were *you* pretty?

MRS. WEBB:

Yes, I was, if I do say it. I was the prettiest girl in town next to Mamie Cartwright.

EMILY:

But, Mama, you've got to say *some*thing about me. Am I pretty enough . . . to get anybody . . . to get people interested in me?

MRS. WEBB:

Emily, you make me tired. Now stop it. You're pretty enough for all normal purposes.—Come along now and bring that bowl with you.

EMILY:

Oh, Mama, you're no help at all.

STAGE MANAGER:

Thank you. Thank you! That'll do. We'll have to interrupt again here. Thank you, Mrs. Webb; thank you, Emily.

MRS. WEBB *and* EMILY *withdraw.*

There are some more things we want to explore about this town.

He comes to the center of the stage. During the following speech the lights gradually dim to darkness, leaving only a spot on him.

I think this is a good time to tell you that the Cartwright interests have just begun building a new bank in Grover's Corners—

had to go to Vermont for the marble, sorry to say. And they've asked a friend of mine what they should put in the cornerstone for people to dig up . . . a thousand years from now. . . . Of course, they've put in a copy of the *New York Times* and a copy of Mr. Webb's *Sentinel.* . . . We're kind of interested in this because some scientific fellas have found a way of painting all that reading matter with a glue—a silicate glue—that'll make it keep a thousand—two thousand years.

We're putting in a Bible . . . and the Constitution of the United States—and a copy of William Shakespeare's plays. What do you say, folks? What do you think?

Y'know—Babylon once had two million people in it, and all we know about 'em is the names of the kings and some copies of wheat contracts . . . and contracts for the sale of slaves. Yet every night all those families sat down to supper, and the father came home from his work, and the smoke went up the chimney,—same as here. And even in Greece and Rome, all we know about the *real* life of the people is what we can piece together out of the joking poems and the comedies they wrote for the theatre back then.

So I'm going to have a copy of this play put in the cornerstone and the people a thousand years from now'll know a few simple facts about us—more than the Treaty of Versailles and the Lindbergh flight.

See what I mean?

So—people a thousand years from now—this is the way we were in the provinces north of New York at the beginning of the twentieth century.—This is the way we were: in our growing up and in our marrying and in our living and in our dying.

A choir partially concealed in the orchestra pit has begun singing "Blessed Be the Tie That Binds."

SIMON STIMSON *stands directing them.*

Two ladders have been pushed onto the stage; they serve as indication of the second story in the Gibbs and Webb houses. GEORGE *and* EMILY *mount them, and apply themselves to their schoolwork.*

DR. GIBBS *has entered and is seated in his kitchen reading.*

Well!—good deal of time's gone by. It's evening.

You can hear choir practice going on in the Congregational Church.

The children are at home doing their schoolwork.

The day's running down like a tired clock.

SIMON STIMSON:

Now look here, everybody. Music come into the world to give pleasure.—Softer! Softer! Get it out of your heads that music's only good when it's loud. You leave loudness to the Methodists. You couldn't beat 'em, even if you wanted to. Now again. Tenors!

GEORGE:

Hssst! Emily!

EMILY:

Hello.

GEORGE:

Hello!

EMILY:

I can't work at all. The moonlight's so *terrible*.

GEORGE:

Emily, did you get the third problem?

EMILY:

Which?

GEORGE:

The *third*?

EMILY:

Why, yes, George—that's the easiest of them all.

GEORGE:

I don't see it. Emily, can you give me a hint?

EMILY:

I'll tell you one thing: the answer's in yards.

GEORGE:

!!! In yards? How do you mean?

EMILY:

In *square* yards.

GEORGE:

Oh . . . in square yards.

EMILY:

Yes, George, don't you see?

GEORGE:

Yeah.

EMILY:

In square yards of *wallpaper*.

GEORGE:

Wallpaper,—oh, I see. Thanks a lot, Emily.

EMILY:

You're welcome. My, isn't the moonlight *terrible*? And choir practice going on.—I think if you hold your breath you can hear the train all the way to Contoocook. Hear it?

GEORGE:

M-m-m—What do you know!

EMILY:

Well, I guess I better go back and try to work.

GEORGE:

Good night, Emily. And thanks.

EMILY:

Good night, George.

SIMON STIMSON:

Before I forget it: how many of you will be able to come in Tuesday afternoon and sing at Fred Hersey's wedding?—show your hands. That'll be fine; that'll be right nice. We'll do the same music we did for Jane Trowbridge's last month.

—Now we'll do: "Art Thou Weary; Art Thou Languid?" It's a question, ladies and gentlemen, make it talk. Ready.

DR. GIBBS:

Oh, George, can you come down a minute?

GEORGE:

Yes, Pa.

He descends the ladder.

DR. GIBBS:

Make yourself comfortable, George; I'll only keep you a minute. George, how old are you?

GEORGE:

I? I'm sixteen, almost seventeen.

DR. GIBBS:

What do you want to do after school's over?

GEORGE:

Why, you know, Pa. I want to be a farmer on Uncle Luke's farm.

DR. GIBBS:

You'll be willing, will you, to get up early and milk and feed the stock . . . and you'll be able to hoe and hay all day?

GEORGE:

Sure, I will. What are you . . . what do you mean, Pa?

DR. GIBBS:

Well, George, while I was in my office today I heard a funny sound . . . and what do you think it was? It was your mother chopping wood. There you see your mother—getting up early; cooking meals all day long; washing and ironing;—and still she has to go out in the back yard and chop wood. I suppose she just got tired of asking you. She just gave up and decided it was easier to do it herself. And you eat her meals, and put on the clothes she keeps nice for you, and you run off and play baseball,—like she's some hired girl we keep around the house but that we don't like very much. Well, I knew all I had to do was call your attention to it. Here's a handkerchief, son. George,

I've decided to raise your spending money twenty-five cents a week. Not, of course, for chopping wood for your mother, because that's a present you give her, but because you're getting older—and I imagine there are lots of things you must find to do with it.

GEORGE:
Thanks, Pa.

DR. GIBBS:
Let's see—tomorrow's your payday. You can count on it—Hmm. Probably Rebecca'll feel she ought to have some more too. Wonder what could have happened to your mother. Choir practice never was as late as this before.

GEORGE:
It's only half past eight, Pa.

DR. GIBBS:
I don't know why she's in that old choir. She hasn't any more voice than an old crow. . . . Traipsin' around the streets at this hour of the night . . . Just about time you retired, don't you think?

GEORGE:
Yes, Pa.

GEORGE *mounts to his place on the ladder.*

Laughter and good nights can be heard on stage left and presently MRS. GIBBS, MRS. SOAMES *and* MRS. WEBB *come down Main Street. When they arrive at the corner of the stage they stop.*

MRS. SOAMES:
Good night, Martha. Good night, Mr. Foster.

MRS. WEBB:

I'll tell Mr. Webb; I *know* he'll want to put it in the paper.

MRS. GIBBS:

My, it's late!

MRS. SOAMES:

Good night, Irma.

MRS. GIBBS:

Real nice choir practice, wa'n't it? Myrtle Webb! Look at that moon, will you! Tsk-tsk-tsk. Potato weather, for sure.

They are silent a moment, gazing up at the moon.

MRS. SOAMES:

Naturally I didn't want to say a word about it in front of those others, but now we're alone—really, it's the worst scandal that ever was in this town!

MRS. GIBBS:

What?

MRS. SOAMES:

Simon Stimson!

MRS. GIBBS:

Now, Louella!

MRS. SOAMES:

But, Julia! To have the organist of a church *drink* and *drunk* year after year. You know he was drunk tonight.

MRS. GIBBS:

Now, Louella! We all know about Mr. Stimson, and we all know about the troubles he's been through, and Dr. Ferguson knows too, and if Dr. Ferguson keeps him on there in his job the only thing the rest of us can do is just not to notice it.

MRS. SOAMES:

Not to notice it! But it's getting worse.

MRS. WEBB:

No, it isn't, Louella. It's getting better. I've been in that choir twice as long as you have. It doesn't happen anywhere near so often. . . . My, I hate to go to bed on a night like this.—I better hurry. Those children'll be sitting up till all hours. Good night, Louella.

They all exchange good nights. She hurries downstage, enters her house and disappears.

MRS. GIBBS:

Can you get home safe, Louella?

MRS. SOAMES:

It's as bright as day. I can see Mr. Soames scowling at the window now. You'd think we'd been to a dance the way the menfolk carry on.

More good nights. MRS. GIBBS *arrives at her home and passes through the trellis into the kitchen.*

MRS. GIBBS:

Well, we had a real good time.

DR. GIBBS:

You're late enough.

MRS. GIBBS:

Why, Frank, it ain't any later 'n usual.

DR. GIBBS:

And you stopping at the corner to gossip with a lot of hens.

MRS. GIBBS:

Now, Frank, don't be grouchy. Come out and smell the heliotrope in the moonlight.

They stroll out arm in arm along the footlights.

Isn't that wonderful? What did you do all the time I was away?

DR. GIBBS:

Oh, I read—as usual. What were the girls gossiping about tonight?

MRS. GIBBS:

Well, believe me, Frank—there is something to gossip about.

DR. GIBBS:

Hmm! Simon Stimson far gone, was he?

MRS. GIBBS:

Worst I've ever seen him. How'll that end, Frank? Dr. Ferguson can't forgive him forever.

DR. GIBBS:

I guess I know more about Simon Stimson's affairs than anybody in this town. Some people ain't made for small-town life. I don't know how that'll end; but there's nothing we can do but just leave it alone. Come, get in.

MRS. GIBBS:

No, not yet . . . Frank, I'm worried about you.

DR. GIBBS:

What are you worried about?

MRS. GIBBS:

I think it's my duty to make plans for you to get a real rest and change. And if I get that legacy, well, I'm going to insist on it.

DR. GIBBS:

Now, Julia, there's no sense in going over that again.

MRS. GIBBS:

Frank, you're just *unreasonable!*

DR. GIBBS:

Starting into the house.

Come on, Julia, it's getting late. First thing you know you'll catch cold. I gave George a piece of my mind tonight. I reckon you'll have your wood chopped for a while anyway. No, no, start getting upstairs.

MRS. GIBBS:

Oh, dear. There's always so many things to pick up, seems like. You know, Frank, Mrs. Fairchild always locks her front door every night. All those people up that part of town do.

DR. GIBBS:

Blowing out the lamp.

They're all getting citified, that's the trouble with them. They haven't got nothing fit to burgle and everybody knows it.

They disappear.

REBECCA *climbs up the ladder beside* GEORGE.

GEORGE:

Get out, Rebecca. There's only room for one at this window. You're always spoiling everything.

REBECCA:

Well, let me look just a minute.

GEORGE:
Use your own window.

REBECCA:
I did, but there's no moon there. . . . George, do you know what I think, do you? I think maybe the moon's getting nearer and nearer and there'll be a big 'splosion.

GEORGE:
Rebecca, you don't know anything. If the moon were getting nearer, the guys that sit up all night with telescopes would see it first and they'd tell about it, and it'd be in all the newspapers.

REBECCA:
George, is the moon shining on South America, Canada and half the whole world?

GEORGE:
Well—prob'ly is.

The STAGE MANAGER *strolls on.*

Pause. The sound of crickets is heard.

STAGE MANAGER:
Nine thirty. Most of the lights are out. No, there's Constable Warren trying a few doors on Main Street. And here comes Editor Webb, after putting his newspaper to bed.

MR. WARREN, *an elderly policeman, comes along Main Street from the right,* MR. WEBB *from the left.*

MR. WEBB:
Good evening, Bill.

CONSTABLE WARREN:
Evenin', Mr. Webb.

MR. WEBB:

Quite a moon!

CONSTABLE WARREN:

Yepp.

MR. WEBB:

All quiet tonight?

CONSTABLE WARREN:

Simon Stimson is rollin' around a little. Just saw his wife movin' out to hunt for him so I looked the other way—there he is now.

> SIMON STIMSON *comes down Main Street from the left, only a trace of unsteadiness in his walk.*

MR. WEBB:

Good evening, Simon . . . Town seems to have settled down for the night pretty well. . . .

> SIMON STIMSON *comes up to him and pauses a moment and stares at him, swaying slightly.*

Good evening . . . Yes, most of the town's settled down for the night, Simon. . . . I guess we better do the same. Can I walk along a ways with you?

> SIMON STIMSON *continues on his way without a word and disappears at the right.*

Good night.

CONSTABLE WARREN:

I don't know how that's goin' to end, Mr. Webb.

MR. WEBB:

Well, he's seen a peck of trouble, one thing after another. . . .

Oh, Bill . . . if you see my boy smoking cigarettes, just give him a word, will you? He thinks a lot of you, Bill.

CONSTABLE WARREN:

I don't think he smokes no cigarettes, Mr. Webb. Leastways, not more'n two or three a year.

MR. WEBB:

Hm . . . I hope not.—Well, good night, Bill.

CONSTABLE WARREN:

Good night, Mr. Webb.

Exit.

MR. WEBB:

Who's that up there? Is that you, Myrtle?

EMILY:

No, it's me, Papa.

MR. WEBB:

Why aren't you in bed?

EMILY:

I don't know. I just can't sleep yet, Papa. The moonlight's so *won*-derful. And the smell of Mrs. Gibbs' heliotrope. Can you smell it?

MR. WEBB:

Hm . . . Yes. Haven't any troubles on your mind, have you, Emily?

EMILY:

Troubles, Papa? *No.*

MR. WEBB:

Well, enjoy yourself, but don't let your mother catch you. Good night, Emily.

EMILY:

Good night, Papa.

MR. WEBB *crosses into the house, whistling "Blessed Be the Tie That Binds" and disappears.*

REBECCA:

I never told you about that letter Jane Crofut got from her minister when she was sick. He wrote Jane a letter and on the envelope the address was like this: It said: Jane Crofut; The Crofut Farm; Grover's Corners; Sutton County; New Hampshire; United States of America.

GEORGE:

What's funny about that?

REBECCA:

But listen, it's not finished: the United States of America; Continent of North America; Western Hemisphere; the Earth; the Solar System; the Universe; the Mind of God—that's what it said on the envelope.

GEORGE:

What do you know!

REBECCA:

And the postman brought it just the same.

GEORGE:

What do you know!

STAGE MANAGER:

That's the end of the First Act, friends. You can go and smoke now, those that smoke.

—⚯—

Act II

The tables and chairs of the two kitchens are still on the stage.
The ladders and the small bench have been withdrawn.
The STAGE MANAGER *has been at his accustomed place*
watching the audience return to its seats.

STAGE MANAGER:

Three years have gone by.

Yes, the sun's come up over a thousand times.

Summers and winters have cracked the mountains a little bit
more and the rains have brought down some of the dirt.

Some babies that weren't even born before have begun talking
regular sentences already; and a number of people who thought
they were right young and spry have noticed that they can't
bound up a flight of stairs like they used to, without their heart
fluttering a little.

All that can happen in a thousand days.

Nature's been pushing and contriving in other ways, too: a
number of young people fell in love and got married.

Yes, the mountain got bit away a few fractions of an inch; millions of gallons of water went by the mill; and here and there a new home was set up under a roof.

Almost everybody in the world gets married,—you know what I mean? In our town there aren't hardly any exceptions. Most everybody in the world climbs into their graves married.

The First Act was called the Daily Life. This act is called Love and Marriage. There's another act coming after this: I reckon you can guess what that's about.

So:

It's three years later. It's 1904.

It's July 7th, just after High School Commencement.

That's the time most of our young people jump up and get married.

Soon as they've passed their last examinations in solid geometry and Cicero's Orations, looks like they suddenly feel themselves fit to be married.

It's early morning. Only this time it's been raining. It's been pouring and thundering.

Mrs. Gibbs' garden, and Mrs. Webb's here: drenched.

All those bean poles and pea vines: drenched.

All yesterday over there on Main Street, the rain looked like curtains being blown along.

Hm . . . it may begin again any minute.

There! You can hear the 5:45 for Boston.

MRS. GIBBS *and* MRS. WEBB *enter their kitchen and start the day as in the First Act.*

And there's Mrs. Gibbs and Mrs. Webb come down to make breakfast, just as though it were an ordinary day. I don't have to point out to the women in my audience that those ladies they see before them, both of those ladies cooked three meals a day—one of 'em for twenty years, the other for forty—and no summer vacation. They brought up two children apiece, washed, cleaned the house,—and *never a nervous breakdown.*

It's like what one of those Middle West poets said: You've got to love life to have life, and you've got to have life to love life. . . . It's what they call a vicious circle.

HOWIE NEWSOME:

Off stage left.

Giddap, Bessie!

STAGE MANAGER:

Here comes Howie Newsome delivering the milk. And there's Si Crowell delivering the papers like his brother before him.

SI CROWELL *has entered hurling imaginary newspapers into doorways;* HOWIE NEWSOME *has come along Main Street with Bessie.*

SI CROWELL:

Morning, Howie.

HOWIE NEWSOME:

Morning, Si.—Anything in the papers I ought to know?

SI CROWELL:

Nothing much, except we're losing about the best baseball pitcher Grover's Corners ever had—George Gibbs.

HOWIE NEWSOME:

Reckon he is.

SI CROWELL:

He could hit and run bases, too.

HOWIE NEWSOME:

Yep. Mighty fine ball player.—Whoa! Bessie! I guess I can stop and talk if I've a mind to!

SI CROWELL:

I don't see how he could give up a thing like that just to get married. Would you, Howie?

HOWIE NEWSOME:

Can't tell, Si. Never had no talent that way.

CONSTABLE WARREN *enters. They exchange good mornings.*

You're up early, Bill.

CONSTABLE WARREN:

Seein' if there's anything I can do to prevent a flood. River's been risin' all night.

HOWIE NEWSOME:

Si Crowell's all worked up here about George Gibbs' retiring from baseball.

CONSTABLE WARREN:

Yes, sir; that's the way it goes. Back in '84 we had a player, Si—even George Gibbs couldn't touch him. Name of Hank Todd.

Went down to Maine and become a parson. Wonderful ball player.—Howie, how does the weather look to you?

HOWIE NEWSOME:

Oh, 'tain't bad. Think maybe it'll clear up for good.

CONSTABLE WARREN *and* SI CROWELL *continue on their way.*

HOWIE NEWSOME *brings the milk first to Mrs. Gibbs' house. She meets him by the trellis.*

MRS. GIBBS:

Good morning, Howie. Do you think it's going to rain again?

HOWIE NEWSOME:

Morning, Mrs. Gibbs. It rained so heavy, I think maybe it'll clear up.

MRS. GIBBS:

Certainly hope it will.

HOWIE NEWSOME:

How much did you want today?

MRS. GIBBS:

I'm going to have a houseful of relations, Howie. Looks to me like I'll need three-a-milk and two-a-cream.

HOWIE NEWSOME:

My wife says to tell you we both hope they'll be very happy, Mrs. Gibbs. Know they *will*.

MRS. GIBBS:

Thanks a lot, Howie. Tell your wife I hope she gits there to the wedding.

HOWIE NEWSOME:

Yes, she'll be there; she'll be there if she kin.

HOWIE NEWSOME *crosses to Mrs. Webb's house.*

Morning, Mrs. Webb.

MRS. WEBB:

Oh, good morning, Mr. Newsome. I told you four quarts of milk, but I hope you can spare me another.

HOWIE NEWSOME:

Yes'm . . . and the two of cream.

MRS. WEBB:

Will it start raining again, Mr. Newsome?

HOWIE NEWSOME:

Well. Just sayin' to Mrs. Gibbs as how it may lighten up. Mrs. Newsome told me to tell you as how we hope they'll both be very happy, Mrs. Webb. Know they *will.*

MRS. WEBB:

Thank you, and thank Mrs. Newsome and we're counting on seeing you at the wedding.

HOWIE NEWSOME:

Yes, Mrs. Webb. We hope to git there. Couldn't miss that. Come on, Bessie.

Exit HOWIE NEWSOME.

DR. GIBBS *descends in shirt sleeves, and sits down at his breakfast table.*

DR. GIBBS:

Well, Ma, the day has come. You're losin' one of your chicks.

MRS. GIBBS:

Frank Gibbs, don't you say another word. I feel like crying every minute. Sit down and drink your coffee.

DR. GIBBS:

The groom's up shaving himself—only there ain't an awful lot to shave. Whistling and singing, like he's glad to leave us.—Every now and then he says "I do" to the mirror, but it don't sound convincing to me.

MRS. GIBBS:

I declare, Frank, I don't know how he'll get along. I've arranged his clothes and seen to it he's put warm things on,—Frank! they're too *young*. Emily won't think of such things. He'll catch his death of cold within a week.

DR. GIBBS:

I was remembering my wedding morning, Julia.

MRS. GIBBS:

Now don't start that, Frank Gibbs.

DR. GIBBS:

I was the scaredest young fella in the State of New Hampshire. I thought I'd make a mistake for sure. And when I saw you comin' down that aisle I thought you were the prettiest girl I'd ever seen, but the only trouble was that I'd never seen you before. There I was in the Congregational Church marryin' a total stranger.

MRS. GIBBS:

And how do you think I felt!—Frank, weddings are perfectly awful things. Farces,—that's what they are!

She puts a plate before him.

Here, I've made something for you.

DR. GIBBS:

Why, Julia Hersey—French toast!

MRS. GIBBS:

'Tain't hard to make and I had to do *some*thing.

Pause. DR. GIBBS *pours on the syrup.*

DR. GIBBS:

How'd you sleep last night, Julia?

MRS. GIBBS:

Well, I heard a lot of the hours struck off.

DR. GIBBS:

Ye-e-s! I get a shock every time I think of George setting out to be a family man—that great gangling thing!—I tell you Julia, there's nothing so terrifying in the world as a *son*. The relation of father and son is the darndest, awkwardest—

MRS. GIBBS:

Well, mother and daughter's no picnic, let me tell you.

DR. GIBBS:

They'll have a lot of troubles, I suppose, but that's none of our business. Everybody has a right to their own troubles.

MRS. GIBBS:

At the table, drinking her coffee, meditatively.

Yes . . . people are meant to go through life two by two. 'Tain't natural to be lonesome.

Pause. DR. GIBBS *starts laughing.*

DR. GIBBS:

Julia, do you know one of the things I was scared of when I married you?

MRS. GIBBS:

Oh, go along with you!

DR. GIBBS:

I was afraid we wouldn't have material for conversation more'n'd last us a few weeks.

Both laugh.

I was afraid we'd run out and eat our meals in silence, that's a fact.—Well, you and I been conversing for twenty years now without any noticeable barren spells.

MRS. GIBBS:

Well,—good weather, bad weather—'tain't very choice, but I always find something to say.

She goes to the foot of the stairs.

Did you hear Rebecca stirring around upstairs?

DR. GIBBS:

No. Only day of the year Rebecca hasn't been managing everybody's business up there. She's hiding in her room.—I got the impression she's crying.

MRS. GIBBS:

Lord's sakes!—This has got to stop.—Rebecca! Rebecca! Come and get your breakfast.

GEORGE *comes rattling down the stairs, very brisk.*

GEORGE:

Good morning, everybody. Only five more hours to live.

Makes the gesture of cutting his throat, and a loud "k-k-k," and starts through the trellis.

MRS. GIBBS:

George Gibbs, where are you going?

GEORGE:

Just stepping across the grass to see my girl.

MRS. GIBBS:

Now, George! You put on your overshoes. It's raining torrents. You don't go out of this house without you're prepared for it.

GEORGE:

Aw, Ma. It's just a *step!*

MRS. GIBBS:

George! You'll catch your death of cold and cough all through the service.

DR. GIBBS:

George, do as your mother tells you!

DR. GIBBS *goes upstairs.*

GEORGE *returns reluctantly to the kitchen and pantomimes putting on overshoes.*

MRS. GIBBS:

From tomorrow on you can kill yourself in all weathers, but while you're in my house you'll live wisely, thank you.— Maybe Mrs. Webb isn't used to callers at seven in the morning.—Here, take a cup of coffee first.

GEORGE:

Be back in a minute.

He crosses the stage, leaping over the puddles.

Good morning, Mother Webb.

MRS. WEBB:

Goodness! You frightened me!—Now, George, you can come in a minute out of the wet, but you know I can't ask you in.

GEORGE:

Why not—?

MRS. WEBB:

George, you know 's well as I do: the groom can't see his bride on his wedding day, not until he sees her in church.

GEORGE:

Aw!—that's just a superstition.—Good morning, Mr. Webb.

Enter MR. WEBB.

MR. WEBB:

Good morning, George.

GEORGE:

Mr. Webb, you don't believe in that superstition, do you?

MR. WEBB:

There's a lot of common sense in some superstitions, George.

He sits at the table, facing right.

MRS. WEBB:

Millions have folla'd it, George, and you don't want to be the first to fly in the face of custom.

GEORGE:

How is Emily?

MRS. WEBB:

She hasn't waked up yet. I haven't heard a sound out of her.

GEORGE:

Emily's *asleep!!!*

MRS. WEBB:

No wonder! We were up 'til all hours, sewing and packing. Now I'll tell you what I'll do; you set down here a minute with Mr. Webb and drink this cup of coffee; and I'll go upstairs and see she doesn't come down and surprise you. There's some bacon, too; but don't be long about it.

Exit MRS. WEBB.

Embarrassed silence.

MR. WEBB *dunks doughnuts in his coffee.*

More silence.

MR. WEBB:

Suddenly and loudly.

Well, George, how are you?

GEORGE:

Startled, choking over his coffee.

Oh, fine, I'm fine.

Pause.

Mr. Webb, what sense could there be in a superstition like that?

MR. WEBB:

Well, you see,—on her wedding morning a girl's head's apt to be full of . . . clothes and one thing and another. Don't you think that's probably it?

GEORGE:

Ye-e-s. I never thought of that.

MR. WEBB:

A girl's apt to be a mite nervous on her wedding day.

Pause.

GEORGE:

I wish a fellow could get married without all that marching up and down.

MR. WEBB:

Every man that's ever lived has felt that way about it, George; but it hasn't been any use. It's the womenfolk who've built up weddings, my boy. For a while now the women have it all their own. A man looks pretty small at a wedding, George. All those good women standing shoulder to shoulder making sure that the knot's tied in a mighty public way.

GEORGE:

But . . . you *believe* in it, don't you, Mr. Webb?

MR. WEBB:

With alacrity.

Oh, yes; *oh, yes.* Don't you misunderstand me, my boy. Marriage is a wonderful thing,—wonderful thing. And don't you forget that, George.

GEORGE:

No, sir.—Mr. Webb, how old were you when you got married?

MR. WEBB:

Well, you see: I'd been to college and I'd taken a little time to get settled. But Mrs. Webb—she wasn't much older than what Emily is. Oh, age hasn't much to do with it, George,—not compared with . . . uh . . . other things.

GEORGE:

What were you going to say, Mr. Webb?

MR. WEBB:

Oh, I don't know.—Was I going to say something?

Pause.

George, I was thinking the other night of some advice my father gave me when I got married. Charles, he said, Charles, start out early showing who's boss, he said. Best thing to do is to give an order, even if it don't make sense; just so she'll learn to obey. And he said: if anything about your wife irritates you—her conversation, or anything—just get up and leave the house. That'll make it clear to her, he said. And, oh, yes! he said never, *never* let your wife know how much money you have, never.

GEORGE:

Well, Mr. Webb . . . I don't think I could . . .

MR. WEBB:

So I took the opposite of my father's advice and I've been happy ever since. And let that be a lesson to you, George, never to ask advice on personal matters.—George, are you going to raise chickens on your farm?

GEORGE:

What?

MR. WEBB:

Are you going to raise chickens on your farm?

GEORGE:

Uncle Luke's never been much interested, but I thought—

MR. WEBB:

A book came into my office the other day, George, on the Philo System of raising chickens. I want you to read it. I'm thinking of beginning in a small way in the back yard, and I'm going to put an incubator in the cellar—

Enter MRS. WEBB.

MRS. WEBB:

Charles, are you talking about that old incubator again? I thought you two'd be talking about things worth while.

MR. WEBB:

Bitingly.

Well, Myrtle, if you want to give the boy some good advice, I'll go upstairs and leave you alone with him.

MRS. WEBB:

Pulling GEORGE *up.*

George, Emily's got to come downstairs and eat her breakfast. She sends you her love but she doesn't want to lay eyes on you. Good-by.

GEORGE:

Good-by.

GEORGE *crosses the stage to his own home, bewildered and crestfallen. He slowly dodges a puddle and disappears into his house.*

MR. WEBB:

Myrtle, I guess you don't know about that older superstition.

MRS. WEBB:

What do you mean, Charles?

MR. WEBB:

Since the cave men: no bridegroom should see his father-in-law on the day of the wedding, or near it. Now remember that.

Both leave the stage.

STAGE MANAGER:

Thank you very much, Mr. and Mrs. Webb.—Now I have to interrupt again here. You see, we want to know how all this began—this wedding, this plan to spend a lifetime together. I'm awfully interested in how big things like that begin.

You know how it is: you're twenty-one or twenty-two and you make some decisions; then whisssh! you're seventy: you've been a lawyer for fifty years, and that white-haired lady at your side has eaten over fifty thousand meals with you.

How do such things begin?

George and Emily are going to show you now the conversation they had when they first knew that . . . that . . . as the saying goes . . . they were meant for one another.

But before they do it I want you to try and remember what it was like to have been very young.

And particularly the days when you were first in love; when you were like a person sleepwalking, and you didn't quite see the street you were in, and didn't quite hear everything that was said to you.

You're just a little bit crazy. Will you remember that, please?

Now they'll be coming out of high school at three o'clock. George has just been elected President of the Junior Class, and as it's June, that means he'll be President of the Senior Class all next year. And Emily's just been elected Secretary and Treasurer.

I don't have to tell you how important that is.

He places a board across the backs of two chairs, which he takes from those at the Gibbs family's table. He brings two high stools from the wings and places them behind the board. Persons sitting on the stools will be facing the audience. This is the counter of Mr. Morgan's drugstore. The sounds of young people's voices are heard off left.

Yepp,—there they are coming down Main Street now.

EMILY, *carrying an armful of—imaginary—schoolbooks, comes along Main Street from the left.*

EMILY:
I can't, Louise. I've got to go home. Good-by. Oh, Ernestine! Ernestine! Can you come over tonight and do Latin? Isn't that Cicero the worst thing—! Tell your mother you *have* to. G'by. G'by, Helen. G'by, Fred.

GEORGE, *also carrying books, catches up with her.*

GEORGE:

Can I carry your books home for you, Emily?

EMILY:

Coolly.

Why . . . uh . . . Thank you. It isn't far.

She gives them to him.

GEORGE:

Excuse me a minute, Emily.—Say, Bob, if I'm a little late, start practice anyway. And give Herb some long high ones.

EMILY:

Good-by, Lizzy.

GEORGE:

Good-by, Lizzy.—I'm awfully glad you were elected, too, Emily.

EMILY:

Thank you.

They have been standing on Main Street, almost against the back wall. They take the first steps toward the audience when GEORGE *stops and says:*

GEORGE:

Emily, why are you mad at me?

EMILY:

I'm not mad at you.

GEORGE:

You've been treating me so funny lately.

EMILY:

Well, since you ask me, I might as well say it right out, George,—

She catches sight of a teacher passing.

Good-by, Miss Corcoran.

GEORGE:

Good-by, Miss Corcoran.—Wha—what is it?

EMILY:

Not scoldingly; finding it difficult to say.

I don't like the whole change that's come over you in the last year. I'm sorry if that hurts your feelings, but I've got to— tell the truth and shame the devil.

GEORGE:

A *change?*—Wha—what do you mean?

EMILY:

Well, up to a year ago I used to like you a lot. And I used to watch you as you did everything . . . because we'd been friends so long . . . and then you began spending all your time at *baseball* . . . and you never stopped to speak to anybody any more. Not even to your own family you didn't . . . and, George, it's a fact, you've got awful conceited and stuck-up, and all the girls say so. They may not say so to your face, but that's what they say about you behind your back, and it hurts me to hear them say it, but I've got to agree with them a little. I'm sorry if it hurts your feelings . . . but I can't be sorry I said it.

GEORGE:

I . . . I'm glad you said it, Emily. I never thought that such a thing was happening to me. I guess it's hard for a fella not to have faults creep into his character.

They take a step or two in silence, then stand still in misery.

EMILY:

I always expect a man to be perfect and I think he should be.

GEORGE:

Oh . . . I don't think it's possible to be perfect, Emily.

EMILY:

Well, my *father* is, and as far as I can see *your* father is. There's no reason on earth why you shouldn't be, too.

GEORGE:

Well, I feel it's the other way round. That men aren't naturally good; but girls are.

EMILY:

Well, you might as well know right now that I'm not perfect. It's not as easy for a girl to be perfect as a man, because we girls are more—more—nervous.—Now I'm sorry I said all that about you. I don't know what made me say it.

GEORGE:

Emily,—

EMILY:

Now I can see it's not the truth at all. And I suddenly feel that it isn't important, anyway.

GEORGE:

Emily . . . would you like an ice-cream soda, or something, before you go home?

EMILY:

Well, thank you . . . I would.

They advance toward the audience and make an abrupt right turn, opening the door of Morgan's drugstore. Under strong emotion, EMILY *keeps her face down.* GEORGE *speaks to some passers-by.*

GEORGE:

Hello, Stew,—how are you?—Good afternoon, Mrs. Slocum.

The STAGE MANAGER, *wearing spectacles and assuming the role of Mr. Morgan, enters abruptly from the right and stands between the audience and the counter of his soda fountain.*

STAGE MANAGER:

Hello, George. Hello, Emily.—What'll you have?—Why, Emily Webb,—what you been crying about?

GEORGE:

He gropes for an explanation.

She . . . she just got an awful scare, Mr. Morgan. She almost got run over by that hardware-store wagon. Everybody says that Tom Huckins drives like a crazy man.

STAGE MANAGER:

Drawing a drink of water.

Well, now! You take a drink of water, Emily. You look all shook up. I tell you, you've got to look both ways before you cross Main Street these days. Gets worse every year.—What'll you have?

EMILY:

I'll have a strawberry phosphate, thank you, Mr. Morgan.

GEORGE:

No, no, Emily. Have an ice-cream soda with me. Two strawberry ice-cream sodas, Mr. Morgan.

STAGE MANAGER:

Working the faucets.

Two strawberry ice-cream sodas, yes sir. Yes, sir. There are a hundred and twenty-five horses in Grover's Corners this minute I'm talking to you. State Inspector was in here yesterday. And now they're bringing in these auto-mo-biles, the best thing to do is to just stay home. Why, I can remember when a dog could go to sleep all day in the middle of Main Street and nothing come along to disturb him.

He sets the imaginary glasses before them.

There they are. Enjoy 'em.

He sees a customer, right.

Yes, Mrs. Ellis. What can I do for you?

He goes out right.

EMILY:

They're so expensive.

GEORGE:

No, no,—don't you think of that. We're celebrating our election. And then do you know what else I'm celebrating?

EMILY:

N-no.

GEORGE:

I'm celebrating because I've got a friend who tells me all the things that ought to be told me.

EMILY:

George, *please* don't think of that. I don't know why I said it. It's not true. You're—

GEORGE:

No, Emily, you stick to it. I'm glad you spoke to me like you did. But you'll *see:* I'm going to change so quick—you bet I'm going to change. And, Emily, I want to ask you a favor.

EMILY:

What?

GEORGE:

Emily, if I go away to State Agriculture College next year, will you write me a letter once in a while?

EMILY:

I certainly will. I certainly will, George . . .

Pause. They start sipping the sodas through the straws.

It certainly seems like being away three years you'd get out of touch with things. Maybe letters from Grover's Corners wouldn't be so interesting after a while. Grover's Corners isn't a very important place when you think of all—New Hampshire; but I think it's a very nice town.

GEORGE:

The day wouldn't come when I wouldn't want to know everything that's happening here. I know *that's* true, Emily.

EMILY:

Well, I'll try to make my letters interesting.

Pause.

GEORGE:

Y'know. Emily, whenever I meet a farmer I ask him if he thinks it's important to go to Agriculture School to be a good farmer.

EMILY:

Why, George—

GEORGE:

Yeah, and some of them say that it's even a waste of time. You can get all those things, anyway, out of the pamphlets the government sends out. And Uncle Luke's getting old,—he's about ready for me to start in taking over his farm tomorrow, if I could.

EMILY:

My!

GEORGE:

And, like you say, being gone all that time . . . in other places and meeting other people . . . Gosh, if anything like that can happen I don't want to go away. I guess new people aren't any better than old ones. I'll bet they almost never are. Emily . . . I feel that you're as good a friend as I've got. I don't need to go and meet the people in other towns.

EMILY:

But, George, maybe it's very important for you to go and learn all that about—cattle judging and soils and those things. . . . Of course, I don't know.

GEORGE:

After a pause, very seriously.

Emily, I'm going to make up my mind right now. I won't go. I'll tell Pa about it tonight.

EMILY:

Why, George, I don't see why you have to decide right now. It's a whole year away.

GEORGE:

Emily, I'm glad you spoke to me about that . . . that fault in my character. What you said was right; but there was *one* thing wrong in it, and that was when you said that for a year I wasn't noticing people, and . . . you, for instance. Why, you say you were watching me when I did everything . . . I was doing the same about you all the time. Why, sure,—I always thought about you as one of the chief people I thought about. I always made sure where you were sitting on the bleachers, and who you were with, and for three days now I've been trying to walk home with you; but something's always got in the way. Yesterday I was standing over against the wall waiting for you, and you walked home with *Miss Corcoran*.

EMILY:

George! . . . Life's awful funny! How could I have known that? Why, I thought—

GEORGE:

Listen, Emily, I'm going to tell you why I'm not going to Agriculture School. I think that once you've found a person that you're very fond of . . . I mean a person who's fond of you, too, and likes you enough to be interested in your character . . .

Well, I think that's just as important as college is, and even
more so. That's what I think.

EMILY:

I think it's awfully important, too.

GEORGE:

Emily.

EMILY:

Y-yes, George.

GEORGE:

Emily, if I *do* improve and make a big change . . . would you
be . . . I mean: *could* you be . . .

EMILY:

I . . . I am now; I always have been.

GEORGE:

Pause.

So I guess this is an important talk we've been having.

EMILY:

Yes . . . yes.

GEORGE:

Takes a deep breath and straightens his back.

Wait just a minute and I'll walk you home.

With mounting alarm he digs into his pockets for the money.

The STAGE MANAGER *enters, right.*

GEORGE, *deeply embarrassed, but direct, says to him:*

Mr. Morgan, I'll have to go home and get the money to pay you for this. It'll only take me a minute.

STAGE MANAGER:

Pretending to be affronted.

What's that? George Gibbs, do you mean to tell me—!

GEORGE:

Yes, but I had reasons, Mr. Morgan.—Look, here's my gold watch to keep until I come back with the money.

STAGE MANAGER:

That's all right. Keep your watch. I'll trust you.

GEORGE:

I'll be back in five minutes.

STAGE MANAGER:

I'll trust you ten years, George,—not a day over.—Got all over your shock, Emily?

EMILY:

Yes, thank you, Mr. Morgan. It was nothing.

GEORGE:

Taking up the books from the counter.

I'm ready.

They walk in grave silence across the stage and pass through the trellis at the Webbs' back door and disappear.

The STAGE MANAGER *watches them go out, then turns to the audience, removing his spectacles.*

STAGE MANAGER:

Well,—

He claps his hands as a signal.

Now we're ready to get on with the wedding.

He stands waiting while the set is prepared for the next scene.

STAGEHANDS *remove the chairs, tables and trellises from the Gibbs and Webb houses.*

They arrange the pews for the church in the center of the stage. The congregation will sit facing the back wall. The aisle of the church starts at the center of the back wall and comes toward the audience.

A small platform is placed against the back wall on which the STAGE MANAGER *will stand later, playing the minister.*

The image of a stained-glass window is cast from a lantern slide upon the back wall.

When all is ready the STAGE MANAGER *strolls to the center of the stage, down front, and, musingly, addresses the audience.*

There are a lot of things to be said about a wedding; there are a lot of thoughts that go on during a wedding.

We can't get them all into one wedding, naturally, and especially not into a wedding at Grover's Corners, where they're awfully plain and short.

In this wedding I play the minister. That gives me the right to say a few more things about it.

For a while now, the play gets pretty serious.

Y'see, some churches say that marriage is a sacrament. I don't quite know what that means, but I can guess. Like Mrs. Gibbs said a few minutes ago: People were made to live two-by-two.

This is a good wedding, but people are so put together that even at a good wedding there's a lot of confusion way down deep in people's minds and we thought that that ought to be in our play, too.

The real hero of this scene isn't on the stage at all, and you know who that is. It's like what one of those European fellas said: every child born into the world is nature's attempt to make a perfect human being. Well, we've seen nature pushing and contriving for some time now. We all know that nature's interested in quantity; but I think she's interested in quality, too,—that's why I'm in the ministry.

And don't forget all the other witnesses at this wedding,— the ancestors. Millions of them. Most of them set out to live two-by-two, also. Millions of them.

Well, that's all my sermon. 'Twan't very long, anyway.

The organ starts playing Handel's "Largo."

The congregation streams into the church and sits in silence.

Church bells are heard.

MRS. GIBBS *sits in the front row, the first seat on the aisle, the right section; next to her are* REBECCA *and* DR. GIBBS.

Across the aisle MRS. WEBB, WALLY *and* MR. WEBB. *A small choir takes its place, facing the audience under the stained-glass window.*

MRS. WEBB, *on the way to her place, turns back and speaks to the audience.*

MRS. WEBB:

I don't know why on earth I should be crying. I suppose there's nothing to cry about. It came over me at breakfast this morning; there was Emily eating her breakfast as she's done for seventeen years and now she's going off to eat it in someone else's house. I suppose that's it.

And Emily! She suddenly said: I can't eat another mouthful, and she put her head down on the table and *she* cried.

She starts toward her seat in the church, but turns back and adds:

Oh, I've got to say it: you know, there's something downright cruel about sending our girls out into marriage this way.

I hope some of her girl friends have told her a thing or two. It's cruel, I know, but I couldn't bring myself to say anything. I went into it blind as a bat myself.

In half-amused exasperation.

The whole world's wrong, that's what's the matter.

There they come.

She hurries to her place in the pew.

GEORGE *starts to come down the right aisle of the theatre, through the audience.*

Suddenly THREE MEMBERS *of his baseball team appear by the right proscenium pillar and start whistling and catcalling to him. They are dressed for the ball field.*

THE BASEBALL PLAYERS:

Eh, George, George! Hast—yaow! Look at him, fellas—he looks scared to death. Yaow! George, don't look so innocent, you old geezer. We know what you're thinking. Don't disgrace the team, big boy. Whoo-oo-oo.

STAGE MANAGER:

All right! All right! That'll do. That's enough of that.

Smiling, he pushes them off the stage. They lean back to shout a few more catcalls.

There used to be an awful lot of that kind of thing at weddings in the old days,—Rome, and later. We're more civilized now,—so they say.

The choir starts singing "Love Divine, All Love Excelling—." GEORGE *has reached the stage. He stares at the congregation a moment, then takes a few steps of withdrawal, toward the right proscenium pillar. His mother, from the front row, seems to have felt his confusion. She leaves her seat and comes down the aisle quickly to him.*

MRS. GIBBS:

George! George! What's the matter?

GEORGE:

Ma, I don't want to grow old. Why's everybody pushing me so?

MRS. GIBBS:

Why, George . . . you wanted it.

GEORGE:

No, Ma, listen to me—

MRS. GIBBS:

No, no, George,—you're a man now.

GEORGE:

Listen, Ma,—for the last time I ask you . . . All I want to do is to be a fella—

MRS. GIBBS:

George! If anyone should hear you! Now stop. Why, I'm ashamed of you!

GEORGE:

He comes to himself and looks over the scene.

What? Where's Emily?

MRS. GIBBS:

Relieved.

George! You gave me such a turn.

GEORGE:

Cheer up, Ma. I'm getting married.

MRS. GIBBS:

Let me catch my breath a minute.

GEORGE:

Comforting her.

Now, Ma, you save Thursday nights. Emily and I are coming over to dinner every Thursday night . . . you'll see. Ma, what are you crying for? Come on; we've got to get ready for this.

MRS. GIBBS, *mastering her emotion, fixes his tie and whispers to him.*

In the meantime, EMILY, *in white and wearing her wedding veil, has come through the audience and mounted onto the stage. She too draws back, frightened, when she sees the congregation in the church. The choir begins: "Blessed Be the Tie That Binds."*

EMILY:

I never felt so alone in my whole life. And George over there, looking so . . . ! I *hate* him. I wish I were dead. Papa! Papa!

MR. WEBB:

Leaves his seat in the pews and comes toward her anxiously.

Emily! Emily! Now don't get upset. . . .

EMILY:

But, Papa,—I don't want to get married. . . .

MR. WEBB:

Sh—sh—Emily. Everything's all right.

EMILY:

Why can't I stay for a while just as I am? Let's go away,—

MR. WEBB:

No, no, Emily. Now stop and think a minute.

EMILY:

Don't you remember that you used to say,—all the time you used to say—all the time: that I was *your* girl! There must be lots of places we can go to. I'll work for you. I could keep house.

MR. WEBB:

Sh . . . You mustn't think of such things. You're just nervous, Emily.

He turns and calls:

George! George! Will you come here a minute?

He leads her toward George.

Why you're marrying the best young fellow in the world. George is a fine fellow.

EMILY:
But Papa,—

MRS. GIBBS *returns unobtrusively to her seat.*

MR. WEBB *has one arm around his daughter. He places his hand on* GEORGE'S *shoulder.*

MR. WEBB:
I'm giving away my daughter, George. Do you think you can take care of her?

GEORGE:
Mr. Webb, I want to . . . I want to try. Emily, I'm going to do my best. I love you, Emily. I need you.

EMILY:
Well, if you love me, help me. All I want is someone to love me.

GEORGE:
I will, Emily. Emily, I'll try.

EMILY:
And I mean for *ever.* Do you hear? For ever and ever.

They fall into each other's arms.

The March from Lohengrin *is heard.*

The STAGE MANAGER, *as* CLERGYMAN, *stands on the box, up center.*

MR. WEBB:

Come, they're waiting for us. Now you know it'll be all right. Come, quick.

GEORGE *slips away and takes his place beside the* STAGE MANAGER-CLERGYMAN.

EMILY *proceeds up the aisle on her father's arm.*

STAGE MANAGER:

Do you, George, take this woman, Emily, to be your wedded wife, to have . . .

MRS. SOAMES *has been sitting in the last row of the congregation.*

She now turns to her neighbors and speaks in a shrill voice. Her chatter drowns out the rest of the clergyman's words.

MRS. SOAMES:

Perfectly lovely wedding! Loveliest wedding I ever saw. Oh, I do love a good wedding, don't you? Doesn't she make a lovely bride?

GEORGE:

I do.

STAGE MANAGER:

Do you, Emily, take this man, George, to be your wedded husband,—

Again his further words are covered by those of MRS. SOAMES.

MRS. SOAMES:

Don't know *when* I've seen such a lovely wedding. But I always cry. Don't know why it is, but I always cry. I just like to see young people happy, don't you? Oh, I think it's lovely.

The ring.

The kiss.

The stage is suddenly arrested into silent tableau.

The STAGE MANAGER, *his eyes on the distance, as though to himself:*

STAGE MANAGER:

I've married over two hundred couples in my day.

Do I believe in it?

I don't know.

M. . . . marries N. . . . millions of them.

The cottage, the go-cart, the Sunday-afternoon drives in the Ford, the first rheumatism, the grandchildren, the second rheumatism, the deathbed, the reading of the will,—

He now looks at the audience for the first time, with a warm smile that removes any sense of cynicism from the next line.

Once in a thousand times it's interesting.

—Well, let's have Mendelssohn's "Wedding March"!

The organ picks up the March.

The BRIDE *and* GROOM *come down the aisle, radiant, but trying to be very dignified.*

MRS. SOAMES:

Aren't they a lovely couple? Oh, I've never been to such a nice wedding. I'm sure they'll be happy. I always say: *happiness,* that's the great thing! The important thing is to be happy.

The BRIDE *and* GROOM *reach the steps leading into the audience. A bright light is thrown upon them. They descend into the auditorium and run up the aisle joyously.*

STAGE MANAGER:

That's all the Second Act, folks. Ten minutes' intermission.

CURTAIN

Act III

During the intermission the audience has seen the stagehands arranging the stage. On the right-hand side, a little right of the center, ten or twelve ordinary chairs have been placed in three openly spaced rows facing the audience.

These are graves in the cemetery.

Toward the end of the intermission the ACTORS *enter and take their places. The front row contains: toward the center of the stage, an empty chair; then* MRS. GIBBS; SIMON STIMSON.

The second row contains, among others, MRS. SOAMES.

The third row has WALLY WEBB.

The dead do not turn their heads or their eyes to right or left, but they sit in a quiet without stiffness. When they speak their tone is matter-of-fact, without sentimentality and, above all, without lugubriousness.

The STAGE MANAGER *takes his accustomed place and waits for the house lights to go down.*

STAGE MANAGER:

This time nine years have gone by, friends—summer, 1913.

Gradual changes in Grover's Corners. Horses are getting rarer.

Farmers coming into town in Fords.

Everybody locks their house doors now at night. Ain't been any burglars in town yet, but everybody's heard about 'em.

You'd be surprised, though—on the whole, things don't change much around here.

This is certainly an important part of Grover's Corners. It's on a hilltop—a windy hilltop—lots of sky, lots of clouds,—often lots of sun and moon and stars.

You come up here, on a fine afternoon and you can see range on range of hills—awful blue they are—up there by Lake Sunapee and Lake Winnipesaukee . . . and way up, if you've got a glass, you can see the White Mountains and Mt. Washington—where North Conway and Conway is. And, of course, our favorite mountain, Mt. Monadnock, 's right here—and all these towns that lie around it: Jaffrey, 'n East Jaffrey, 'n Peterborough, 'n Dublin; and

Then pointing down in the audience.

there, quite a ways down, is Grover's Corners.

Yes, beautiful spot up here. Mountain laurel and li-lacks. I often wonder why people like to be buried in Woodlawn and Brooklyn when they might pass the same time up here in New Hampshire.

Over there—

Pointing to stage left.

are the old stones,—1670, 1680. Strong-minded people that come a long way to be independent. Summer people walk

around there laughing at the funny words on the tombstones
. . . it don't do any harm. And genealogists come up from
Boston—get paid by city people for looking up their ancestors.
They want to make sure they're Daughters of the American
Revolution and of the *Mayflower*.. . . Well, I guess that don't do
any harm, either. Wherever you come near the human race,
there's layers and layers of nonsense. . . .

Over there are some Civil War veterans. Iron flags on their
graves . . . New Hampshire boys . . . had a notion that the
Union ought to be kept together, though they'd never seen
more than fifty miles of it themselves. All they knew was the
name, friends—the United States of America. The United
States of America. And they went and died about it.

This here is the new part of the cemetery. Here's your friend
Mrs. Gibbs. 'N let me see—Here's Mr. Stimson, organist at the
Congregational Church. And Mrs. Soames who enjoyed the
wedding so—you remember? Oh, and a lot of others. And Editor Webb's boy, Wallace, whose appendix burst while he was on
a Boy Scout trip to Crawford Notch.

Yes, an awful lot of sorrow has sort of quieted down up here.

People just wild with grief have brought their relatives up to
this hill. We all know how it is . . . and then time . . . and
sunny days . . . and rainy days . . . 'n snow . . . We're all glad
they're in a beautiful place and we're coming up here ourselves when our fit's over.

Now there are some things we all know, but we don't take'm
out and look at'm very often. We all know that *something* is
eternal. And it ain't houses and it ain't names, and it ain't earth,
and it ain't even the stars . . . everybody knows in their bones

that *something* is eternal, and that something has to do with human beings. All the greatest people ever lived have been telling us that for five thousand years and yet you'd be surprised how people are always losing hold of it. There's something way down deep that's eternal about every human being.

Pause.

You know as well as I do that the dead don't stay interested in us living people for very long. Gradually, gradually, they lose hold of the earth . . . and the ambitions they had . . . and the pleasures they had . . . and the things they suffered . . . and the people they loved.

They get weaned away from earth—that's the way I put it,— weaned away.

And they stay here while the earth part of 'em burns away, burns out; and all that time they slowly get indifferent to what's goin' on in Grover's Corners.

They're waitin'. They're waitin' for something that they feel is comin'. Something important, and great. Aren't they waitin' for the eternal part in them to come out clear?

Some of the things they're going to say maybe'll hurt your feel-ings—but that's the way it is: mother'n daughter . . . husband 'n wife . . . enemy 'n enemy . . . money 'n miser . . . all those ter-ribly important things kind of grow pale around here. And what's left when memory's gone, and your identity, Mrs. Smith?

He looks at the audience a minute, then turns to the stage.

Well! There are some *living* people. There's Joe Stoddard, our undertaker, supervising a new-made grave. And here comes a Grover's Corners boy, that left town to go out West.

JOE STODDARD *has hovered about in the background.* SAM
CRAIG *enters left, wiping his forehead from the exertion. He
carries an umbrella and strolls front.*

SAM CRAIG:

Good afternoon, Joe Stoddard.

JOE STODDARD:

Good afternoon, good afternoon. Let me see now: do I know
you?

SAM CRAIG:

I'm Sam Craig.

JOE STODDARD:

Gracious sakes' alive! Of all people! I should'a knowed you'd
be back for the funeral. You've been away a long time, Sam.

SAM CRAIG:

Yes, I've been away over twelve years. I'm in business out in
Buffalo now, Joe. But I was in the East when I got news of my
cousin's death, so I thought I'd combine things a little and
come and see the old home. You look well.

JOE STODDARD:

Yes, yes, can't complain. Very sad, our journey today, Samuel.

SAM CRAIG:

Yes.

JOE STODDARD:

Yes, yes. I always say I hate to supervise when a young person is
taken. They'll be here in a few minutes now. I had to come here
early today—my son's supervisin' at the home.

SAM CRAIG:

Reading stones.

Old Farmer McCarty, I used to do chores for him—after school. He had the lumbago.

JOE STODDARD:

Yes, we brought Farmer McCarty here a number of years ago now.

SAM CRAIG:

Staring at Mrs. Gibbs' knees.

Why, this is my Aunt Julia . . . I'd forgotten that she'd . . . of course, of course.

JOE STODDARD:

Yes, Doc Gibbs lost his wife two-three years ago . . . about this time. And today's another pretty bad blow for him, too.

MRS. GIBBS:

To Simon Stimson: in an even voice.

That's my sister Carey's boy, Sam . . . Sam Craig.

SIMON STIMSON:

I'm always uncomfortable when *they're* around.

MRS. GIBBS:

Simon.

SAM CRAIG:

Do they choose their own verses much, Joe?

JOE STODDARD:

No . . . not usual. Mostly the bereaved pick a verse.

SAM CRAIG:

Doesn't sound like Aunt Julia. There aren't many of those Hersey sisters left now. Let me see: where are . . . I wanted to look at my father's and mother's . . .

JOE STODDARD:

Over there with the Craigs . . . Avenue F.

SAM CRAIG:

Reading Simon Stimson's epitaph.

He was organist at church, wasn't he?—Hm, drank a lot, we used to say.

JOE STODDARD:

Nobody was supposed to know about it. He'd seen a peck of trouble.

Behind his hand.

Took his own life, y' know?

SAM CRAIG:

Oh, did he?

JOE STODDARD:

Hung himself in the attic. They tried to hush it up, but of course it got around. He chose his own epy-taph. You can see it there. It ain't a verse exactly.

SAM CRAIG:

Why, it's just some notes of music—what is it?

JOE STODDARD:

Oh, I wouldn't know. It was wrote up in the Boston papers at the time.

SAM CRAIG:

Joe, what did she die of?

JOE STODDARD:

Who?

SAM CRAIG:

My cousin.

JOE STODDARD:

Oh, didn't you know? Had some trouble bringing a baby into the world. 'Twas her second, though. There's a little boy 'bout four years old.

SAM CRAIG:

Opening his umbrella.

The grave's going to be over there?

JOE STODDARD:

Yes, there ain't much more room over here among the Gibbses, so they're opening up a whole new Gibbs section over by Avenue B. You'll excuse me now. I see they're comin'.

From left to center, at the back of the stage, comes a procession. FOUR MEN *carry a casket, invisible to us. All the rest are under umbrellas. One can vaguely see:* DR. GIBBS, GEORGE, *the* WEBBS, *etc. They gather about a grave in the back center of the stage, a little to the left of center.*

MRS. SOAMES:

Who is it, Julia?

MRS. GIBBS:

Without raising her eyes.

My daughter-in-law, Emily Webb.

MRS. SOAMES:

A little surprised, but no emotion.

Well, I declare! The road up here must have been awful muddy. What did she die of, Julia?

MRS. GIBBS:

In childbirth.

MRS. SOAMES:

Childbirth.

Almost with a laugh.

I'd forgotten all about that. My, wasn't life awful—

With a sigh.

and wonderful.

SIMON STIMSON:

With a sideways glance.

Wonderful, was it?

MRS. GIBBS:

Simon! Now, remember!

MRS. SOAMES:

I remember Emily's wedding. Wasn't it a lovely wedding! And I remember her reading the class poem at Graduation Exercises. Emily was one of the brightest girls ever graduated from High School. I've heard Principal Wilkins say so time after time. I called on them at their new farm, just before I died. Perfectly beautiful farm.

A WOMAN FROM AMONG THE DEAD:

It's on the same road we lived on.

A MAN AMONG THE DEAD:

Yepp, right smart farm.

They subside. The group by the grave starts singing "Blessed Be the Tie That Binds."

A WOMAN AMONG THE DEAD:

I always liked that hymn. I was hopin' they'd sing a hymn.

Pause. Suddenly EMILY *appears from among the umbrellas. She is wearing a white dress. Her hair is down her back and tied by a white ribbon like a little girl. She comes slowly, gazing wonderingly at the dead, a little dazed.*

She stops halfway and smiles faintly. After looking at the mourners for a moment, she walks slowly to the vacant chair beside Mrs. Gibbs and sits down.

EMILY:

To them all, quietly, smiling.

Hello.

MRS. SOAMES:

Hello, Emily.

A MAN AMONG THE DEAD:

Hello, M's Gibbs.

EMILY:

Warmly.

Hello, Mother Gibbs.

MRS. GIBBS:

Emily.

EMILY:

Hello.

With surprise.

It's raining.

Her eyes drift back to the funeral company.

MRS. GIBBS:

Yes . . . They'll be gone soon, dear. Just rest yourself.

EMILY:

It seems thousands and thousands of years since I . . . Papa remembered that that was my favorite hymn.

Oh, I wish I'd been here a long time. I don't like being new here.—How do you do, Mr. Stimson?

SIMON STIMSON:

How do you do, Emily.

EMILY *continues to look about her with a wondering smile; as though to shut out from her mind the thought of the funeral company she starts speaking to Mrs. Gibbs with a touch of nervousness.*

EMILY:

Mother Gibbs, George and I have made that farm into just the best place you ever saw. We thought of you all the time. We wanted to show you the new barn and a great long ce-ment drinking fountain for the stock. We bought that out of the money you left us.

MRS. GIBBS:

I did?

EMILY:

Don't you remember, Mother Gibbs—the legacy you left us? Why, it was over three hundred and fifty dollars.

MRS. GIBBS:

Yes, yes, Emily.

EMILY:

Well, there's a patent device on the drinking fountain so that it never overflows, Mother Gibbs, and it never sinks below a certain mark they have there. It's fine.

Her voice trails off and her eyes return to the funeral group.

It won't be the same to George without me, but it's a lovely farm.

Suddenly she looks directly at Mrs. Gibbs.

Live people don't understand, do they?

MRS. GIBBS:

No, dear—not very much.

EMILY:

They're sort of shut up in little boxes, aren't they? I feel as though I knew them last a thousand years ago . . . My boy is spending the day at Mrs. Carter's.

She sees MR. CARTER *among the dead.*

Oh, Mr. Carter, my little boy is spending the day at your house.

MR. CARTER:

Is he?

EMILY:

Yes, he loves it there.—Mother Gibbs, we have a Ford, too. Never gives any trouble. I don't drive, though. Mother Gibbs,

when does this feeling go away?—Of being . . . one of *them*?
How long does it . . . ?

MRS. GIBBS:

Sh! dear. Just wait and be patient.

EMILY:

With a sigh.

I know.—Look, they're finished. They're going.

MRS. GIBBS:

Sh—.

> *The umbrellas leave the stage.* DR. GIBBS *has come over to his
> wife's grave and stands before it a moment.* EMILY *looks up at
> his face.* MRS. GIBBS *does not raise her eyes.*

EMILY:

Look! Father Gibbs is bringing some of my flowers to you. He
looks just like George, doesn't he? Oh, Mother Gibbs, I never
realized before how troubled and how . . . how in the dark live
persons are. Look at him. I loved him so. From morning till
night, that's all they are—troubled.

> DR. GIBBS *goes off.*

THE DEAD:

Little cooler than it was.—Yes, that rain's cooled it off a little.
Those northeast winds always do the same thing, don't they?
If it isn't a rain, it's a three-day blow.—

> *A patient calm falls on the stage. The* STAGE MANAGER
> *appears at his proscenium pillar, smoking.* EMILY *sits up
> abruptly with an idea.*

EMILY:

But, Mother Gibbs, one can go back; one can go back there again . . . into living. I feel it. I know it. Why just then for a moment I was thinking about . . . about the farm . . . and for a minute I *was* there, and my baby was on my lap as plain as day.

MRS. GIBBS:

Yes, of course you can.

EMILY:

I can go back there and live all those days over again . . . why not?

MRS. GIBBS:

All I can say is, Emily, don't.

EMILY:

She appeals urgently to the stage manager.

But it's true, isn't it? I can go and live . . . back there . . . again.

STAGE MANAGER:

Yes, some have tried—but they soon come back here.

MRS. GIBBS:

Don't do it, Emily.

MRS. SOAMES:

Emily, don't. It's not what you think it'd be.

EMILY:

But I won't live over a sad day. I'll choose a happy one—I'll choose the day I first knew that I loved George. Why should that be painful?

THEY *are silent. Her question turns to the stage manager.*

STAGE MANAGER:

You not only live it; but you watch yourself living it.

EMILY:

Yes?

STAGE MANAGER:

And as you watch it, you see the thing that they—down there—never know. You see the future. You know what's going to happen afterwards.

EMILY:

But is that—painful? Why?

MRS. GIBBS:

That's not the only reason why you shouldn't do it, Emily. When you've been here longer you'll see that our life here is to forget all that, and think only of what's ahead, and be ready for what's ahead. When you've been here longer you'll understand.

EMILY:

Softly.

But, Mother Gibbs, how can I *ever* forget that life? It's all I know. It's all I had.

MRS. SOAMES:

Oh, Emily. It isn't wise. Really, it isn't.

EMILY:

But it's a thing I must know for myself. I'll choose a happy day, anyway.

MRS. GIBBS:

No!—At least, choose an unimportant day. Choose the least important day in your life. It will be important enough.

EMILY:

To herself.

Then it can't be since I was married; or since the baby was born.

To the stage manager, eagerly.

I can choose a birthday at least, can't I?—I choose my twelfth birthday.

STAGE MANAGER:

All right. February 11th, 1899. A Tuesday.—Do you want any special time of day?

EMILY:

Oh, I want the whole day.

STAGE MANAGER:

We'll begin at dawn. You remember it had been snowing for several days; but it had stopped the night before, and they had begun clearing the roads. The sun's coming up.

EMILY:

With a cry; rising.

There's Main Street . . . why, that's Mr. Morgan's drugstore before he changed it! . . . And there's the livery stable.

The stage at no time in this act has been very dark; but now the left half of the stage gradually becomes very bright—the brightness of a crisp winter morning. EMILY *walks toward Main Street.*

STAGE MANAGER:

Yes, it's 1899. This is fourteen years ago.

EMILY:

Oh, that's the town I knew as a little girl. And, *look,* there's the old white fence that used to be around our house. Oh, I'd forgotten that! Oh, I love it so! Are they inside?

STAGE MANAGER:

Yes, your mother'll be coming downstairs in a minute to make breakfast.

EMILY:

Softly.

Will she?

STAGE MANAGER:

And you remember: your father had been away for several days; he came back on the early-morning train.

EMILY:

No . . . ?

STAGE MANAGER:

He'd been back to his college to make a speech—in western New York, at Clinton.

EMILY:

Look! There's Howie Newsome. There's our policeman. But he's *dead;* he *died.*

The voices of HOWIE NEWSOME, CONSTABLE WARREN *and* JOE CROWELL, JR., *are heard at the left of the stage.* EMILY *listens in delight.*

HOWIE NEWSOME:

Whoa, Bessie!—Bessie! 'Morning, Bill.

CONSTABLE WARREN:

Morning, Howie.

HOWIE NEWSOME:

You're up early.

CONSTABLE WARREN:

Been rescuin' a party; darn near froze to death, down by Polish Town thar. Got drunk and lay out in the snowdrifts. Thought he was in bed when I shook'm.

EMILY:

Why, there's Joe Crowell. . . .

JOE CROWELL:

Good morning, Mr. Warren. 'Morning, Howie.

MRS. WEBB *has appeared in her kitchen, but* EMILY *does not see her until she calls.*

MRS. WEBB:

Chil-*dren!* Wally! Emily! . . . Time to get up.

EMILY:

Mama, I'm here! Oh! how young Mama looks! I didn't know Mama was ever that young.

MRS. WEBB:

You can come and dress by the kitchen fire, if you like; but hurry.

HOWIE NEWSOME *has entered along Main Street and brings the milk to Mrs. Webb's door.*

Good morning, Mr. Newsome. Whhhh—it's cold.

HOWIE NEWSOME:

Ten below by my barn, Mrs. Webb.

MRS. WEBB:

Think of it! Keep yourself wrapped up.

She takes her bottles in, shuddering.

EMILY:

With an effort.

Mama, I can't find my blue hair ribbon anywhere.

MRS. WEBB:

Just open your eyes, dear, that's all. I laid it out for you special—on the dresser, there. If it were a snake it would bite you.

EMILY:

Yes, yes . . .

She puts her hand on her heart. MR. WEBB *comes along Main
Street, where he meets* CONSTABLE WARREN. *Their movements
and voices are increasingly lively in the sharp air.*

MR. WEBB:

Good morning, Bill.

CONSTABLE WARREN:

Good morning, Mr. Webb. You're up early.

MR. WEBB:

Yes, just been back to my old college in New York State.
Been any trouble here?

CONSTABLE WARREN:

Well, I was called up this mornin' to rescue a Polish fella—
darn near froze to death he was.

MR. WEBB:

We must get it in the paper.

CONSTABLE WARREN:

'Twan't much.

EMILY:

Whispers.

Papa.

MR. WEBB *shakes the snow off his feet and enters his house.*
CONSTABLE WARREN *goes off, right.*

MR. WEBB:

Good morning, Mother.

MRS. WEBB:

How did it go, Charles?

MR. WEBB:

Oh, fine, I guess. I told'm a few things.—Everything all right
here?

MRS. WEBB:

Yes—can't think of anything that's happened, special. Been
right cold. Howie Newsome says it's ten below over to his barn.

MR. WEBB:

Yes, well, it's colder than that at Hamilton College. Students'
ears are falling off. It ain't Christian.—Paper have any mistakes in it?

MRS. WEBB:

None that I noticed. Coffee's ready when you want it.

He starts upstairs.

Charles! Don't forget, it's Emily's birthday. Did you remember to get her something?

MR. WEBB:

Patting his pocket.

Yes, I've got something here.

Calling up the stairs.

Where's my girl? Where's my birthday girl?

He goes off left.

MRS. WEBB:

Don't interrupt her now, Charles. You can see her at breakfast. She's slow enough as it is. Hurry up, children! It's seven o'clock. Now, I don't want to call you again.

EMILY:

Softly, more in wonder than in grief.

I can't bear it. They're so young and beautiful. Why did they ever have to get old? Mama, I'm here. I'm grown up. I love you all, everything.—I can't look at everything hard enough.

She looks questioningly at the STAGE MANAGER, *saying or suggesting: "Can I go in?" He nods briefly. She crosses to the inner door to the kitchen, left of her mother, and as though entering the room, says, suggesting the voice of a girl of twelve:*

Good morning, Mama.

MRS. WEBB:

Crossing to embrace and kiss her; in her characteristic matter-of-fact manner.

Well, now, dear, a very happy birthday to my girl and many happy returns. There are some surprises waiting for you on the kitchen table.

EMILY:

Oh, Mama, you *shouldn't* have.

She throws an anguished glance at the stage manager.

I can't—I can't.

MRS. WEBB:

Facing the audience, over her stove.

But birthday or no birthday, I want you to eat your breakfast good and slow. I want you to grow up and be a good strong girl.

That in the blue paper is from your Aunt Carrie; and I reckon you can guess who brought the post-card album. I found it on the doorstep when I brought in the milk—George Gibbs . . . must have come over in the cold pretty early . . . right nice of him.

EMILY:

To herself.

Oh, George! I'd forgotten that. . . .

MRS. WEBB:

Chew that bacon good and slow. It'll help keep you warm on a cold day.

EMILY:

With mounting urgency.

Oh, Mama, just look at me one minute as though you really saw me. Mama, fourteen years have gone by. I'm dead. You're a grandmother, Mama. I married George Gibbs, Mama. Wally's dead, too. Mama, his appendix burst on a camping trip to North Conway. We felt just terrible about it—don't you remember? But, just for a moment now we're all together. Mama, just for a moment we're happy. *Let's look at one another.*

MRS. WEBB:

That in the yellow paper is something I found in the attic among your grandmother's things. You're old enough to wear it now, and I thought you'd like it.

EMILY:

And this is from you. Why, Mama, it's just lovely and it's just what I wanted. It's beautiful!

She flings her arms around her mother's neck. Her MOTHER *goes on with her cooking, but is pleased.*

MRS. WEBB:

Well, I hoped you'd like it. Hunted all over. Your Aunt Norah couldn't find one in Concord, so I had to send all the way to Boston.

Laughing.

Wally has something for you, too. He made it at manual-training class and he's very proud of it. Be sure you make a big fuss about it.—Your father has a surprise for you, too; don't know what it is myself. Sh—here he comes.

MR. WEBB:

Off stage.

Where's my girl? Where's my birthday girl?

EMILY:

In a loud voice to the stage manager.

I can't. I can't go on. It goes so fast. We don't have time to look at one another.

She breaks down sobbing.

The lights dim on the left half of the stage. MRS. WEBB *disappears.*

I didn't realize. So all that was going on and we never noticed. Take me back—up the hill—to my grave. But first: Wait! One more look.

Good-by, Good-by, world. Good-by, Grover's Corners . . . Mama and Papa. Good-by to clocks ticking . . . and Mama's sunflowers. And food and coffee. And new-ironed dresses and hot baths . . . and sleeping and waking up. Oh, earth, you're too wonderful for anybody to realize you.

She looks toward the stage manager and asks abruptly, through her tears:

Do any human beings ever realize life while they live it?—every, every minute?

STAGE MANAGER:

No.

Pause.

The saints and poets, maybe—they do some.

EMILY:

I'm ready to go back.

She returns to her chair beside Mrs. Gibbs.

Pause.

MRS. GIBBS:

Were you happy?

EMILY:

No . . . I should have listened to you. That's all human beings are! Just blind people.

MRS. GIBBS:

Look, it's clearing up. The stars are coming out.

EMILY:

Oh, Mr. Stimson, I should have listened to them.

SIMON STIMSON:

With mounting violence; bitingly.

Yes, now you know. Now you know! That's what it was to be alive. To move about in a cloud of ignorance; to go up and down trampling on the feelings of those . . . of those about you. To spend and waste time as though you had a million years. To be always at the mercy of one self-centered passion, or another. Now you know—that's the happy existence you wanted to go back to. Ignorance and blindness.

MRS. GIBBS:

Spiritedly.

Simon Stimson, that ain't the whole truth and you know it. Emily, look at that star. I forget its name.

A MAN AMONG THE DEAD:

My boy Joel was a sailor,—knew 'em all. He'd set on the porch evenings and tell 'em all by name. Yes, sir, wonderful!

ANOTHER MAN AMONG THE DEAD:

A star's mighty good company.

A WOMAN AMONG THE DEAD:

Yes. Yes, 'tis.

SIMON STIMSON:

Here's one of *them* coming.

THE DEAD:

That's funny. 'Tain't no time for one of them to be here.—Goodness sakes.

EMILY:

Mother Gibbs, it's George.

MRS. GIBBS:

Sh, dear. Just rest yourself.

EMILY:

It's George.

GEORGE *enters from the left, and slowly comes toward them.*

A MAN FROM AMONG THE DEAD:

And my boy, Joel, who knew the stars—he used to say it took millions of years for that speck o' light to git to the earth. Don't seem like a body could believe it, but that's what he used to say—millions of years.

GEORGE *sinks to his knees then falls full length at Emily's feet.*

A WOMAN AMONG THE DEAD:
Goodness! That ain't no way to behave!

MRS. SOAMES:
He ought to be home.

EMILY:
Mother Gibbs?

MRS. GIBBS:
Yes, Emily?

EMILY:
They don't understand, do they?

MRS. GIBBS:
No, dear. They don't understand.

The STAGE MANAGER *appears at the right, one hand on a dark curtain which he slowly draws across the scene.*

In the distance a clock is heard striking the hour very faintly.

STAGE MANAGER:
Most everybody's asleep in Grover's Corners. There are a few lights on: Shorty Hawkins, down at the depot, has just watched the Albany train go by. And at the livery stable somebody's setting up late and talking.—Yes, it's clearing up. There are the stars—doing their old, old crisscross journeys in the sky. Scholars haven't settled the matter yet, but they seem to think there are no living beings up there. Just chalk . . . or fire. Only this one is straining away, straining away all the time to make something of itself. The strain's so bad that every sixteen hours everybody lies down and gets a rest.

He winds his watch.

Hm. . . . Eleven o'clock in Grover's Corners.—You get a good rest, too. Good night.

THE END

The Skin of Our Teeth

A Play in Three Acts

———✺———

The first performance of The Skin of Our Teeth *took place at the* Shubert Theatre in New Haven, Connecticut, on October 15, 1942. It opened in New York at the Plymouth Theatre on November 18. It was produced by Michael Myerberg and directed by Elia Kazan. Sabina was played by Tallulah Bankhead, Mr. and Mrs. Antrobus by Fredric March and Florence Eldridge, the Antrobus children by Montgomery Clift and Frances Heflin, the Fortune Teller by Florence Reed. The scenery was designed by Albert Johnson, the costumes by Mary Percy Schenck.

The London production opened at the Phoenix Theatre on May 16, 1945. It was presented by H. M. Tennent Ltd. and directed by Sir Laurence Olivier. Sabina was played by Vivien Leigh, Mr. and Mrs. Antrobus by Cecil Parker (later by George Devine) and Joan Young (later by Esther Somers), the Antrobus children by Terry Morgan and Pamela Conroy, the Fortune Teller by Ena Burrill. The scenery and costumes were designed by Roger Furse. On a tour of Australia and New Zealand in 1948, the role of Mr. Antrobus was played by Sir Laurence Olivier.

In a revival produced by the American National Theatre and Academy for presentation in Paris in June, 1955, as a part of the Festival "Salut à la France," and later presented in a number of cities in the United States, Sabina was played by Mary Martin, Mr. and Mrs. Antrobus by George Abbott and Helen Hayes, and the Fortune Teller by Florence Reed. The play was directed by Alan Schneider.

CHARACTERS (in the order of their appearance)

ANNOUNCER	MISS E. MUSE
SABINA	T. MUSE
MR. FITZPATRICK	MISS M. MUSE
MRS. ANTROBUS	TWO USHERS
DINOSAUR	TWO DRUM MAJORETTES
MAMMOTH	FORTUNE TELLER
TELEGRAPH BOY	TWO CHAIR PUSHERS
GLADYS	SIX CONVEENERS
HENRY	BROADCAST OFFICIAL
MR. ANTROBUS	DEFEATED CANDIDATE
DOCTOR	MR. TREMAYNE
PROFESSOR	HESTER
JUDGE	IVY
HOMER	FRED BAILEY

Act I. Home, Excelsior, New Jersey.
Act II. Atlantic City Boardwalk.
Act III. Home, Excelsior, New Jersey.

—⋙—

Act I

A projection screen in the middle of the curtain. The first lantern slide: the name of the theatre, and the words: NEWS EVENTS OF THE WORLD. An ANNOUNCER'S *voice is heard.*

ANNOUNCER:
The management takes pleasure in bringing to you—The News Events of the World:

Slide of the sun appearing above the horizon.

Freeport, Long Island.

The sun rose this morning at 6:32 a.m. This gratifying event was first reported by Mrs. Dorothy Stetson of Freeport, Long Island, who promptly telephoned the Mayor.

The Society for Affirming the End of the World at once went into a special session and postponed the arrival of that event for TWENTY-FOUR HOURS.

All honor to Mrs. Stetson for her public spirit.

New York City:

> *Slide of the front doors of the theatre in which this play is*
> *playing; three cleaning* WOMEN *with mops and pails.*

The X Theatre. During the daily cleaning of this theatre a
number of lost objects were collected as usual by Mesdames
Simpson, Pateslewski, and Moriarty.

Among these objects found today was a wedding ring,
inscribed: To Eva from Adam. Genesis II:18.

The ring will be restored to the owner or owners, if their credentials are satisfactory.

Tippehatchee, Vermont:

> *Slide representing a glacier.*

The unprecedented cold weather of this summer has produced a condition that has not yet been satisfactorily
explained. There is a report that a wall of ice is moving
southward across these counties. The disruption of commu-
nications by the cold wave now crossing the country has rendered exact information difficult, but little credence is given
to the rumor that the ice had pushed the Cathedral of Mon-
treal as far as St. Albans, Vermont.

For further information see your daily papers.

Excelsior, New Jersey:

> *Slide of a modest suburban home.*

The home of Mr. George Antrobus, the inventor of the
wheel. The discovery of the wheel, following so closely on the
discovery of the lever, has centered the attention of the coun-

try on Mr. Antrobus of this attractive suburban residence district. This is his home, a commodious seven-room house, conveniently situated near a public school, a Methodist church, and a firehouse; it is right handy to an A. and P.

Slide of MR. ANTROBUS *on his front steps, smiling and lifting his straw hat. He holds a wheel.*

Mr. Antrobus, himself. He comes of very old stock and has made his way up from next to nothing.

It is reported that he was once a gardener, but left that situation under circumstances that have been variously reported.

Mr. Antrobus is a veteran of foreign wars, and bears a number of scars, front and back.

Slide of MRS. ANTROBUS, *holding some roses.*

This is Mrs. Antrobus, the charming and gracious president of the Excelsior Mothers' Club.

Mrs. Antrobus is an excellent needlewoman; it is she who invented the apron on which so many interesting changes have been rung since.

Slide of the FAMILY *and* SABINA.

Here we see the Antrobuses with their two children, Henry and Gladys, and friend. The friend in the rear, is Lily Sabina, the maid.

I know we all want to congratulate this typical American family on its enterprise. We all wish Mr. Antrobus a successful future. Now the management takes you to the interior of this home for a brief visit.

Curtain rises. Living room of a commuter's home. SABINA — *straw-blonde, over-rouged—is standing by the window back center, a feather duster under her elbow.*

SABINA:

Oh, oh, oh! Six o'clock and the master not home yet.

Pray God nothing serious has happened to him crossing the Hudson River. If anything happened to him, we would certainly be inconsolable and have to move into a less desirable residence district.

The fact is I don't know what'll become of us. Here it is the middle of August and the coldest day of the year. It's simply freezing; the dogs are sticking to the sidewalks; can anybody explain that? No.

But I'm not surprised. The whole world's at sixes and sevens, and why the house hasn't fallen down about our ears long ago is a miracle to me.

A fragment of the right wall leans precariously over the stage. SABINA *looks at it nervously and it slowly rights itself.*

Every night this same anxiety as to whether the master will get home safely: whether he'll bring home anything to eat. In the midst of life we are in the midst of death, a truer word was never said.

The fragment of scenery flies up into the lofts. SABINA *is struck dumb with surprise, shrugs her shoulders and starts dusting* MR. ANTROBUS' *chair, including the under side.*

Of course, Mr. Antrobus is a very fine man, an excellent husband and father, a pillar of the church, and has all the best interests of the community at heart. Of course, every muscle goes tight every time he passes a policeman; but what I think is that there are certain charges that ought not to be made, and I think I may add, ought not to be allowed to be made; we're all human; who isn't?

She dusts MRS. ANTROBUS' *rocking chair.*

Mrs. Antrobus is as fine a woman as you could hope to see. She lives only for her children; and if it would be any benefit to her children she'd see the rest of us stretched out dead at her feet without turning a hair,—that's the truth. If you want to know anything more about Mrs. Antrobus, just go and look at a tigress, and look hard.

As to the children—

Well, Henry Antrobus is a real, clean-cut American boy. He'll graduate from High School one of these days, if they make the alphabet any easier.—Henry, when he has a stone in his hand, has a perfect aim; he can hit anything from a bird to an older brother—Oh! I didn't mean to say that!—but it certainly was an unfortunate accident, and it was very hard getting the police out of the house.

Mr. and Mrs. Antrobus' daughter is named Gladys. She'll make some good man a good wife some day, if he'll just come down off the movie screen and ask her.

So here we are!

We've managed to survive for some time now, catch as catch can, the fat and the lean, and if the dinosaurs don't trample us to death, and if the grasshoppers don't eat up our garden, we'll all live to see better days, knock on wood.

Each new child that's born to the Antrobuses seems to them to be sufficient reason for the whole universe's being set in motion; and each new child that dies seems to them to have been spared a whole world of sorrow, and what the end of it will be is still very much an open question.

We've rattled along, hot and cold, for some time now—

A portion of the wall above the door, right, flies up into the air and disappears.

—and my advice to you is not to inquire into why or whither, but just enjoy your ice cream while it's on your plate,—that's my philosophy.

Don't forget that a few years ago we came through the depression by the skin of our teeth! One more tight squeeze like that and where will we be?

This is a cue line. SABINA *looks angrily at the kitchen door and repeats:*

. . . we came through the depression by the skin of our teeth; one more tight squeeze like that and where will we be?

Flustered, she looks through the opening in the right wall; then goes to the window and reopens the Act.

Oh, oh, oh! Six o'clock and the master not home yet. Pray God nothing has happened to him crossing the Hudson. Here it is the middle of August and the coldest day of the year. It's simply freezing; the dogs are sticking. One more tight squeeze like that and where will we be?

VOICE:

Off stage.

Make up something! Invent something!

SABINA:

Well . . . uh . . . this certainly is a fine American home . . . and— uh . . . everybody's very happy . . . and—uh . . .

Suddenly flings pretense to the winds and coming down stage says with indignation:

I can't invent any words for this play, and I'm glad I can't. I hate this play and every word in it.

As for me, I don't understand a single word of it, anyway,— all about the troubles the human race has gone through, there's a subject for you.

Besides, the author hasn't made up his silly mind as to whether we're all living back in caves or in New Jersey today, and that's the way it is all the way through.

Oh—why can't we have plays like we used to have—*Peg o' My Heart,* and *Smilin' Thru,* and *The Bat*—good entertainment with a message you can take home with you?

I took this hateful job because I had to. For two years I've sat up in my room living on a sandwich and a cup of tea a day, waiting for better times in the theatre. And look at me now: I—I who've played *Rain* and *The Barretts of Wimpole Street* and *First Lady*—God in Heaven!

The STAGE MANAGER *puts his head out from the hole in the scenery.*

MR. FITZPATRICK:

Miss Somerset!! Miss Somerset!

SABINA:

Oh! Anyway!—nothing matters! It'll all be the same in a hundred years.

Loudly.

We came through the depression by the skin of our teeth,— that's true!—one more tight squeeze like that and where will we be?

Enter MRS. ANTROBUS, *a mother.*

MRS. ANTROBUS:

Sabina, you've let the fire go out.

SABINA:

In a lather.

One-thing-and-another; don't-know-whether-my-wits-are- upside-or-down; might-as-well-be-dead-as-alive-in-a-house- all-sixes-and-sevens. . . .

MRS. ANTROBUS:

You've let the fire go out. Here it is the coldest day of the year right in the middle of August, and you've let the fire go out.

SABINA:

Mrs. Antrobus, I'd like to give my two weeks' notice, Mrs. An- trobus. A girl like I can get a situation in a home where they're rich enough to have a fire in every room, Mrs. Antrobus, and a girl don't have to carry the responsibility of the whole house on her two shoulders. And a home without children, Mrs. Antro- bus, because children are a thing only a parent can stand, and a truer word was never said; and a home, Mrs. Antrobus, where the master of the house don't pinch decent, self-respecting girls when he meets them in a dark corridor. I mention no names and make no charges. So you have my notice, Mrs. Antrobus. I hope that's perfectly clear.

MRS. ANTROBUS:

You've let the fire go out!—Have you milked the mammoth?

SABINA:

I don't understand a word of this play.—Yes, I've milked the mammoth.

MRS. ANTROBUS:

Until Mr. Antrobus comes home we have no food and we have no fire. You'd better go over to the neighbors and borrow some fire.

SABINA:

Mrs. Antrobus! I can't! I'd die on the way, you know I would. It's worse than January. The dogs are sticking to the sidewalks. I'd die.

MRS. ANTROBUS:

Very well, I'll go.

SABINA:

Even more distraught, coming forward and sinking on her knees.

You'd never come back alive; we'd all perish; if you weren't here, we'd just perish. How do we know Mr. Antrobus'll be back? We don't know. If you go out, I'll just kill myself.

MRS. ANTROBUS:

Get up, Sabina.

SABINA:

Every night it's the same thing. Will he come back safe, or won't he? Will we starve to death, or freeze to death, or boil to death or will we be killed by burglars? I don't know why we go on living. I don't know why we go on living at all. It's easier being dead.

She flings her arms on the table and buries her head in them. In each of the succeeding speeches she flings her head up—and sometimes her hands—then quickly buries her head again.

MRS. ANTROBUS:

The same thing! Always throwing up the sponge, Sabina. Always announcing your own death. But give you a new hat— or a plate of ice cream—or a ticket to the movies, and you want to live forever.

SABINA:

You don't care whether we live or die; all you care about is those children. If it would be any benefit to them you'd be glad to see us all stretched out dead.

MRS. ANTROBUS:

Well, maybe I would.

SABINA:

And what do they care about? Themselves—that's all they care about.

Shrilly.

They make fun of you behind your back. Don't tell me: they're ashamed of you. Half the time, they pretend they're someone else's children. Little thanks you get from them.

MRS. ANTROBUS:

I'm not asking for any thanks.

SABINA:

And Mr. Antrobus—you don't understand *him*. All that work he does—trying to discover the alphabet and the multiplication table. Whenever he tries to learn anything you fight against it.

MRS. ANTROBUS:

Oh, Sabina, I know you.

When Mr. Antrobus raped you home from your Sabine hills, he did it to insult me.

He did it for your pretty face, and to insult me.

You were the new wife, weren't you?

For a year or two you lay on your bed all day and polished the nails on your hands and feet:

You made puff-balls of the combings of your hair and you blew them up to the ceiling.

And I washed your underclothes and I made you chicken broths.

I bore children and between my very groans I stirred the cream that you'd put on your face.

But I knew you wouldn't last.

You didn't last.

SABINA:

But it was I who encouraged Mr. Antrobus to make the alphabet. I'm sorry to say it, Mrs. Antrobus, but you're not a beautiful woman, and you can never know what a man could do if he tried. It's girls like I who inspire the multiplication table.

I'm sorry to say it, but you're not a beautiful woman, Mrs. Antrobus, and that's the God's truth.

MRS. ANTROBUS:
And you didn't last—you sank to the kitchen. And what do you do there? *You let the fire go out!*

No wonder to you it seems easier being dead.

Reading and writing and counting on your fingers is all very well in their way,—but I keep the home going.

MRS. ANTROBUS:
—There's that dinosaur on the front lawn again.—Shoo! Go away. Go away.

The baby DINOSAUR *puts his head in the window.*

DINOSAUR:
It's cold.

MRS. ANTROBUS:
You go around to the back of the house where you belong.

DINOSAUR:
It's cold.

The DINOSAUR *disappears.* MRS. ANTROBUS *goes calmly out.*

SABINA *slowly raises her head and speaks to the audience. The central portion of the center wall rises, pauses, and disappears into the loft.*

SABINA:

Now that you audience are listening to this, too, I understand it a little better.

I wish eleven o'clock were here; I don't want to be dragged
through this whole play again.

> The TELEGRAPH BOY *is seen entering along the back wall of
> the stage from the right. She catches sight of him and calls:*

Mrs. Antrobus! Mrs. Antrobus! Help! There's a strange man
coming to the house. He's coming up the walk, help!

> *Enter* MRS. ANTROBUS *in alarm, but efficient.*

MRS. ANTROBUS:

Help me quick!

> *They barricade the door by piling the furniture against it.*

Who is it? What do you want?

TELEGRAPH BOY:

A telegram for Mrs. Antrobus from Mr. Antrobus in the city.

SABINA:

Are you sure, are you sure? Maybe it's just a trap!

MRS. ANTROBUS:

I know his voice, Sabina. We can open the door.

> *Enter the* TELEGRAPH BOY, *12 years old, in uniform. The*
> DINOSAUR *and* MAMMOTH *slip by him into the room and
> settle down front right.*

I'm sorry we kept you waiting. We have to be careful, you
know.

To the ANIMALS.

Hm! . . . Will you be quiet?

They nod.

Have you had your supper?

They nod.

Are you *ready* to come in?

They nod.

Young man, have you any fire with you? Then light the grate, will you?

He nods, produces something like a briquet; and kneels by the imagined fireplace, footlights center. Pause.

What are people saying about this cold weather?

He makes a doubtful shrug with his shoulders.

Sabina, take this stick and go and light the stove.

SABINA:

Like I told you, Mrs. Antrobus; two weeks. That's the law. I hope that's perfectly clear.

Exit.

MRS. ANTROBUS:

What about this cold weather?

TELEGRAPH BOY:

Lowered eyes.

Of course, I don't know anything . . . but they say there's a wall of ice moving down from the North, that's what they say. We can't get Boston by telegraph, and they're burning pianos in Hartford.

. . . It moves everything in front of it, churches and post offices and city halls.

I live in Brooklyn myself.

MRS. ANTROBUS:
What are people doing about it?

TELEGRAPH BOY:
Well . . . uh . . . Talking, mostly.

Or just what you'd do a day in February.

There are some that are trying to go South and the roads are crowded; but you can't take old people and children very far in a cold like this.

MRS. ANTROBUS:
—What's this telegram you have for me?

TELEGRAPH BOY:
Fingertips to his forehead.

If you wait just a minute; I've got to remember it.

The ANIMALS *have left their corner and are nosing him. Presently they take places on either side of him, leaning against his hips, like heraldic beasts.*

This telegram was flashed from Murray Hill to University Heights! And then by puffs of smoke from University Heights to Staten Island.

And then by lantern from Staten Island to Plainfield, New Jersey. What hath God wrought!

He clears his throat.

"To Mrs. Antrobus, Excelsior, New Jersey:

My dear wife, will be an hour late. Busy day at the office. Don't worry the children about the cold just keep them warm burn everything except Shakespeare."

Pause.

MRS. ANTROBUS:

Men!—He knows I'd burn ten Shakespeares to prevent a child of mine from having one cold in the head. What does it say next?

Enter SABINA.

TELEGRAPH BOY:

"Have made great discoveries today have separated em from en."

SABINA:

I know what that is, that's the alphabet, yes it is. Mr. Antrobus is just the cleverest man. Why, when the alphabet's finished, we'll be able to tell the future and everything.

TELEGRAPH BOY:

Then listen to this: "Ten tens make a hundred semi-colon consequences far-reaching."

Watches for effect.

MRS. ANTROBUS:

The earth's turning to ice, and all he can do is to make up new numbers.

TELEGRAPH BOY:

Well, Mrs. Antrobus, like the head man at our office said: a few more discoveries like that and we'll be worth freezing.

MRS. ANTROBUS:

What does he say next?

TELEGRAPH BOY:

I . . . I can't do this last part very well.

He clears his throat and sings.

"Happy w'dding ann'vers'ry to you, Happy ann'vers'ry to you—"

The ANIMALS *begin to howl soulfully;* SABINA *screams with pleasure.*

MRS. ANTROBUS:

Dolly! Frederick! Be quiet.

TELEGRAPH BOY:

Above the din.

"Happy w'dding ann'vers'ry, dear Eva; happy w'dding ann'vers'ry to you."

MRS. ANTROBUS:

Is that in the telegram? Are they singing telegrams now?

He nods.

The earth's getting so silly no wonder the sun turns cold.

SABINA:

Mrs. Antrobus, I want to take back the notice I gave you. Mrs. Antrobus, I don't want to leave a house that gets such interesting telegrams and I'm sorry for anything I said. I really am.

MRS. ANTROBUS:

Young man, I'd like to give you something for all this trouble; Mr. Antrobus isn't home yet and I have no money and no food in the house—

TELEGRAPH BOY:

Mrs. Antrobus . . . I don't like to . . . appear to . . . ask for anything, but . . .

MRS. ANTROBUS:

What is it you'd like?

TELEGRAPH BOY:

Do you happen to have an old needle you could spare? My wife just sits home all day thinking about needles.

SABINA:

Shrilly.

We only got two in the house. Mrs. Antrobus, you know we only got two in the house.

MRS. ANTROBUS:

After a look at SABINA *taking a needle from her collar.*

Why yes, I can spare this.

TELEGRAPH BOY:

Lowered eyes.

Thank you, Mrs. Antrobus. Mrs. Antrobus, can I ask you something else? I have two sons of my own; if the cold gets worse, what should I do?

SABINA:

I think we'll all perish, that's what I think. Cold like this in August is just the end of the whole world.

Silence.

MRS. ANTROBUS:

I don't know. After all, what does one do about anything? Just keep as warm as you can. And don't let your wife and children see that you're worried.

TELEGRAPH BOY:

Yes. . . . Thank you, Mrs. Antrobus. Well, I'd better be going. —Oh, I forgot! There's one more sentence in the telegram. "Three cheers have invented the wheel."

MRS. ANTROBUS:

A wheel? What's a wheel?

TELEGRAPH BOY:

I don't know. That's what it said. The sign for it is like this. Well, goodbye.

The WOMEN *see him to the door, with goodbyes and injunctions to keep warm.*

SABINA:

Apron to her eyes, wailing.

Mrs. Antrobus, it looks to me like all the nice men in the world are already married; I don't know why that is.

Exit.

MRS. ANTROBUS:

Thoughtful; to the ANIMALS.

Do you ever remember hearing tell of any cold like this in August?

The ANIMALS *shake their heads.*

From your grandmothers or anyone?

They shake their heads.

Have you any suggestions?

They shake their heads.

She pulls her shawl around, goes to the front door and opening it an inch calls:

HENRY. GLADYS. CHILDREN. Come right in and get warm. No, no, when mama says a thing she means it.

Henry! HENRY. Put down that stone. You know what happened last time.

Shriek.

HENRY! Put down that stone!

Gladys! Put down your dress!! Try and be a lady.

The CHILDREN *bound in and dash to the fire. They take off their winter things and leave them in heaps on the floor.*

GLADYS:

Mama, I'm hungry. Mama, why is it so cold?

HENRY:

At the same time.

Mama, why doesn't it snow? Mama, when's supper ready?

Maybe, it'll snow and we can make snowballs.

GLADYS:

Mama, it's so cold that in one more minute I just couldn't of stood it.

MRS. ANTROBUS:

Settle down, both of you, I want to talk to you.

> *She draws up a hassock and sits front center over the orchestra pit before the imaginary fire. The* CHILDREN *stretch out on the floor, leaning against her lap. Tableau by Raphael. The* ANIMALS *edge up and complete the triangle.*

It's just a cold spell of some kind. Now listen to what I'm saying:

When your father comes home I want you to be extra quiet.

He's had a hard day at the office and I don't know but what he may have one of his moods.

I just got a telegram from him very happy and excited, and you know what that means. Your father's temper's uneven; I guess you know that.

> *Shriek.*

Henry! Henry!

Why—why can't you remember to keep your hair down over your forehead? You must keep that scar covered up. Don't you know that when your father sees it he loses all control over himself? He goes crazy. He wants to die.

> *After a moment's despair she collects herself decisively, wets the hem of her apron in her mouth and starts polishing his forehead vigorously.*

Lift your head up. Stop squirming. Blessed me, sometimes I think that it's going away—and then there it is: just as red as ever.

HENRY:

Mama, today at school two teachers forgot and called me by my old name. They forgot, Mama. You'd better write another letter to the principal, so that he'll tell them I've changed my name. Right out in class they called me: Cain.

MRS. ANTROBUS:
Putting her hand on his mouth, too late; hoarsely.

Don't say it.

Polishing feverishly.

If you're good they'll forget it. Henry, you didn't hit anyone . . . today, did you?

HENRY:
Oh . . . no-o-o!

MRS. ANTROBUS:
Still working, not looking at Gladys.

And, Gladys, I want you to be especially nice to your father tonight. You know what he calls you when you're good—his little angel, his little star. Keep your dress down like a little lady. And keep your voice nice and low. Gladys Antrobus!! What's that red stuff you have on your face?

Slaps her.

You're a filthy detestable child!

Rises in real, though temporary, repudiation and despair.

Get away from me, both of you! I wish I'd never seen sight or sound of you. Let the cold come! I can't stand it. I don't want to go on.

She walks away.

GLADYS:
Weeping.

All the girls at school do, Mama.

MRS. ANTROBUS:
Shrieking.

I'm through with you, that's all!—Sabina! Sabina!—Don't you know your father'd go crazy if he saw that paint on your face? Don't you know your father thinks you're perfect? Don't you know he couldn't live if he didn't think you were perfect?—Sabina!

Enter SABINA.

SABINA:
Yes, Mrs. Antrobus!

MRS. ANTROBUS:
Take this girl out into the kitchen and wash her face with the scrubbing brush.

MR. ANTROBUS:
Outside, roaring.

"I've been working on the railroad, all the livelong day . . . etc."

The ANIMALS *start running around in circles, bellowing.*
SABINA *rushes to the window.*

MRS. ANTROBUS:

Sabina, what's that noise outside?

SABINA:

Oh, it's a drunken tramp. It's a giant, Mrs. Antrobus. We'll all be killed in our beds, I know it!

MRS. ANTROBUS:

Help me quick. Quick. Everybody.

Again they stack all the furniture against the door. MR. ANTROBUS *pounds and bellows.*

Who is it? What do you want?—Sabina, have you any boiling water ready?—Who is it?

MR. ANTROBUS:

Broken-down camel of a pig's snout, open this door.

MRS. ANTROBUS:

God be praised! It's your father.—Just a minute, George!—Sabina, clear the door, quick. Gladys, come here while I clean your nasty face!

MR. ANTROBUS:

She-bitch of a goat's gizzard, I'll break every bone in your body. Let me in or I'll tear the whole house down.

MRS. ANTROBUS:

Just a minute, George, something's the matter with the lock.

MR. ANTROBUS:

Open the door or I'll tear your livers out. I'll smash your brains on the ceiling, and Devil take the hindmost.

MRS. ANTROBUS:

Now, you can open the door, Sabina. I'm ready.

The door is flung open. Silence. MR. ANTROBUS—*face of a Keystone Comedy Cop—stands there in fur cap and blanket. His arms are full of parcels, including a large stone wheel with a center in it. One hand carries a railroad man's lantern. Suddenly he bursts into joyous roar.*

MR. ANTROBUS:

Well, how's the whole crooked family?

Relief. Laughter. Tears. Jumping up and down. ANIMALS *cavorting.* ANTROBUS *throws the parcels on the ground. Hurls his cap and blanket after them. Heroic embraces. Melee of* HUMANS *and* ANIMALS, SABINA *included.*

I'll be scalded and tarred if a man can't get a little welcome when he comes home. Well, Maggie, you old gunny-sack, how's the broken down old weather hen?—Sabina, old fish-bait, old skunkpot.—And the children,—how've the little smellers been?

GLADYS:

Papa, Papa, Papa, Papa, Papa.

MR. ANTROBUS:

How've they been, Maggie?

MRS. ANTROBUS:

Well, I must say, they've been as good as gold. I haven't had to raise my voice once. I don't know what's the matter with them.

ANTROBUS:

Kneeling before GLADYS.

Papa's little weasel, eh?—Sabina, there's some food for you.—
Papa's little gopher?

GLADYS:

Her arm around his neck.

Papa, you're always teasing me.

ANTROBUS:

And Henry? Nothing rash today, I hope. Nothing rash?

HENRY:

No, Papa.

ANTROBUS:

Roaring.

Well that's good, that's good—I'll bet Sabina let the fire go
out.

SABINA:

Mr. Antrobus, I've given my notice. I'm leaving two weeks
from today. I'm sorry, but I'm leaving.

ANTROBUS:

Roar.

Well, if you leave now you'll freeze to death, so go and cook the
dinner.

SABINA:

Two weeks, that's the law.

Exit.

ANTROBUS:

Did you get my telegram?

MRS. ANTROBUS:

Yes.—What's a wheel?

He indicates the wheel with a glance. HENRY *is rolling it around the floor. Rapid, hoarse interchange:* MRS. ANTROBUS: *What does this cold weather mean? It's below freezing.* ANTROBUS: *Not before the children!* MRS. ANTROBUS: *Shouldn't we do something about it?—start off, move?* ANTROBUS: *Not before the children!!! He gives* HENRY *a sharp slap.*

HENRY:

Papa, you hit me!

ANTROBUS:

Well, remember it. That's to make you remember today. Today. The day the alphabet's finished; and the day that we *saw* the hundred—the hundred, the hundred, the hundred, the hundred, the hundred—there's no end to 'em.

I've had a day at the office!

Take a look at that wheel, Maggie—when I've got that to rights: you'll see a sight.

There's a reward there for all the walking you've done.

MRS. ANTROBUS:

How do you mean?

ANTROBUS:

On the hassock looking into the fire; with awe.

Maggie, we've reached the top of the wave. There's not much more to be done. We're there!

MRS. ANTROBUS:
Cutting across his mood sharply.

And the ice?

ANTROBUS:
The ice!

HENRY:
Playing with the wheel.

Papa, you could put a chair on this.

ANTROBUS:
Broodingly.

Ye-e-s, any booby can fool with it now,—but I thought of it first.

MRS. ANTROBUS:
Children, go out in the kitchen. I want to talk to your father alone.

The CHILDREN *go out.*

ANTROBUS *has moved to his chair up left. He takes the goldfish bowl on his lap; pulls the canary cage down to the level of his face. Both the* ANIMALS *put their paws up on the arm of his chair.* MRS. ANTROBUS *faces him across the room, like a judge.*

MRS. ANTROBUS:
Well?

ANTROBUS:

Shortly.

It's cold.—How things been, eh? Keck, keck, keck.—And you, Millicent?

MRS. ANTROBUS:

I know it's cold.

ANTROBUS:

To the canary.

No spilling of sunflower seed, eh? No singing after lights-out, y'know what I mean?

MRS. ANTROBUS:

You can try and prevent us freezing to death, can't you? You can do something? We can start moving. Or we can go on the animals' backs?

ANTROBUS:

The best thing about animals is that they don't talk much.

MAMMOTH:

It's cold.

ANTROBUS:

Eh, eh, eh! Watch that!—

—By midnight we'd turn to ice. The roads are full of people now who can scarcely lift a foot from the ground. The grass out in front is like iron,—which reminds me, I have another needle for you.—The people up north—where are they?

Frozen . . . crushed. . . .

MRS. ANTROBUS:

Is that what's going to happen to us?—Will you answer me?

ANTROBUS:

I don't know. I don't know anything. Some say that the ice is going slower. Some say that it's stopped. The sun's growing cold. What can I do about that? Nothing we can do but burn everything in the house, and the fenceposts and the barn. Keep the fire going. When we have no more fire, we die.

MRS. ANTROBUS:

Well, why didn't you say so in the first place?

MRS. ANTROBUS *is about to march off when she catches sight of two* REFUGEES, *men, who have appeared against the back wall of the theatre and who are soon joined by others.*

REFUGEES:

Mr. Antrobus! Mr. Antrobus! Mr. An-nn-tro-bus!

MRS. ANTROBUS:

Who's that? Who's that calling you?

ANTROBUS:

Clearing his throat guiltily.

Hm—let me see.

Two REFUGEES *come up to the window.*

REFUGEE:

Could we warm our hands for a moment, Mr. Antrobus. It's very cold, Mr. Antrobus.

ANOTHER REFUGEE:

Mr. Antrobus, I wonder if you have a piece of bread or something that you could spare.

Silence. They wait humbly. MRS. ANTROBUS *stands rooted to the spot. Suddenly a knock at the door, then another hand knocking in short rapid blows.*

MRS. ANTROBUS:

Who are these people? Why, they're all over the front yard.

What have they come *here* for?

Enter SABINA.

SABINA:

Mrs. Antrobus! There are some tramps knocking at the back door.

MRS. ANTROBUS:

George, tell these people to go away. Tell them to move right along. I'll go and send them away from the back door. Sabina, come with me.

She goes out energetically.

ANTROBUS:

Sabina! Stay here! I have something to say to you.

He goes to the door and opens it a crack and talks through it.

Ladies and gentlemen! I'll have to ask you to wait a few minutes longer. It'll be all right . . . while you're waiting you might each one pull up a stake of the fence. We'll need them all for the fireplace. There'll be coffee and sandwiches in a moment.

SABINA *looks out door over his shoulder and suddenly extends her arm pointing, with a scream.*

SABINA:

Mr. Antrobus, what's that??—that big white thing? Mr. Antrobus, it's ICE. It's ICE!!

ANTROBUS:

Sabina, I want you to go in the kitchen and make a lot of coffee. Make a whole pail full.

SABINA:

Pail full!!

ANTROBUS:

With gesture.

And sandwiches . . . piles of them . . . like this.

SABINA:

Mr. An . . . !!

Suddenly she drops the play, and says in her own person as MISS SOMERSET, *with surprise.*

Oh, *I* see what this part of the play means now! This means refugees.

She starts to cross to the proscenium.

Oh, I don't like it. I don't like it.

She leans against the proscenium and bursts into tears.

ANTROBUS:

Miss Somerset!

Voice of the STAGE MANAGER.

Miss Somerset!

SABINA:

Energetically, to the audience.

Ladies and gentlemen! Don't take this play serious. The world's not coming to an end. You know it's not. People exaggerate!

Most people really have enough to eat and a roof over their heads. Nobody actually starves—you can always eat grass or something. That ice-business—why, it was a long, long time ago. Besides they were only savages. Savages don't love their families—not like we do.

ANTROBUS *and* STAGE MANAGER:

Miss Somerset!!

There is renewed knocking at the door.

SABINA:

All right. I'll say the lines, but I won't think about the play.

Enter MRS. ANTROBUS.

SABINA:

Parting thrust at the audience.

And I advise *you* not to think about the play, either.

Exit SABINA.

MRS. ANTROBUS:

George, these tramps say that you asked them to come to the house. What does this mean?

Knocking at the door.

ANTROBUS:

Just . . . uh. . . . There are a few friends, Maggie, I met on the road. Real nice, real useful people. . . .

MRS. ANTROBUS:

Back to the door.

Now, don't you ask them in!

George Antrobus, not another soul comes in here over my dead body.

ANTROBUS:

Maggie, there's a doctor there. Never hurts to have a good doctor in the house. We've lost a peck of children, one way and another. You can never tell when a child's throat will get stopped up. What you and I have seen—!!!

He puts his fingers on his throat, and imitates diphtheria.

MRS. ANTROBUS:

Well, just one person then, the Doctor. The others can go right along the road.

ANTROBUS:

Maggie, there's an old man, particular friend of mine—

MRS. ANTROBUS:

I won't listen to you—

ANTROBUS:

It was he that really started off the A.B.C.'s.

MRS. ANTROBUS:

I don't care if he perishes. We can do without reading or writing. We can't do without food.

ANTROBUS:

Then let the ice come!! Drink your coffee!! I don't want any coffee if I can't drink it with some good people.

MRS. ANTROBUS:

Stop shouting. Who else is there trying to push us off the cliff?

ANTROBUS:

Well, there's the man . . . who makes all the laws. Judge Moses!

MRS. ANTROBUS:

Judges can't help us now.

ANTROBUS:

And if the ice melts? . . . and if we pull through? Have you and I been able to bring up Henry? What have we done?

MRS. ANTROBUS:

Who are those old women?

ANTROBUS:

Coughs.

Up in town there are nine sisters. There are three or four of them here. They're sort of music teachers . . . and one of them recites and one of them—

MRS. ANTROBUS:

That's the end. A singing troupe! Well, take your choice, live or die. Starve your own children before your face.

ANTROBUS:

Gently.

These people don't take much. They're used to starving.

They'll sleep on the floor.

Besides, Maggie, listen: no, listen:

Who've we got in the house, but Sabina? Sabina's always afraid the worst will happen. Whose spirits can she keep up? Maggie, these people never give up. They think they'll live and work forever.

MRS. ANTROBUS:

Walks slowly to the middle of the room.

All right, let them in. Let them in. You're master here.

Softly.

—But these animals must go. Enough's enough. They'll soon be big enough to push the walls down, anyway. Take them away.

ANTROBUS:

Sadly.

All right. The dinosaur and mammoth—! Come on, baby, come on Frederick. Come for a walk. That's a good little fellow.

DINOSAUR:

It's cold.

ANTROBUS:

Yes, nice cold fresh air. Bracing.

He holds the door open and the ANIMALS *go out. He beckons to his friends. The* REFUGEES *are typical elderly out-of-works from the streets of New York today.* JUDGE MOSES *wears a skull cap.* HOMER *is a blind beggar with a guitar. The seedy crowd shuffles in and waits humbly and expectantly.* ANTROBUS *introduces them to his wife who bows to each with a stately bend of her head.*

Make yourself at home, Maggie, this the doctor . . . m . . . Coffee'll be here in a minute. . . . Professor, this is my wife. . . . And: . . . Judge . . . Maggie, you know the Judge.

An old blind man with a guitar.

Maggie, you know . . . you know Homer?—Come right in, Judge.—

Miss Muse—are some of your sisters here? Come right in. . . . Miss E. Muse; Miss T. Muse, Miss M. Muse.

MRS. ANTROBUS:

Pleased to meet you.

Just . . . make yourself comfortable. Supper'll be ready in a minute.

She goes out, abruptly.

ANTROBUS:

Make yourself at home, friends. I'll be right back.

He goes out.

The REFUGEES *stare about them in awe. Presently several voices start whispering "Homer! Homer!" All take it up.* HOMER *strikes a chord or two on his guitar, then starts to speak:*

HOMER:

Μῆνιν ἄειδε, θεὰ, Πηληϊάδεω Ἀχιλῆος,
οὐλομένην, ἥ μυρί’ Ἀχαιοῖς ἄλγε’ ἔθηκεν,
πολλὰς δ’ ἰφθίμους ψυχὰς—

HOMER'S *face shows he is lost in thought and memory and the words die away on his lips. The* REFUGEES *likewise nod in dreamy recollection. Soon the whisper "Moses, Moses!" goes around. An aged Jew parts his beard and recites dramatically:*

MOSES:

בְּרֵאשִׁית בָּרָא אֱלֹהִים אֵת הַשָּׁמַיִם וְאֵת הָאָרֶץ: וְהָאָרֶץ הָיְתָה תֹהוּ
וָבֹהוּ וְחֹשֶׁךְ עַל־פְּנֵי תְהוֹם וְרוּחַ אֱלֹהִים מְרַחֶפֶת עַל־פְּנֵי הַמָּיִם:

*The same dying away of the words take place, and on the part
of the* REFUGEES *the same retreat into recollection. Some of
them murmur, "Yes, yes."*

The mood is broken by the abrupt entrance of MR. *and* MRS.
ANTROBUS *and* SABINA *bearing platters of sandwiches and a
pail of coffee.* SABINA *stops and stares at the guests.*

MR. ANTROBUS:
Sabina, pass the sandwiches.

SABINA:
I thought I was working in a respectable house that had
respectable guests. I'm giving my notice, Mr. Antrobus: two
weeks, that's the law.

MR. ANTROBUS:
Sabina! Pass the sandwiches.

SABINA:
Two weeks, that's the law.

MR. ANTROBUS:
There's the law. That's Moses.

SABINA:
Stares.

The Ten Commandments—FAUGH!!—(*To Audience*)

That's the worst line I've ever had to say on any stage.

ANTROBUS:

I think the best thing to do is just not to stand on ceremony, but pass the sandwiches around from left to right.—Judge, help yourself to one of these.

MRS. ANTROBUS:

The roads are crowded, I hear?

THE GUESTS:

All talking at once.

Oh, ma'am, you can't imagine. . . . You can hardly put one foot before you . . . people are trampling one another.

Sudden silence.

MRS. ANTROBUS:

Well, you know what I think it is,—I think it's sun-spots!

THE GUESTS:

Discreet hubbub.

Oh, you're right, Mrs. Antrobus . . . that's what it is. . . . That's what I was saying the other day.

Sudden silence.

ANTROBUS:

Well, I don't believe the whole world's going to turn to ice.

All eyes are fixed on him, waiting.

I can't believe it. Judge! Have we worked for nothing? Professor! Have we just failed in the whole thing?

MRS. ANTROBUS:

It is certainly very strange—well fortunately on both sides of the family we come of very hearty stock.—Doctor, I want you to meet my children. They're eating their supper now. And of course I want them to meet you.

MISS M. MUSE:

How many children have you, Mrs. Antrobus?

MRS. ANTROBUS:

I have two,—a boy and a girl.

MOSES:

Softly.

I understood you had two sons, Mrs. Antrobus.

MRS. ANTROBUS *in blind suffering; she walks toward the foot lights.*

MRS. ANTROBUS:

In a low voice.

Abel, Abel, my son, my son, Abel, my son, Abel, Abel, my son.

The REFUGEES *move with few steps toward her as though in comfort murmuring words in Greek, Hebrew, German, et cetera.*

*A piercing shriek from the kitchen,—*SABINA'S *voice.*

All heads turn.

ANTROBUS:

What's that?

SABINA *enters, bursting with indignation, pulling on her gloves.*

SABINA:

Mr. Antrobus—that son of yours, that boy Henry Antrobus—I don't stay in this house another moment!—He's not fit to live among respectable folks and that's a fact.

MRS. ANTROBUS:

Don't say another word, Sabina. I'll be right back.

Without waiting for an answer she goes past her into the kitchen.

SABINA:

Mr. Antrobus, Henry has thrown a stone again and if he hasn't killed the boy that lives next door, I'm very much mistaken. He finished his supper and went out to play; and I heard such a fight; and then I saw it. I saw it with my own eyes. And it looked to me like stark murder.

MRS. ANTROBUS *appears at the kitchen door, shielding* HENRY *who follows her. When she steps aside, we see on* HENRY'S *forehead a large ochre and scarlet scar in the shape of a C.* MR. ANTROBUS *starts toward him. A pause.* HENRY *is heard saying under his breath:*

HENRY:

He was going to take the wheel away from me. He started to throw a stone at me first.

MRS. ANTROBUS:

George, it was just a boyish impulse. Remember how young he is.

Louder, in an urgent wail.

George, he's only four thousand years old.

SABINA:

And everything was going along so nicely!

Silence. ANTROBUS *goes back to the fireplace.*

ANTROBUS:

Put out the fire! Put out all the fires.

Violently.

No wonder the sun grows cold.

He starts stamping on the fireplace.

MRS. ANTROBUS:

Doctor! Judge! Help me!—George, have you lost your mind?

ANTROBUS:

There is no mind. We'll not try to live.

To the guests.

Give it up. Give up trying.

MRS. ANTROBUS *seizes him.*

SABINA:

Mr. Antrobus! I'm downright ashamed of you.

MRS. ANTROBUS:

George, have some more coffee.—Gladys! Where's Gladys gone?

GLADYS *steps in, frightened.*

GLADYS:

Here I am, mama.

MRS. ANTROBUS:

Go upstairs and bring your father's slippers. How could you forget a thing like that, when you know how tired he is?

ANTROBUS *sits in his chair. He covers his face with his hands.*
MRS. ANTROBUS *turns to the* REFUGEES:

Can't some of you sing? It's your business in life to sing, isn't it? Sabina!

Several of the women clear their throats tentatively, and with frightened faces gather around HOMER'S *guitar. He establishes a few chords. Almost inaudibly they start singing, led by* SABINA: *"Jingle Bells."* MRS. ANTROBUS *continues to* ANTROBUS *in a low voice, while taking off his shoes:*

George, remember all the other times. When the volcanoes came right up in the front yard.

And the time the grasshoppers ate every single leaf and blade of grass, and all the grain and spinach you'd grown with your own hands. And the summer there were earthquakes every night.

ANTROBUS:

Henry! Henry!

Puts his hand on his forehead.

Myself. All of us, we're covered with blood.

MRS. ANTROBUS:

Then remember all the times you were pleased with him and when you were proud of yourself.—Henry! Henry! Come here and recite to your father the multiplication table that you do so nicely.

> HENRY *kneels on one knee beside his father and starts whispering the multiplication table.*

HENRY:
Finally.

Two times six is twelve; three times six is eighteen—I don't think I know the sixes.

> *Enter* GLADYS *with the slippers.* MRS. ANTROBUS *makes stern gestures to her: Go in there and do your best. The* GUESTS *are now singing "Tenting Tonight."*

GLADYS:
Putting slippers on his feet.

Papa . . . papa . . . I was very good in school today. Miss Conover said right out in class that if all the girls had as good manners as Gladys Antrobus, that the world would be a very different place to live in.

MRS. ANTROBUS:
You recited a piece at assembly, didn't you? Recite it to your father.

GLADYS:
Papa, do you want to hear what I recited in class?

> *Fierce directorial glance from her mother.*

"THE STAR" by Henry Wadsworth LONGFELLOW.

MRS. ANTROBUS:
Wait!!! The fire's going out. There isn't enough wood!

Henry, go upstairs and bring down the chairs and start breaking up the beds.

Exit HENRY. *The singers return to "Jingle Bells," still very softly.*

GLADYS:

Look, Papa, here's my report card. Lookit. Conduct A! Look, Papa. Papa, do you want to hear the Star, by Henry Wadsworth Longfellow? Papa, you're not mad at me, are you?—I know it'll get warmer. Soon it'll be just like spring, and we can go to a picnic at the Hibernian Picnic Grounds like you always like to do, don't you remember? Papa, just look at me once.

Enter HENRY *with some chairs.*

ANTROBUS:

You recited in assembly, did you?

She nods eagerly.

You didn't forget it?

GLADYS:

No!!! I was perfect.

Pause. Then ANTROBUS *rises, goes to the front door and opens it. The* REFUGEES *draw back timidly; the song stops; he peers out of the door, then closes it.*

ANTROBUS:

With decision, suddenly.

Build up the fire. It's cold. Build up the fire. We'll do what we can. Sabina, get some more wood. Come around the fire, everybody. At least the young ones may pull through. Henry, have you eaten something?

HENRY:

Yes, papa.

ANTROBUS:

Gladys, have you had some supper?

GLADYS:

I ate in the kitchen, papa.

ANTROBUS:

If you do come through this—what'll you be able to do? What do you know? Henry, did you take a good look at that wheel?

HENRY:

Yes, papa.

ANTROBUS:

Sitting down in his chair.

Six times two are—

HENRY:

—twelve; six times three are eighteen; six times four are—Papa, it's hot and cold. It makes my head all funny. It makes me sleepy.

ANTROBUS:

Gives him a cuff.

Wake up. I don't care if your head is sleepy. Six times four are twenty-four. Six times five are—

HENRY:

Thirty. Papa!

ANTROBUS:

Maggie, put something into Gladys' head on the chance she can use it.

MRS. ANTROBUS:

What do you mean, George?

ANTROBUS:

Six times six are thirty-six.

Teach her the beginning of the Bible.

GLADYS:

But, Mama, it's so cold and close.

HENRY *has all but drowsed off. His father slaps him sharply and the lesson goes on.*

MRS. ANTROBUS:

"In the beginning God created the heavens and the earth; and the earth was waste and void; and the darkness was upon the face of the deep—"

The singing starts up again louder. SABINA *has returned with wood.*

SABINA:

After placing wood on the fireplace comes down to the foot- lights and addresses the audience:

Will you please start handing up your chairs? We'll need everything for this fire. Save the human race.—Ushers, will you pass the chairs up here? Thank you.

HENRY:

Six times nine are fifty-four; six times ten are sixty.

In the back of the auditorium the sound of chairs being ripped up can be heard. USHERS *rush down the aisles with chairs and hand them over.*

GLADYS:

"And God called the light Day and the darkness he called Night."

SABINA:

Pass up your chairs, everybody. Save the human race.

CURTAIN

—∽∾∽—

Act II

*Toward the end of the intermission, though with the houselights
still up, lantern slide projections begin to appear on the curtain.
Timetables for trains leaving Pennsylvania Station for Atlantic
City. Advertisements of Atlantic City hotels, drugstores, churches,
rug merchants; fortune tellers, Bingo parlors.*

    When the house-lights go down, the voice of an ANNOUNCER
is heard.

ANNOUNCER:
The Management now brings you the News Events of the
World. Atlantic City, New Jersey:

    *Projection of a chrome postcard of the waterfront, trimmed
    in mica with the legend: FUN AT THE BEACH.*

This great convention city is playing host this week to the
anniversary convocation of that great fraternal order,—the
Ancient and Honorable Order of Mammals, Subdivision
Humans. This great fraternal, militant and burial society is

celebrating on the Boardwalk, ladies and gentlemen, its six hundred thousandth Annual Convention.

It has just elected its president for the ensuing term,—

Projection of MR. *and* MRS. ANTROBUS *posed as they will be shown a few moments later.*

Mr. George Antrobus of Excelsior, New Jersey. We show you President Antrobus and his gracious and charming wife, every inch a mammal. Mr. Antrobus has had a long and chequered career. Credit has been paid to him for many useful enterprises including the introduction of the lever, of the wheel and the brewing of beer. Credit has been also extended to President Antrobus's gracious and charming wife for many practical suggestions, including the hem, the gore, and the gusset; and the novelty of the year,—frying in oil. Before we show you Mr. Antrobus accepting the nomination, we have an important announcement to make. As many of you know, this great celebration of the Order of the Mammals has received delegations from the other rival Orders,— or shall we say: esteemed concurrent Orders: the WINGS, the FINS, the SHELLS, and so on. These Orders are holding their conventions also, in various parts of the world, and have sent representatives to our own, two of a kind.

Later in the day we will show you President Antrobus broadcasting his words of greeting and congratulation to the collected assemblies of the whole natural world.

Ladies and Gentlemen! We give you President Antrobus!

The screen becomes a Transparency. MR. ANTROBUS *stands beside a pedestal;* MRS. ANTROBUS *is seated wearing a corsage of orchids.* ANTROBUS *wears an untidy Prince Albert; spats;*

from a red rosette in his buttonhole hangs a fine long purple ribbon of honor. He wears a gay lodge hat,—something between a fez and a legionnaire's cap.

ANTROBUS:

Fellow-mammals, fellow-vertebrates, fellow-humans, I thank you. Little did my dear parents think,—when they told me to stand on my own two feet,—that I'd arrive at this place.

My friends, we have come a long way.

During this week of happy celebration it is perhaps not fitting that we dwell on some of the difficult times we have been through. The dinosaur is extinct—

Applause.

—the ice has retreated; and the common cold is being pursued by every means within our power.

MRS. ANTROBUS *sneezes, laughs prettily, and murmurs: "I beg your pardon."*

In our memorial service yesterday we did honor to all our friends and relatives who are no longer with us, by reason of cold, earthquakes, plagues and . . . and . . .

Coughs.

differences of opinion.

As our Bishop so ably said . . . uh . . . so ably said. . . .

MRS. ANTROBUS:
Closed lips.

Gone, but not forgotten.

ANTROBUS:

'They are gone, but not forgotten.'

I think I can say, I think I can prophesy with complete . . . uh
. . . with complete. . . .

MRS. ANTROBUS:

Confidence.

ANTROBUS:

Thank you, my dear,—With complete lack of confidence, that a
new day of security is about to dawn.

The watchword of the closing year was: Work. I give you the
watchword for the future: Enjoy Yourselves.

MRS. ANTROBUS:

George, sit down!

ANTROBUS:

Before I close, however, I wish to answer one of those unjust
and malicious accusations that were brought against me during this last electoral campaign.

Ladies and gentlemen, the charge was made that at various
points in my career I leaned toward joining some of the rival
orders,—that's a lie.

As I told reporters of the *Atlantic City Herald,* I do not deny
that a few months before my birth I hesitated between . . . uh
. . . between pinfeathers and gill-breathing,—and so did many
of us here,—but for the last million years I have been vivipa-
rous, hairy and diaphragmatic.

Applause. Cries of 'Good old Antrobus,' 'The Prince chap!'
'Georgie,' etc.

ANNOUNCER:

Thank you. Thank you very much, Mr. Antrobus.

Now I know that our visitors will wish to hear a word from that gracious and charming mammal, Mrs. Antrobus, wife and mother,—Mrs. Antrobus!

MRS. ANTROBUS *rises, lays her program on her chair, bows and says:*

MRS. ANTROBUS:

Dear friends, I don't really think I should say anything. After all, it was my husband who was elected and not I. Perhaps, as president of the Women's Auxiliary Bed and Board Society,— I had some notes here, oh, yes, here they are:—I should give a short report from some of our committees that have been meeting in this beautiful city.

Perhaps it may interest you to know that it has at last been decided that the tomato is edible. Can you all hear me? The tomato *is* edible.

A delegate from across the sea reports that the thread woven by the silkworm gives a cloth . . . I have a sample of it here . . . can you see it? smooth, elastic. I should say that it's rather attractive,—though personally I prefer less shiny surfaces. Should the windows of a sleeping apartment be open or shut? I know all mothers will follow our debates on this matter with close interest. I am sorry to say that the most expert authorities have not yet decided. It does seem to me that the night air would be bound to be unhealthy for our children, but there are many distinguished authorities on both sides. Well, I could go on talking forever,—as Shakespeare says: a woman's work is seldom done; but I think I'd better join my husband in saying thank you, and sit down. Thank you.

She sits down.

ANNOUNCER:
Oh, Mrs. Antrobus!

MRS. ANTROBUS:
Yes?

ANNOUNCER:
We understand that you are about to celebrate a wedding anniversary. I know our listeners would like to extend their felicitations and hear a few words from you on that subject.

MRS. ANTROBUS:
I have been asked by this kind gentleman . . . yes, my friends, this Spring Mr. Antrobus and I will be celebrating our five thousandth wedding anniversary.

I don't know if I speak for my husband, but I can say that, as for me, I regret every moment of it.

Laughter of confusion.

I beg your pardon. What I *mean* to say is that I do not regret one moment of it. I hope none of you catch my cold. We have two children. We've always had two children, though it hasn't always been the same two. But as I say, we have two fine children, and we're very grateful for that. Yes, Mr. Antrobus and I have been married five thousand years. Each wedding anniversary reminds me of the times when there were no weddings. We had to crusade for marriage. Perhaps there are some women within the sound of my voice who remember that crusade and

those struggles; we fought for it, didn't we? We chained ourselves to lampposts and we made disturbances in the Senate,—
anyway, at last we women got the ring.

A few men helped us, but I must say that most men blocked
our way at every step: they said we were unfeminine.

I only bring up these unpleasant memories, because I see
some signs of backsliding from that great victory.

Oh, my fellow mammals, keep hold of that.

My husband says that the watchword for the year is Enjoy
Yourselves. I think that's very open to misunderstanding. My
watchword for the year is: Save the Family. It's held together
for over five thousand years: Save it! Thank you.

ANNOUNCER:
Thank you, Mrs. Antrobus.

The transparency disappears.

We had hoped to show you the Beauty Contest that took
place here today.

President Antrobus, an experienced judge of pretty girls,
gave the title of Miss Atlantic City 1942, to Miss Lily-Sabina
Fairweather, charming hostess of our Boardwalk Bingo Parlor.

Unfortunately, however, our time is up, and I must take you
to some views of the Convention City and conveeners,—
enjoying themselves.

A burst of music; the curtain rises.

The Boardwalk. The audience is sitting in the ocean. A handrail of scarlet cord stretches across the front of the stage. A ramp—also with scarlet hand rail—descends to the right corner of the orchestra pit where a great scarlet beach umbrella or a cabana stands. Front and right stage left are benches facing the sea; attached to each bench is a street-lamp.

The only scenery is two cardboard cut-outs six feet high, representing shops at the back of the stage. Reading from left to right they are: SALT WATER TAFFY: FORTUNE TELLER; then the blank space; BINGO PARLOR; TURKISH BATH. They have practical doors, that of the Fortune Teller's being hung with bright gypsy curtains.

By the left proscenium and rising from the orchestra pit is the weather signal; it is like the mast of a ship with cross bars. From time to time black discs are hung on it to indicate the storm and hurricane warnings. Three roller chairs, pushed by melancholy NEGROES *file by empty. Throughout the act they traverse the stage in both directions.*

From time to time, CONVEENERS, *dressed like* MR. ANTROBUS, *cross the stage. Some walk sedately by; others engage in inane horseplay. The old gypsy* FORTUNE TELLER *is seated at the door of her shop, smoking a corncob pipe.*

From the Bingo Parlor comes the voice of the CALLER.

BINGO CALLER:
A-Nine; A-Nine. C-Twenty-six; C-Twenty-six.

A-Four; A-Four. B-Twelve.

CHORUS:

Back-stage.

Bingo!!!

The front of the Bingo Parlor shudders, rises a few feet in the air and returns to the ground trembling.

FORTUNE TELLER:

Mechanically, to the unconscious back of a passerby, pointing with her pipe.

Bright's disease! Your partner's deceiving you in that Kansas City deal. You'll have six grandchildren. Avoid high places.

She rises and shouts after another:

Cirrhosis of the liver!

SABINA *appears at the door of the Bingo Parlor. She hugs about her a blue raincoat that almost conceals her red bathing suit. She tries to catch the* FORTUNE TELLER'S *attention.*

SABINA:

Ssssst! Esmeralda! Ssssst!

FORTUNE TELLER:

Keck!

SABINA:

Has President Antrobus come along yet?

FORTUNE TELLER:

No, no, no. Get back there. Hide yourself.

SABINA:

I'm afraid I'll miss him. Oh, Esmeralda, if I fail in this, I'll die; I know I'll die. President Antrobus!!! And I'll be his wife! If it's the last thing I'll do, I'll be Mrs. George Antrobus.—Esmeralda, tell me my future.

FORTUNE TELLER:

Keck!

SABINA:

All right, I'll tell *you* my future.

Laughing dreamily and tracing it out with one finger on the palm of her hand.

I've won the Beauty Contest in Atlantic City,—well, I'll win the Beauty Contest of the whole world. I'll take President Antrobus away from that wife of his. Then I'll take every man away from his wife. I'll turn the whole earth upside down.

FORTUNE TELLER:

Keck!

SABINA:

When all those husbands just think about me they'll get dizzy. They'll faint in the streets. They'll have to lean against lampposts.—Esmeralda, who was Helen of Troy?

FORTUNE TELLER:

Furiously.

Shut your foolish mouth. When Mr. Antrobus comes along you can see what you can do. Until then,—go away.

SABINA *laughs. As she returns to the door of her Bingo Parlor a group of* CONVEENERS *rush over and smother her with attentions: "Oh, Miss Lily, you know me. You've known me for years."*

SABINA:

Go away, boys, go away. I'm after bigger fry than you are.— Why, Mr. Simpson!! How *dare* you!! I expect that even you nobodies must have girls to amuse you; but where you find them and what you do with them, is of absolutely no interest to me.

Exit. The CONVEENERS *squeal with pleasure and stumble in after her.*

The FORTUNE TELLER *rises, puts her pipe down on the stool, unfurls her voluminous skirts, gives a sharp wrench to her bodice and strolls towards the audience, swinging her hips like a young woman.*

FORTUNE TELLER:

I tell the future. Keck. Nothing easier. Everybody's future is in their face. Nothing easier.

But who can tell your past,—eh? Nobody!

Your youth,—where did it go? It slipped away while you weren't looking. While you were asleep. While you were drunk? Puh! You're like our friends, Mr. and Mrs. Antrobus; you lie awake nights trying to know your past. What did it mean? What was it trying to say to you?

Think! Think! Split your heads. I can't tell the past and neither can you. If anybody tries to tell you the past, take my word for it, they're charlatans! Charlatans! But I can tell the future.

She suddenly barks at a passing chair-pusher.

Apoplexy!

She returns to the audience.

Nobody listens.—Keck! I see a face among you now—I won't embarrass him by pointing him out, but, listen, it may be you: Next year the watchsprings inside you will crumple up. Death by regret,—Type Y. It's in the corners of your mouth. You'll decide that you should have lived for pleasure, but that you missed it. Death by regret,—Type Y. . . . Avoid mirrors. You'll try to be angry,—but no!—no anger.

Far forward, confidentially.

And now what's the immediate future of our friends, the Antrobuses? Oh, you've seen it as well as I have, keck,—that dizziness of the head; that Great Man dizziness? The inventor of beer and gunpowder. The sudden fits of temper and then the long stretches of inertia? "I'm a sultan; let my slave-girls fan me?"

You know as well as I what's coming. Rain. Rain. Rain in floods. The deluge. But first you'll see shameful things— shameful things. Some of you will be saying: "Let him drown. He's not worth saving. Give the whole thing up." I can see it in your faces. But you're wrong. Keep your doubts and despairs to yourselves.

Again there'll be the narrow escape. The survival of a handful. From destruction,—total destruction.

She points sweeping with her hand to the stage.

Even of the animals, a few will be saved: two of a kind, male and female, two of a kind.

The heads of CONVEENERS *appear about the stage and in the orchestra pit, jeering at her.*

CONVEENERS:

Charlatan! Madam Kill-joy! Mrs. Jeremiah! Charlatan!

FORTUNE TELLER:

And *you!* Mark my words before it's too late. Where'll *you* be?

CONVEENERS:

The croaking raven. Old dust and ashes. Rags, bottles, sacks.

FORTUNE TELLER:

Yes, stick out your tongues. You can't stick your tongues out far enough to lick the death-sweat from your foreheads. It's too late to work now—bail out the flood with your soup spoons. You've had your chance and you've lost.

CONVEENERS:

Enjoy yourselves!!!

They disappear. The FORTUNE TELLER *looks off left and puts her finger on her lip.*

FORTUNE TELLER:

They're coming—the Antrobuses. Keck. Your hope. Your despair. Your selves.

Enter from the left, MR. *and* MRS. ANTROBUS *and* GLADYS.

MRS. ANTROBUS:

Gladys Antrobus, stick your stummick in.

GLADYS:

But it's easier this way.

MRS. ANTROBUS:

Well, it's too bad the new president has such a clumsy daughter, that's all I can say. Try and be a lady.

FORTUNE TELLER:

Aijah! That's been said a hundred billion times.

MRS. ANTROBUS:

Goodness! Where's Henry? He was here just a minute ago. Henry!

Sudden violent stir. A roller-chair appears from the left. About it are dancing in great excitement HENRY *and a* NEGRO CHAIR-PUSHER.

HENRY:

Slingshot in band.

I'll put your eye out. I'll make you yell, like you never yelled before.

NEGRO:

At the same time.

Now, I warns you. I warns you. If you make me mad, you'll get hurt.

ANTROBUS:

Henry! What is this? Put down that slingshot.

MRS. ANTROBUS:

At the same time.

Henry! HENRY! Behave yourself.

FORTUNE TELLER:

That's right, young man. There are too many people in the world as it is. Everybody's in the way, except one's self.

HENRY:

All I wanted to do was—have some fun.

NEGRO:

Nobody can't touch my chair, nobody, without I allow 'em to. You get clean away from me and you get away fast.

He pushes his chair off, muttering.

ANTROBUS:

What were you doing, Henry?

HENRY:

Everybody's always getting mad. Everybody's always trying to push you around. I'll make him sorry for this; I'll make him sorry.

ANTROBUS:

Give me that slingshot.

HENRY:

I won't. I'm sorry I came to this place. I wish I weren't here. I wish I weren't anywhere.

MRS. ANTROBUS:

Now, Henry, don't get so excited about nothing. I declare I don't know what we're going to do with you. Put your sling-shot in your pocket, and don't try to take hold of things that don't belong to you.

ANTROBUS:

After this you can stay home. I wash my hands of you.

MRS. ANTROBUS:

Come now, let's forget all about it. Everybody take a good breath of that sea air and calm down.

A passing CONVEENER *bows to* ANTROBUS *who nods to him.*

Who was that you spoke to, George?

ANTROBUS:

Nobody, Maggie. Just the candidate who ran against me in the election.

MRS. ANTROBUS:

The man who ran against you in the election!!

She turns and waves her umbrella after the disappearing CONVEENER.

My husband didn't speak to you and he never will speak to you.

ANTROBUS:

Now, Maggie.

MRS. ANTROBUS:

After those lies you told about him in your speeches! Lies, that's what they were.

GLADYS AND HENRY:

Mama, everybody's looking at you. Everybody's laughing at you.

MRS. ANTROBUS:

If you must know, my husband's a SAINT, a downright SAINT, and you're not fit to speak to him on the street.

ANTROBUS:

Now, Maggie, now, Maggie, that's enough of that.

MRS. ANTROBUS:

George Antrobus, you're a perfect worm. If you won't stand up for yourself, I will.

GLADYS:

Mama, you just act awful in public.

MRS. ANTROBUS:

Laughing.

Well, I must say I enjoyed it. I feel better. Wish his wife had been there to hear it. Children, what do you want to do?

GLADYS:

Papa, can we ride in one of those chairs? Mama, I want to ride in one of those chairs.

MRS. ANTROBUS:

No, sir. If you're tired you just sit where you are. We have no money to spend on foolishness.

ANTROBUS:

I guess we have money enough for a thing like that. It's one of the things you do at Atlantic City.

MRS. ANTROBUS:

Oh, we have? I tell you it's a miracle my children have shoes to stand up in. I didn't think I'd ever live to see them pushed around in chairs.

ANTROBUS:

We're on a vacation, aren't we? We have a right to some treats, I guess. Maggie, some day you're going to drive me crazy.

MRS. ANTROBUS:

All right, go. I'll just sit here and laugh at you. And you can give me my dollar right in my hand. Mark my words, a rainy day is coming. There's a rainy day ahead of us. I feel it in my bones. Go on, throw your money around. I can starve. I've starved before. I know how.

A CONVEENER *puts his head through Turkish Bath window, and says with raised eyebrows:*

CONVEENER:
Hello, George. How are ya? I see where you brought the WHOLE family along.

MRS. ANTROBUS:
And what do you mean by that?

CONVEENER *withdraws head and closes window.*

ANTROBUS:
Maggie, I tell you there's a limit to what I can stand. God's Heaven, haven't I worked *enough?* Don't I get *any* vacation? Can't I even give my children so much as a ride in a roller-chair?

MRS. ANTROBUS:
Putting out her hand for raindrops.

Anyway, it's going to rain very soon and you have your broadcast to make.

ANTROBUS:
Now, Maggie, I warn you. A man can stand a family only just so long. I'm warning you.

Enter SABINA *from the Bingo-Parlor. She wears a flounced red silk bathing suit, 1905. Red stockings, shoes, parasol. She bows demurely to* ANTROBUS *and starts down the ramp.* ANTROBUS *and the* CHILDREN *stare at her.* ANTROBUS *bows gallantly.*

MRS. ANTROBUS:

Why, George Antrobus, how can you say such a thing! You have the best family in the world.

ANTROBUS:

Good morning, Miss Fairweather.

SABINA *finally disappears behind the beach umbrella or in a cabana in the orchestra pit.*

MRS. ANTROBUS:

Who on earth was that you spoke to, George?

ANTROBUS:

Complacent; mock-modest.

Hm . . . m . . . just a . . . solambaka keray.

MRS. ANTROBUS:

What? I can't understand you.

GLADYS:

Mama, wasn't she beautiful?

HENRY:

Papa, introduce her to me.

MRS. ANTROBUS:

Children, will you be quiet while I ask your father a simple question?—Who did you say it was, George?

ANTROBUS:

Why-uh . . . a friend of mine. Very nice refined girl.

MRS. ANTROBUS:

I'm waiting.

ANTROBUS:

Maggie, that's the girl I gave the prize to in the beauty contest,—that's Miss Atlantic City 1942.

MRS. ANTROBUS:

Hm! She looked like Sabina to me.

HENRY:

At the railing.

Mama, the life-guard knows her, too. Mama, he knows her well.

ANTROBUS:

Henry, come here.—She's a very nice girl in every way and the sole support of her aged mother.

MRS. ANTROBUS:

So was Sabina, so was Sabina; and it took a wall of ice to open your eyes about Sabina.—Henry, come over and sit down on this bench.

ANTROBUS:

She's a very different matter from Sabina. Miss Fairweather is a college graduate, Phi Beta Kappa.

MRS. ANTROBUS:

Henry, you sit here by mama. Gladys—

ANTROBUS:

Sitting.

Reduced circumstances have required her taking a position as hostess in a Bingo Parlor; but there isn't a girl with higher principles in the country.

MRS. ANTROBUS:

Well, let's not talk about it.—Henry, I haven't seen a whale yet.

ANTROBUS:

She speaks seven languages and has more culture in her little finger than you've acquired in a lifetime.

MRS. ANTROBUS:

Assumed amiability.

All right, all right, George. I'm glad to know there are such superior girls in the Bingo Parlors.—Henry, what's that?

Pointing at the storm signal, which has one black disk.

HENRY:

What is it, Papa?

ANTROBUS:

What? Oh, that's the storm signal. One of those black disks means bad weather; two means storm; three means hurricane; and four means the end of the world.

As they watch it a second black disk rolls into place

MRS. ANTROBUS:

Goodness! I'm going this very minute to buy you all some raincoats.

GLADYS:

Putting her cheek against her father's shoulder.

Mama, don't go yet. I like sitting this way. And the ocean coming in and coming in. Papa, don't you like it?

MRS. ANTROBUS:

Well, there's only one thing I lack to make me a perfectly happy woman: I'd like to see a whale.

HENRY:

Mama, we saw two. Right out there. They're delegates to the convention. I'll find you one.

GLADYS:

Papa, ask me something. Ask me a question.

ANTROBUS:

Well . . . how big's the ocean?

GLADYS:

Papa, you're teasing me. It's—three-hundred and sixty million square-miles—and—it—covers—three-fourths—of—the—earth's—surface—and—its—deepest-place—is—five—and—a—half—miles—deep—and—its—average—depth—is—twelve—thousand-feet. No, Papa, ask me something hard, real hard.

MRS. ANTROBUS:

Rising.

Now I'm going off to buy those raincoats. I think that bad weather's going to get worse and worse. I hope it doesn't come before your broadcast. I should think we have about an hour or so.

HENRY:

I hope it comes and zzzzzz everything before it. I hope it—

MRS. ANTROBUS:

Henry!—George, I think . . . maybe, it's one of those storms that are just as bad on land as on the sea. When you're just as safe and safer in a good stout boat.

HENRY:

There's a boat out at the end of the pier.

MRS. ANTROBUS:

Well, keep your eye on it. George, you shut your eyes and get a good rest before the broadcast.

ANTROBUS:

Thundering Judas, do I have to be told when to open and shut my eyes? Go and buy your raincoats.

MRS. ANTROBUS:

Now, children, you have ten minutes to walk around. Ten minutes. And, Henry: control yourself. Gladys, stick by your brother and don't get lost.

They run off.

MRS. ANTROBUS:

Will you be all right, George?

CONVEENERS *suddenly stick their heads out of the Bingo Parlor and Salt Water Taffy store, and voices rise from the orchestra pit.*

CONVEENERS:

George. Geo-r-r-rge! George! Leave the old hen-coop at home, George. Do-mes-ticated Georgie!

MRS. ANTROBUS:

Shaking her umbrella.

Low common oafs! That's what they are. Guess a man has a right to bring his wife to a convention, if he wants to.

She starts off.

What's the matter with a family, I'd like to know. What else have they got to offer?

Exit. ANTROBUS *has closed his eyes. The* FORTUNE TELLER *comes out of her shop and goes over to the left proscenium. She leans against it watching* SABINA *quizzically.*

FORTUNE TELLER:

Heh! Here she comes!

SABINA:

Loud whisper.

What's he doing?

FORTUNE TELLER:

Oh, he's ready for you. Bite your lips, dear, take a long breath and come on up.

SABINA:

I'm nervous. My whole future depends on this. I'm nervous.

FORTUNE TELLER:

Don't be a fool. What more could you want? He's forty-five. His head's a little dizzy. He's just been elected president. He's never known any other woman than his wife. Whenever he looks at her he realizes that she knows every foolish thing he's ever done.

SABINA:

Still whispering.

I don't know why it is, but every time I start one of these I'm nervous.

The FORTUNE TELLER *stands in the center of the stage watching the following:*

FORTUNE TELLER:

You make me tired.

SABINA:

First tell me my fortune.

The FORTUNE TELLER *laughs drily and makes the gesture of brushing away a nonsensical question.* SABINA *coughs and says:*

Oh, Mr. Antrobus,—dare I speak to you for a moment?

ANTROBUS:

What?—Oh, certainly, certainly, Miss Fairweather.

SABINA:

Mr. Antrobus . . . I've been so unhappy. I've wanted . . . I've wanted to make sure that you don't think that I'm the kind of girl who goes out for beauty contests.

FORTUNE TELLER:

That's the way!

ANTROBUS:

Oh, I understand. I understand perfectly.

FORTUNE TELLER:

Give it a little more. Lean on it.

SABINA:

I knew you would. My mother said to me this morning: Lily, she said, that fine Mr. Antrobus gave you the prize because he saw at once that you weren't the kind of girl who'd go in for a thing like that. But, honestly, Mr. Antrobus, in this world, honestly, a good girl doesn't know where to turn.

FORTUNE TELLER:

Now you've gone too far.

ANTROBUS:

My dear Miss Fairweather!

SABINA:

You wouldn't know how hard it is. With that lovely wife and daughter you have. Oh, I think Mrs. Antrobus is the finest woman I ever saw. I wish I were like her.

ANTROBUS:

There, there. There's . . . uh . . . room for all kinds of people in the world, Miss Fairweather.

SABINA:

How wonderful of you to say that. How generous!—Mr. Antrobus, have you a moment free? . . . I'm afraid I may be a little conspicuous here . . . could you come down, for just a moment, to my beach cabana . . . ?

ANTROBUS:

Why-uh . . . yes, certainly . . . for a moment . . . just for a moment.

SABINA:

There's a deck chair there. Because: you know you *do* look tired. Just this morning my mother said to me: Lily, she said,

I hope Mr. Antrobus is getting a good rest. His fine strong face has deep deep lines in it. Now isn't it true, Mr. Antrobus: you work too hard?

FORTUNE TELLER:

Bingo!

She goes into her shop.

SABINA:

Now you will just stretch out. No, I shan't say a word, not a word. I shall just sit there,—privileged. That's what I am.

ANTROBUS:

Taking her hand.

Miss Fairweather . . . you'll . . . spoil me.

SABINA:

Just a moment. I have something I wish to say to the audience.—Ladies and gentlemen. I'm not going to play this particular scene tonight. It's just a short scene and we're going to skip it. But I'll tell you what takes place and then we can continue the play from there on. Now in this scene—

ANTROBUS:

Between his teeth.

But, Miss Somerset!

SABINA:

I'm sorry. I'm sorry. But I have to skip it. In this scene, I talk to Mr. Antrobus, and at the end of it he decides to leave his wife, get a divorce at Reno and marry me. That's all.

ANTROBUS:

Fitz!—Fitz!

SABINA:

So that now I've told you we can jump to the end of it,— where you say:

Enter in fury MR. FITZPATRICK, *the stage manager.*

MR. FITZPATRICK:

Miss Somerset, we insist on your playing this scene.

SABINA:

I'm sorry, Mr. Fitzpatrick, but I can't and I won't. I've told the audience all they need to know and now we can go on.

Other ACTORS *begin to appear on the stage, listening.*

MR. FITZPATRICK:

And *why* can't you play it?

SABINA:

Because there are some lines in that scene that would hurt some people's feelings and I don't think the theatre is a place where people's feelings ought to be hurt.

MR. FITZPATRICK:

Miss Somerset, you can pack up your things and go home. I shall call the understudy and I shall report you to Equity.

SABINA:

I sent the understudy up to the corner for a cup of coffee and if Equity tries to penalize me I'll drag the case right up to the Supreme Court. Now listen, everybody, there's no need to get excited.

MR. FITZPATRICK *AND* ANTROBUS:

Why can't you play it . . . what's the matter with the scene?

SABINA:

Well, if you must know, I have a personal guest in the audience tonight. Her life hasn't been exactly a happy one. I wouldn't have my friend hear some of these lines for the whole world. I don't suppose it occurred to the author that some other women might have gone through the experience of losing their husbands like this. Wild horses wouldn't drag from me the details of my friend's life, but . . . well, they'd been married twenty years, and before he got rich, why, she'd done the washing and everything.

MR. FITZPATRICK:

Miss Somerset, your friend will forgive you. We must play this scene.

SABINA:

Nothing, nothing will make me say some of those lines . . . about "a man outgrows a wife every seven years" and . . . and that one about "the Mohammedans being the only people who looked the subject square in the face." Nothing.

MR. FITZPATRICK:

Miss Somerset! Go to your dressing room. I'll *read* your lines.

SABINA:

Now everybody's nerves are on edge.

MR. ANTROBUS:

Skip the scene.

MR. FITZPATRICK *and the other* ACTORS *go off.*

SABINA:

Thank you. I knew you'd understand. We'll do just what I said. So Mr. Antrobus is going to divorce his wife and marry me. Mr.

Antrobus, you say: "It won't be easy to lay all this before my wife."

The ACTORS *withdraw.* ANTROBUS *walks about, his hand to his forehead muttering:*

ANTROBUS:

Wait a minute. I can't get back into it as easily as all that. "My wife is a very obstinate woman." Hm . . . then you say . . . hm . . . Miss Fairweather, I mean Lily, it won't be easy to lay all this before my wife. It'll hurt her feelings a little.

SABINA:

Listen, George: *other* people haven't got feelings. Not in the same way that we have,—we who are presidents like you and prize-winners like me. Listen, other people haven't got feelings; they just imagine they have. Within two weeks they go back to playing bridge and going to the movies.

Listen, dear: everybody in the world except a few people like you and me are just people of straw. Most people have no insides at all. Now that you're president you'll see that. Listen, darling, there's a kind of secret society at the top of the world,—like you and me,—that know this. The world was made for us. What's life anyway? Except for two things, plea-sure and power, what is life? Boredom! Foolishness. You know it is. Except for those two things, life's nau-se-at-ing. So,— come here!

She moves close. They kiss.

So.

Now when your wife comes, it's really very simple; just tell her.

ANTROBUS:

Lily, Lily: you're a wonderful woman.

SABINA:

Of course I am.

They enter the cabana and it hides them from view. Distant roll of thunder. A third black disk appears on the weather signal. Distant thunder is heard. MRS. ANTROBUS *appears carrying parcels. She looks about, seats herself on the bench left, and fans herself with her handkerchief. Enter* GLADYS *right, followed by two* CONVEENERS. *She is wearing red stockings.*

MRS. ANTROBUS:

Gladys!

GLADYS:

Mama, here I am.

MRS. ANTROBUS:

Gladys Antrobus!!! Where did you get those dreadful things?

GLADYS:

Wha-a-t? Papa liked the color.

MRS. ANTROBUS:

You go back to the hotel this minute!

GLADYS:

I won't. I won't. Papa liked the color.

MRS. ANTROBUS:

All right. All right. You stay here. I've a good mind to let your father see you that way. You stay right here.

GLADYS:

I . . . I don't want to stay if . . . if you don't think he'd like it.

MRS. ANTROBUS:

Oh . . . it's all one to me. I don't care what happens. I don't care if the biggest storm in the whole world comes. Let it come.

She folds her hands.

Where's your brother?

GLADYS:

In a small voice.

He'll be here.

MRS. ANTROBUS:

Will he? Well, let him get into trouble. I don't care. I don't know where your father is, I'm sure.

Laughter from the cabana.

GLADYS:

Leaning over the rail.

I think he's . . . Mama, he's talking to the lady in the red dress.

MRS. ANTROBUS:

Is that so?

Pause.

We'll wait till he's through. Sit down here beside me and stop fidgeting . . . what are you crying about?

Distant thunder. She covers GLADYS'S *stockings with a raincoat.*

GLADYS:

You don't like my stockings.

Two CONVEENERS *rush in with a microphone on a standard and various paraphernalia. The* FORTUNE TELLER *appears at the door of her shop. Other characters gradually gather.*

BROADCAST OFFICIAL:

Mrs. Antrobus! Thank God we've found you at last. Where's Mr. Antrobus? We've been hunting everywhere for him. It's about time for the broadcast to the conventions of the world.

MRS. ANTROBUS:

Calm.

I expect he'll be here in a minute.

BROADCAST OFFICIAL:

Mrs. Antrobus, if he doesn't show up in time, I hope you will consent to broadcast in his place. It's the most important broadcast of the year.

SABINA *enters from cabana followed by* ANTROBUS.

MRS. ANTROBUS:

No, I shan't. I haven't one single thing to say.

BROADCAST OFFICIAL:

Then won't you help us find him, Mrs. Antrobus? A storm's coming up. A hurricane. A deluge!

SECOND CONVEENER:

Who has sighted ANTROBUS *over the rail.*

Joe! Joe! Here he is.

BROADCAST OFFICIAL:

In the name of God, Mr. Antrobus, you're on the air in five minutes. Will you kindly please come and test the instrument? That's all we ask. If you just please begin the alphabet slowly.

ANTROBUS, *with set face, comes ponderously up the ramp. He stops at the point where his waist is level with the stage and speaks authoritatively to the* OFFICIALS.

ANTROBUS:

I'll be ready when the time comes. Until then, move away. Go away. I have something I wish to say to my wife.

BROADCASTING OFFICIAL:
Whimpering.

Mr. Antrobus! This is the most important broadcast of the year.

The OFFICIALS *withdraw to the edge of the stage.* SABINA *glides up the ramp behind* ANTROBUS.

SABINA:
Whispering.

Don't let her argue. Remember arguments have nothing to do with it.

ANTROBUS:

Maggie, I'm moving out of the hotel. In fact, I'm moving out of everything. For good. I'm going to marry Miss Fair-weather. I shall provide generously for you and the children. In a few years you'll be able to see that it's all for the best. That's all I have to say.

BROADCAST OFFICIAL:	BINGO ANNOUNCER:
Mr. Antrobus! I hope you'll be ready. This is the most important broadcast of the year.	A—nine; A—nine. D—forty-two; D—forty-two. C—thirty; C-thirty. B—seventeen; B—seventeen. C—forty; C-forty.

GLADYS:	CHORUS:
What did Papa say, Mama? I didn't hear what papa said.	Bingo!!

BROADCAST OFFICIAL:

Mr. Antrobus. All we want to do is test your voice with the alphabet.

ANTROBUS:

Go away. Clear out.

MRS. ANTROBUS:

Composedly with lowered eyes.

George, I can't talk to you until you wipe those silly red marks off your face.

ANTROBUS:

I think there's nothing to talk about. I've said what I have to say.

SABINA:

Splendid!!

ANTROBUS:

You're a fine woman, Maggie, but . . . but a man has his own life to lead in the world.

MRS. ANTROBUS:

Well, after living with you for five thousand years I guess I have a right to a word or two, haven't I?

ANTROBUS:

To SABINA.

What can I answer to that?

SABINA:

Tell her that conversation would only hurt her feelings. It's-kinder-in-the-long-run-to-do-it-short-and-quick.

ANTROBUS:

I want to spare your feelings in every way I can, Maggie.

BROADCAST OFFICIAL:

Mr. Antrobus, the hurricane signal's gone up. We could begin right now.

MRS. ANTROBUS:

Calmly, almost dreamily.

I didn't marry you because you were perfect. I didn't even marry you because I loved you. I married you because you gave me a promise.

She takes off her ring and looks at it.

That promise made up for your faults. And the promise I gave you made up for mine. Two imperfect people got married and it was the promise that made the marriage.

ANTROBUS:

Maggie, . . . I was only nineteen.

MRS. ANTROBUS:

She puts her ring back on her finger.

And when our children were growing up, it wasn't a house that protected them; and it wasn't our love, that protected them—it was that promise.

And when that promise is broken—this can happen!

With a sweep of the hand she removes the raincoat from GLADYS' *stockings.*

ANTROBUS:

Stretches out his arm, apoplectic.

Gladys!! Have you gone crazy? Has everyone gone crazy?

Turning on SABINA.

You did this. You gave them to her.

SABINA:

I never said a word to her.

ANTROBUS:

To GLADYS.

You go back to the hotel and take those horrible things off.

GLADYS:

Pert.

Before I go, I've got something to tell you,—it's about Henry.

MRS. ANTROBUS:

Claps her hands peremptorily.

Stop your noise,—I'm taking her back to the hotel, George. Before I go I have a letter. . . . I have a message to throw into the ocean.

Fumbling in her handbag.

Where is the plagued thing? Here it is.

She flings something—invisible to us—far over the heads of the audience to the back of the auditorium.

It's a bottle. And in the bottle's a letter. And in the letter is written all the things that a woman knows.

It's never been told to any man and it's never been told to any woman, and if it finds its destination, a new time will come. We're not what books and plays say we are. We're not what advertisements say we are. We're not in the movies and we're not on the radio.

We're not what you're all told and what you think we are:

We're ourselves. And if any man can find one of us he'll learn why the whole universe was set in motion. And if any man harm any one of us, his soul—the only soul he's got—had better be at the bottom of that ocean,—and that's the only way to put it. Gladys, come here. We're going back to the hotel.

She drags GLADYS *firmly off by the hand, but* GLADYS *breaks away and comes down to speak to her father.*

SABINA:

Such goings-on. Don't give it a minute's thought.

GLADYS:

Anyway, I think you ought to know that Henry hit a man with a stone. He hit one of those colored men that push the chairs and the man's very sick. Henry ran away and hid and some policemen are looking for him very hard. And I don't care a bit if you don't want to have anything to do with mama and me, because I'll never like you again and I hope nobody ever likes you again,—so there!

She runs off. ANTROBUS *starts after her.*

ANTROBUS:

I . . . I have to go and see what I can do about this.

SABINA:

You stay right here. Don't you go now while you're excited. Gracious sakes, all these things will be forgotten in a hundred years. Come, now, you're on the air. Just say anything,—it doesn't matter what. Just a lot of birds and fishes and things.

BROADCAST OFFICIAL:

Thank you, Miss Fairweather. Thank you very much. Ready, Mr. Antrobus.

ANTROBUS:

Touching the microphone.

What is it, what is it? Who am I talking to?

BROADCAST OFFICIAL:

Why, Mr. Antrobus! To our order and to all the other orders.

ANTROBUS:

Raising his head.

What are all those birds doing?

BROADCAST OFFICIAL:

Those are just a few of the birds. Those are the delegates to our convention,—two of a kind.

ANTROBUS:

Pointing into the audience.

Look at the water. Look at them all. Those fishes jumping. The children should see this!—There's Maggie's whales!! Here are your whales, Maggie!!

BROADCAST OFFICIAL:

I hope you're ready, Mr. Antrobus.

ANTROBUS:

And look on the beach! You didn't tell me these would be here!

SABINA:

Yes, George. Those are the animals.

BROADCAST OFFICIAL:

Busy with the apparatus.

Yes, Mr. Antrobus, those are the vertebrates. We hope the lion will have a word to say when you're through. Step right up, Mr. Antrobus, we're ready. We'll just have time before the storm.

Pause. In a hoarse whisper:

They're wait-ing.

It has grown dark. Soon after he speaks a high whistling noise begins. Strange veering lights start whirling about the stage. The other characters disappear from the stage.

ANTROBUS:

Friends. Cousins. Four score and ten billion years ago our forefather brought forth upon this planet the spark of life,—

He is drowned out by thunder. When the thunder stops the FORTUNE TELLER *is seen standing beside him.*

FORTUNE TELLER:

Antrobus, there's not a minute to be lost. Don't you see the four disks on the weather signal? Take your family into that boat at the end of the pier.

ANTROBUS:

My family? I have no family. Maggie! Maggie! They won't come.

FORTUNE TELLER:

They'll come.—Antrobus! Take these animals into that boat with you. All of them,—two of each kind.

SABINA:

George, what's the matter with you? This is just a storm like any other storm.

ANTROBUS:

Maggie!

SABINA:

Stay with me, we'll go . . .

Losing conviction.

This is just another thunderstorm,—isn't it? Isn't it?

ANTROBUS:

Maggie!!!

MRS. ANTROBUS *appears beside him with* GLADYS.

MRS. ANTROBUS:
Matter-of-fact.

Here I am and here's Gladys.

ANTROBUS:
Where've you been? Where have you been? Quick, we're going into that boat out there.

MRS. ANTROBUS:
I know we are. But I haven't found Henry.

She wanders off into the darkness calling "Henry!"

SABINA:
Low urgent babbling, only occasionally raising her voice.

I don't believe it. I don't believe it's anything at all. I've seen hundreds of storms like this.

FORTUNE TELLER:
There's no time to lose. Go. Push the animals along before you. Start a new world. Begin again.

SABINA:
Esmeralda! George! Tell me,—is it really serious?

ANTROBUS:
Suddenly very busy.

Elephants first. Gently, gently.—Look where you're going.

GLADYS:
Leaning over the ramp and striking an animal on the back.

Stop it or you'll be left behind!

ANTROBUS:

Is the Kangaroo there? *There* you are! Take those turtles in your pouch, will you?

To some other animals, pointing to his shoulder.

Here! You jump up here. You'll be trampled on.

GLADYS:

To her father, pointing below.

Papa, look,—the snakes!

MRS. ANTROBUS:

I can't find Henry. Hen-ry!

ANTROBUS:

Go along. Go along. Climb on their backs.—Wolves! Jackals, —whatever you are,—tend to your own business!

GLADYS:

Pointing, tenderly.

Papa,—look.

SABINA:

Mr. Antrobus—take me with you. Don't leave me here. I'll work. I'll help. I'll do anything.

THREE CONVEENERS *cross the stage, marching with a banner.*

CONVEENERS:

George! What are you scared of?—George! Fellas, it looks like rain.—"Maggie, where's my umbrella?"—George, setting up for Barnum and Bailey.

ANTROBUS:

Again catching his wife's hand.

Come on now, Maggie,—the pier's going to break any minute.

MRS. ANTROBUS:

I'm not going a step without Henry. Henry!

GLADYS:

On the ramp.

Mama! Papa! Hurry. The pier's cracking, Mama. It's going to break.

MRS. ANTROBUS:

Henry! Cain! CAIN!

HENRY *dashes into the stage and joins his mother.*

HENRY:

Here I am, Mama.

MRS. ANTROBUS:

Thank God!—now come quick.

HENRY:

I didn't think you wanted me.

MRS. ANTROBUS:

Quick!

She pushes him down before her into the aisle.

SABINA:

All the ANTROBUSES *are now in the theater aisle.* SABINA *stands at the top of the ramp.*

Mrs. Antrobus, take me. Don't you remember me? I'll work. I'll help. Don't leave me here!

MRS. ANTROBUS:

Impatiently, but as though it were of no importance.

Yes, yes. There's a lot of work to be done. Only hurry.

FORTUNE TELLER:

Now dominating the stage. To SABINA *with a grim smile.*

Yes, go—back to the kitchen with you.

SABINA:

Half-down the ramp. To FORTUNE TELLER.

I don't know why my life's always being interrupted—just when everything's going fine!!

She dashes up the aisle.

Now the CONVENEERS *emerge doing a serpentine dance on the stage. They jeer at the* FORTUNE TELLER.

CONVENEERS:

Get a canoe—there's not a minute to be lost! Tell me my future, Mrs. Croaker.

FORTUNE TELLER:

Paddle in the water, boys—enjoy yourselves.

VOICE FROM THE BINGO PARLOR:

A-nine; A-nine. C-Twenty-four. C-Twenty-four.

CONVENEERS:

Rags, bottles, and sacks.

FORTUNE TELLER:

Go back and climb on your roofs. Put rags in the cracks under your doors.—Nothing will keep out the flood. You've had your chance. You've had your day. You've failed. You've lost.

VOICE FROM THE BINGO PARLOR:

B-fifteen. B-Fifteen.

FORTUNE TELLER:

Shading her eyes and looking out to sea.

They're safe. George Antrobus! Think it over! A new world to make.—think it over!

CURTAIN

Act III

Just before the curtain rises, two sounds are heard from the stage: a cracked bugle call.

The curtain rises on almost total darkness. Almost all the flats composing the walls of MR. ANTROBUS'S *house, as of Act I, are up, but they lean helter-skelter against one another, leaving irregular gaps. Among the flats missing are two in the back wall, leaving the frames of the window and door crazily out of line. Off stage, back right, some red Roman fire is burning. The bugle call is repeated. Enter* SABINA *through the tilted door. She is dressed as a Napoleonic camp follower, "la fille du regiment," in begrimed reds and blues.*

SABINA:

Mrs. Antrobus! Gladys! Where are you?

The war's over. The war's over. You can come out. The peace treaty's been signed.

Where are they?—Hmpf! Are they dead, too? Mrs. Annnn-trobus! Glaaaadus! Mr. Antrobus'll be here this afternoon. I just saw him downtown. Huuuurry and put things in order. He says that now that the war's over we'll all have to settle down and be perfect.

> *Enter* MR. FITZPATRICK, *the stage manager, followed by the whole company, who stand waiting at the edges of the stage.* MR. FITZPATRICK *tries to interrupt* SABINA.

MR. FITZPATRICK:

Miss Somerset, we have to stop a moment.

SABINA:

They may be hiding out in the back—

MR. FITZPATRICK:

Miss Somerset! We have to stop a moment.

SABINA:

What's the matter?

MR. FITZPATRICK:

There's an explanation we have to make to the audience.— Lights, please.

> *To the actor who plays* MR. ANTROBUS,

Will you explain the matter to the audience?

> *The lights go up. We now see that a balcony or elevated runway has been erected at the back of the stage, back of the wall of the Antrobus house. From its extreme right and left ends ladder-like steps descend to the floor of the stage.*

ANTROBUS:

Ladies and gentlemen, an unfortunate accident has taken place back stage. Perhaps I should say *another* unfortunate accident.

SABINA:

I'm sorry. I'm sorry.

ANTROBUS:

The management feels, in fact, we all feel that you are due an apology. And now we have to ask your indulgence for the most serious mishap of all. Seven of our actors have . . . have been taken ill. Apparently, it was something they ate. I'm not exactly clear what happened.

> *All the* ACTORS *start to talk at once.* ANTROBUS *raises his hand.*

Now, now—not all at once. Fitz, do you know what it was?

MR. FITZPATRICK:

Why, it's perfectly clear. These seven actors had dinner together, and they ate something that disagreed with them.

SABINA:

Disagreed with them!!! They have ptomaine poisoning. They're in Bellevue Hospital this very minute in agony. They're having their stomachs pumped out this very minute, in perfect agony.

ANTROBUS:

Fortunately, we've just heard they'll all recover.

SABINA:

It'll be a miracle if they do, a downright miracle. It was the lemon meringue pie.

ACTORS:

It was the fish . . . it was the canned tomatoes . . . it was the fish.

SABINA:

It was the lemon meringue pie. I saw it with my own eyes; it had blue mould all over the bottom of it.

ANTROBUS:

Whatever it was, they're in no condition to take part in this performance. Naturally, we haven't enough understudies to fill all those roles; but we do have a number of splendid volunteers who have kindly consented to help us out. These friends have watched our rehearsals, and they assure me that they know the lines and the business very well. Let me introduce them to you—my dresser, Mr. Tremayne,—himself a distinguished Shakespearean actor for many years; our wardrobe mistress, Hester; Miss Somerset's maid, Ivy; and Fred Bailey, captain of the ushers in this theatre.

These persons bow modestly. IVY *and* HESTER *are colored girls.*

Now this scene takes place near the end of the act. And I'm sorry to say we'll need a short rehearsal, just a short run-through. And as some of it takes place in the auditorium, we'll have to keep the curtain up. Those of you who wish can go out in the lobby and smoke some more. The rest of you can listen to us, or . . . or just talk quietly among yourselves, as you choose. Thank you. Now will you take it over, Mr. Fitzpatrick?

MR. FITZPATRICK:

Thank you.—Now for those of you who are listening perhaps I should explain that at the end of this act, the men have come back from the War and the family's settled down in the house. And the author wants to show the hours of the night passing by over their heads, and the planets crossing the sky . . . uh . . . over their heads. And he says—this is hard to explain—that each of the hours of the night is a philosopher, or a great thinker. Eleven o'clock, for instance, is Aristotle. And nine o'clock is Spinoza. Like that. I don't suppose it means anything. It's just a kind of poetic effect.

SABINA:

Not mean anything! Why, it certainly does. Twelve o'clock goes by saying those wonderful things. I think it means that when people are asleep they have all those lovely thoughts, much better than when they're awake.

IVY:

Excuse me, I think it means,—excuse me, Mr. Fitzpatrick—

SABINA:

What were you going to say, Ivy?

IVY:

Mr. Fitzpatrick, you let my father come to a rehearsal; and my father's a Baptist minister, and he said that the author meant that—just like the hours and stars go by over our heads at night, in the same way the ideas and thoughts of the great men are in the air around us all the time and they're working on us, even when we don't know it.

MR. FITZPATRICK:

Well, well, maybe that's it. Thank you, Ivy. Anyway,—the hours of the night are philosophers. My friends, are you ready? Ivy, can you be eleven o'clock? "This good estate of the mind possessing its object in energy we call divine." Aristotle.

IVY:

Yes, sir. I know that and I know twelve o'clock and I know nine o'clock.

MR. FITZPATRICK:

Twelve o'clock? Mr. Tremayne, the Bible.

TREMAYNE:

Yes.

MR. FITZPATRICK:

Ten o'clock? Hester,—Plato?

She nods eagerly.

Nine o'clock, Spinoza,—Fred?

BAILEY:

Yes, *sir.*

FRED BAILEY *picks up a great gilded cardboard numeral IX and starts up the steps to the platform.* MR. FITZPATRICK *strikes his forehead.*

MR. FITZPATRICK:

The planets!! We forgot all about the planets.

SABINA:

O my God! The planets! Are they sick too?

ACTORS *nod.*

MR. FITZPATRICK:

Ladies and gentlemen, the planets are singers. Of course, we can't replace them, so you'll have to imagine them singing in this scene. Saturn sings from the orchestra pit down here. The Moon is way up there. And Mars with a red lantern in his hand, stands in the aisle over there—Tz-tz-tz. It's too bad; it all makes a very fine effect. However! Ready—nine o'clock: Spinoza.

BAILEY:

Walking slowly across the balcony, left to right.

"After experience had taught me that the common occurrences of daily life are vain and futile—"

FITZPATRICK:

Louder, Fred. "And I saw that all the objects of my desire and fear—"

BAILEY:

"And I saw that all the objects of my desire and fear were in themselves nothing good nor bad save insofar as the mind was affected by them—"

FITZPATRICK:

Do you know the rest? All right. Ten o'clock. Hester. Plato.

HESTER:

"Then tell me, O Critias, how will a man choose the ruler that shall rule over him? Will he not—"

FITZPATRICK:

Thank you. Skip to the end, Hester.

HESTER:

". . . can be multiplied a thousand fold in its effects among the citizens."

FITZPATRICK:

Thank you.—Aristotle, Ivy?

IVY:

"This good estate of the mind possessing its object in energy we call divine. This we mortals have occasionally and it is this energy which is pleasantest and best. But God has it always.

It is wonderful in us; but in Him how much more wonderful."

FITZPATRICK:

Midnight. Midnight, Mr. Tremayne. That's right,—you've done it before.—All right, everybody. You know what you have to do.—Lower the curtain. House lights up. Act Three of THE SKIN OF OUR TEETH.

As the curtain descends he is heard saying:

You volunteers, just wear what you have on. Don't try to put on the costumes today.

House lights go down. The Act begins again. The Bugle call. Curtain rises. Enter SABINA.

SABINA:

Mrs. Antrobus! Gladys! Where are you? The war's over.— You've heard all this—

She gabbles the main points.

Where—are—they? Are—they—dead, too, et cetera. I—just— saw—Mr.—Antrobus—down town, et cetera.

Slowing up:

He says that now that the war's over we'll all have to settle down and be perfect. They may be hiding out in the back somewhere. Mrs. An-tro-bus.

She wanders off. It has grown lighter.

A trapdoor is cautiously raised and MRS. ANTROBUS *emerges waist-high and listens. She is disheveled and worn; she wears a tattered dress and a shawl half covers her head. She talks down through the trapdoor.*

MRS. ANTROBUS:

It's getting light. There's still something burning over there—Newark, or Jersey City. What? Yes, I could swear I heard some-·one moving about up here. But I can't see anybody. I say: I can't see anybody.

She starts to move about the stage. GLADYS' *head appears at the trapdoor. She is holding a* BABY.

GLADYS:

Oh, Mama. Be careful.

MRS. ANTROBUS:

Now, Gladys, you stay out of sight.

GLADYS:

Well, let me stay here just a minute. I want the baby to get some of this fresh air.

MRS. ANTROBUS:

All right, but keep your eyes open. I'll see what I can find. I'll have a good hot plate of soup for you before you can say Jack Robinson. Gladys Antrobus! Do you know what I think I see? There's old Mr. Hawkins sweeping the sidewalk in front of his A. and P. store. Sweeping it with a broom. Why, he must have gone crazy, like the others! I see some other people moving about, too.

GLADYS:

Mama, come back, come back.

MRS. ANTROBUS *returns to the trapdoor and listens.*

MRS. ANTROBUS:

Gladys, there's something in the air. Everybody's movement's sort of different. I see some women walking right out in the middle of the street.

SABINA'S VOICE:

Mrs. An-tro-bus!

MRS. ANTROBUS AND GLADYS:

What's that?!!

SABINA'S VOICE:

Glaaaadys! Mrs. An-tro-bus!

Enter SABINA.

MRS. ANTROBUS:

Gladys, that's Sabina's voice as sure as I live.—Sabina! Sabina!
—Are you *alive*?!!

SABINA:

Of course, I'm alive. How've you girls been?—*Don't* try and
kiss me. I never want to kiss another human being as long as I
live. Sh-sh, there's nothing to get emotional about. Pull yourself together, the war's over. Take a deep breath,—the war's
over.

MRS. ANTROBUS:

The war's over!! I don't believe you. I don't believe you. I can't
believe you.

GLADYS:

Mama!

SABINA:

Who's that?

MRS. ANTROBUS:

That's Gladys and her baby. I don't believe you. Gladys, Sabina
says the war's over. Oh, Sabina.

SABINA:

Leaning over the BABY.

Goodness! Are there any babies left in the world! Can it *see?* And can it cry and everything?

GLADYS:

Yes, he can. He notices everything very well.

SABINA:

Where on earth did you get it? Oh, I won't ask.—Lord, I've lived all these seven years around camp and I've forgotten how to behave.—Now we've got to think about the men coming home.—Mrs. Antrobus, go and wash your face, I'm ashamed of you. Put your best clothes on. Mr. Antrobus'll be here this afternoon. I just saw him downtown.

MRS. ANTROBUS AND GLADYS:

He's alive!! He'll be here!! Sabina, you're not joking?

MRS. ANTROBUS:

And Henry?

SABINA:

Dryly.

Yes, Henry's alive, too, that's what they say. Now don't stop to talk. Get yourselves fixed up. Gladys, you look terrible. Have you any decent clothes?

SABINA *has pushed them toward the trapdoor.*

MRS. ANTROBUS:

Half down.

Yes, I've something to wear just for this very day. But, Sabina,— who won the war?

SABINA:

Don't stop now,—just wash your face.

A whistle sounds in the distance.

Oh, my God, what's that silly little noise?

MRS. ANTROBUS:

Why, it sounds like . . . it sounds like what used to be the noon whistle at the shoe-polish factory.

Exit.

SABINA:

That's what it is. Seems to me like peacetime's coming along pretty fast—shoe polish!

GLADYS:

Half down.

Sabina, how soon after peacetime begins does the milkman start coming to the door?

SABINA:

As soon as he catches a cow. Give him time to catch a cow, dear.

Exit GLADYS. SABINA *walks about a moment, thinking.*

Shoe polish! My, I'd forgotten what peacetime was like.

She shakes her head, then sits down by the trapdoor and starts talking down the hole.

Mrs. Antrobus, guess what I saw Mr. Antrobus doing this morning at dawn. He was tacking up a piece of paper on the door of the Town Hall. You'll die when you hear: it was a recipe for grass soup, for a grass soup that doesn't give you the diarrhea. Mr. Antrobus is still thinking up new things.—He told me to give you his love. He's got all sorts of ideas for peacetime, he says. No more laziness and idiocy, he says. And oh, yes! Where are his books? What? Well, pass them up. The first thing he wants to see are his books. He says if you've burnt those books, or if the rats have eaten them, he says it isn't worthwhile starting over again. Everybody's going to be beautiful, he says, and diligent, and very intelligent.

A hand reaches up with two volumes.

What language is that? Pu-u-gh,—mold! And he's got such plans for you, Mrs. Antrobus. You're going to study history and algebra—and so are Gladys and I—and philosophy. You should hear him talk:

Taking two more volumes.

Well, these are in English, anyway.—To hear him talk, seems like he expects you to be a combination, Mrs. Antrobus, of a saint and a college professor, and a dancehall hostess, if you know what I mean.

Two more volumes.

Ugh. German!

She is lying on the floor; one elbow bent, her cheek on her hand, meditatively.

Yes, peace will be here before we know it. In a week or two we'll be asking the Perkinses in for a quiet evening of bridge. We'll turn on the radio and hear how to be big successes with a new toothpaste. We'll trot down to the movies and see how girls with wax faces live—all *that* will begin again. Oh, Mrs. Antrobus, God forgive me but I enjoyed the war. Everybody's at their best in wartime. I'm sorry it's over. And, oh, I forgot! Mr. Antrobus sent you another message—can you hear me?—

Enter HENRY, *blackened and sullen. He is wearing torn overalls, but has one gaudy admiral's epaulette hanging by a thread from his right shoulder, and there are vestiges of gold and scarlet braid running down his left trouser leg. He stands listening.*

Listen! Henry's never to put foot in this house again, he says. He'll kill Henry on sight, if he sees him.

You don't know about Henry??? Well, where have you been? What? Well, Henry rose right to the top. Top of *what?* Listen, I'm telling you. Henry rose from corporal to captain, to major, to general.—I don't know how to say it, but the enemy is *Henry;* Henry *is* the enemy. Everybody knows that.

HENRY:

He'll kill me, will he?

SABINA:

Who are *you?* I'm not afraid of you. The war's over.

HENRY:

I'll kill him so fast. I've spent seven years trying to find him; the others I killed were just substitutes.

SABINA:

Goodness! It's Henry!—

He makes an angry gesture.

Oh, I'm not afraid of you. The war's over, Henry Antrobus, and you're not any more important than any other unem-

ployed. You go away and hide yourself, until we calm your
father down.

HENRY:

The first thing to do is to burn up those old books; it's the
ideas he gets out of those old books that . . . that makes the
whole world so you can't live in it.

*He reels forward and starts kicking the books about, but
suddenly falls down in a sitting position.*

SABINA:

You leave those books alone!! Mr. Antrobus is looking forward to them a-special.—Gracious sakes, Henry, you're so
tired you can't stand up. Your mother and sister'll be here in
a minute and we'll think what to do about you.

HENRY:

What did they ever care about me?

SABINA:

There's that old whine again. All you people think you're not
loved enough, nobody loves you. Well, you start being lovable and we'll love you.

HENRY:

Outraged.

I don't want anybody to love me.

SABINA:

Then stop talking about it all the time.

HENRY:

I *never* talk about it. The last thing I want is anybody to pay
any attention to me.

SABINA:

I can hear it behind every word you say.

HENRY:

I want everybody to hate me.

SABINA:

Yes, you've decided that's second best, but it's still the same thing.—Mrs. Antrobus! Henry's here. He's so tired he can't stand up.

> MRS. ANTROBUS *and* GLADYS, *with her* BABY, *emerge. They are dressed as in Act I.* MRS. ANTROBUS *carries some objects in her apron, and* GLADYS *has a blanket over her shoulder.*

MRS. ANTROBUS AND GLADYS:

Henry! Henry! Henry!

HENRY:

Glaring at them.

Have you anything to eat?

MRS. ANTROBUS:

Yes, I have, Henry. I've been saving it for this very day,—two good baked potatoes. No! Henry! one of them's for your father. Henry!! Give me that other potato back this minute.

> SABINA *sidles up behind him and snatches the other potato away.*

SABINA:

He's so dog-tired he doesn't know what he's doing.

MRS. ANTROBUS:

Now you just rest there, Henry, until I can get your room ready. Eat that potato good and slow, so you can get all the nourishment out of it.

HENRY:

You all might as well know right now that I haven't come back here to live.

MRS. ANTROBUS:

Sh. . . . I'll put this coat over you. Your room's hardly damaged at all. Your football trophies are a little tarnished, but Sabina and I will polish them up tomorrow.

HENRY:

Did you hear me? I don't live here. I don't belong to anybody.

MRS. ANTROBUS:

Why, how can you say a thing like that! You certainly do belong right here. Where else would you want to go? Your forehead's feverish, Henry, seems to me. You'd better give me that gun, Henry. You won't need that any more.

GLADYS:

Whispering.

Look, he's fallen asleep already, with his potato half-chewed.

SABINA:

Puh! The terror of the world.

MRS. ANTROBUS:

Sabina, you mind your own business, and start putting the room to rights.

HENRY *has turned his face to the back of the sofa.* MRS. ANTROBUS *gingerly puts the revolver in her apron pocket, then helps* SABINA. SABINA *has found a rope hanging from the ceiling. Grunting, she hangs all her weight on it, and as she pulls the walls begin to move into their right places.* MRS. ANTROBUS *brings the overturned tables, chairs and hassock into the positions of Act 1.*

SABINA:

That's all we do—always beginning again! Over and over again. Always beginning again.

She pulls on the rope and a part of the wall moves into place. She stops. Meditatively:

How do we know that it'll be any better than before? Why do we go on pretending? Some day the whole earth's going to have to turn cold anyway, and until that time all these other things'll be happening again: it will be more wars and more walls of ice and floods and earthquakes.

MRS. ANTROBUS:

Sabina!! Stop arguing and go on with your work.

SABINA:

All right. I'll go on just out of *habit,* but I won't believe in it.

MRS. ANTROBUS:

Aroused.

Now, Sabina. I've let you talk long enough. I don't want to hear any more of it. Do I have to explain to you what everybody knows,—everybody who keeps a home going? Do I have to say to you what nobody should ever *have* to say, because they can read it in each other's eyes?

Now listen to me:

MRS. ANTROBUS *takes hold of the rope.*

I could live for seventy years in a cellar and make soup out of grass and bark, without ever doubting that this world has a work to do and will do it.

Do you hear me?

SABINA:

Frightened.

Yes, Mrs. Antrobus.

MRS. ANTROBUS:

Sabina, do you see this house,—216 Cedar Street,—do you see it?

SABINA:

Yes, Mrs. Antrobus.

MRS. ANTROBUS:

Well, just to have known this house is to have seen the idea of what we can do someday if we keep our wits about us. Too many people have suffered and died for my children for us to start reneging now. So we'll start putting this house to rights. Now, Sabina, go and see what you can do in the kitchen.

SABINA:

Kitchen! Why is it that however far I go away, I always find myself back in the kitchen?

Exit.

MRS. ANTROBUS:

Still thinking over her last speech, relaxes and says with a reminiscent smile:

Goodness gracious, wouldn't you know that my father was a parson? It was just like I heard his own voice speaking and he's been dead five thousand years. There! I've gone and almost waked Henry up.

HENRY:

Talking in his sleep, indistinctly.

Fellows . . . what have they done for us? . . . Blocked our way at every step. Kept everything in their own hands. And you've stood it. When are you going to wake up?

MRS. ANTROBUS:

Sh, Henry. Go to sleep. Go to sleep. Go to sleep.—Well, that looks better. Now let's go and help Sabina.

GLADYS:

Mama, I'm going out into the backyard and hold the baby right up in the air. And show him that we don't have to be afraid any more.

Exit GLADYS *to the kitchen.*

MRS. ANTROBUS *glances at* HENRY, *exits into kitchen.* HENRY *thrashes about in his sleep. Enter* ANTROBUS, *his arms full of bundles, chewing the end of a carrot. He has a slight limp. Over the suit of Act I he is wearing an overcoat too long for him, its skirts trailing on the ground. He lets his bundles fall and stands looking about. Presently his attention is fixed on* HENRY, *whose words grow clearer.*

HENRY:

All right! What have you got to lose? What have they done for us? That's right—nothing. Tear everything down. I don't care what you smash. We'll begin again and we'll show 'em.

ANTROBUS *takes out his revolver and holds it pointing downwards. With his back towards the audience he moves toward the footlights.*

HENRY'S *voice grows louder and he wakes with a start. They stare at one another. Then* HENRY *sits up quickly. Throughout the following scene* HENRY *is played, not as a misunderstood or misguided young man, but as a representation of strong unreconciled evil.*

All right! Do something.

Pause.

Don't think I'm afraid of you, either. All right, do what you were going to do. Do it.

Furiously.

Shoot me, I tell you. You don't have to think I'm any relation of yours. I haven't got any father or any mother, or brothers or sisters. And I don't want any. And what's more I haven't got anybody over me; and I never will have. I'm alone, and that's all I want to be: alone. So you can shoot me.

ANTROBUS:

You're the last person I wanted to see. The sight of you dries up all my plans and hopes. I wish I were back at war still, because it's easier to fight you than to live with you. War's a pleasure— do you hear me?—War's a pleasure compared to what faces us now: trying to build up a peacetime with you in the middle of it.

ANTROBUS *walks up to the window.*

HENRY:

I'm not going to be a part of any peacetime of yours. I'm going a long way from here and make my own world that's fit for a man to live in. Where a man can be free, and have a chance, and do what he wants to do in his own way.

ANTROBUS:

His attention arrested; thoughtfully. He throws the gun out of the window and turns with hope.

. . . Henry, let's try again.

HENRY:

Try what? Living *here*?—Speaking polite downtown to all the old men like you? Standing like a sheep at the street corner until the red light turns to green? Being a good boy and a good sheep, like all the stinking ideas you get out of your books? Oh, no. I'll make a world, and I'll show you.

ANTROBUS:

Hard.

How can you make a world for people to live in, unless you've first put order in yourself? Mark my words: I shall continue fighting you until my last breath as long as you mix up your idea of liberty with your idea of hogging everything for yourself. I shall have no pity on you. I shall pursue you to the far corners of the earth. You and I want the same thing; but until you think of it as something that everyone has a right to, you are my deadly enemy and I will destroy you.—I hear your mother's voice in the kitchen. Have you seen her?

HENRY:

I have no mother. Get it into your head. I don't belong here. I have nothing to do here. I have no home.

ANTROBUS:

Then why did you come here? With the whole world to choose from, why did you come to this one place: 216 Cedar Street, Excelsior, New Jersey. . . . Well?

HENRY:

What if I did? What if I wanted to look at it once more, to see if—

ANTROBUS:

Oh, you're related, all right—When your mother comes in you must behave yourself. Do you hear me?

HENRY:

Wildly.

What is this?—*must behave* yourself. Don't you say *must* to me.

ANTROBUS:

Quiet!

Enter MRS. ANTROBUS *and* SABINA.

HENRY:

Nobody can say *must* to me. All my life everybody's been crossing me,—everybody, everything, all of you. I'm going to be free, even if I have to kill half the world for it. Right now, too. Let me get my hands on his throat. I'll show him.

He advances toward ANTROBUS. *Suddenly,* SABINA *jumps between them and calls out in her own person:*

SABINA:

Stop! Stop! Don't play this scene. You know what happened last night. Stop the play.

The men fall back, panting. HENRY *covers his face with his hands.*

Last night you almost strangled him. You became a regular savage. Stop it!

HENRY:

It's true. I'm sorry. I don't know what comes over me. I have nothing against him personally. I respect him very much . . . I

. . . I admire him. But something comes over me. It's like I become fifteen years old again. I . . . I . . . listen: my own father used to whip me and lock me up every Saturday night. I never had enough to eat. He never let me have enough money to buy decent clothes. I was ashamed to go downtown. I never could go to the dances. My father and my uncle put rules in the way of everything I wanted to do. They tried to prevent my living at all.—I'm sorry. I'm sorry.

MRS. ANTROBUS:
Quickly.

No, go on. Finish what you were saying. Say it all.

HENRY:
In this scene it's as though I were back in High School again. It's like I had some big emptiness inside me,—the emptiness of being hated and blocked at every turn. And the emptiness fills up with the one thought that you have to strike and fight and kill. Listen, it's as though you have to kill somebody else so as not to end up killing yourself.

SABINA:
That's not true. I knew your father and your uncle and your mother. You imagined all that. Why, they did everything they could for you. How can you say things like that? They didn't lock you up.

HENRY:
They did. They did. They wished I hadn't been born.

SABINA:
That's not true.

ANTROBUS:

In his own person, with self-condemnation, but cold and proud.

Wait a minute. I have something to say, too. It's not wholly his fault that he wants to strangle me in this scene. It's my fault, too. He wouldn't feel that way unless there were something in me that reminded him of all that. He talks about an emptiness. Well, there's an emptiness in me, too. Yes,—work, work, work,—that's all I do. I've ceased to *live*. No wonder he feels that anger coming over him.

MRS. ANTROBUS:

There! At least you've said it.

SABINA:

We're all just as wicked as we can be, and that's the God's truth.

MRS. ANTROBUS:

Nods a moment, then comes forward; quietly:

Come. Come and put your head under some cold water.

SABINA:

In a whisper.

I'll go with him. I've known him a long while. You have to go on with the play. Come with me.

HENRY *starts out with* SABINA, *but turns at the exit and says to* ANTROBUS:

HENRY:

Thanks. Thanks for what you said. I'll be all right tomorrow. I won't lose control in that place. I promise.

Exeunt HENRY *and* SABINA.

ANTROBUS *starts toward the front door, fastens it.*

MRS. ANTROBUS: *goes up stage and places the chair close to table.*

MRS. ANTROBUS:

George, do I see you limping?

ANTROBUS:

Yes, a little. My old wound from the other war started smarting again. I can manage.

MRS. ANTROBUS:

Looking out of the window.

Some lights are coming on,—the first in seven years. People are walking up and down looking at them. Over in Hawkins' open lot they've built a bonfire to celebrate the peace. They're dancing around it like scarecrows.

ANTROBUS:

A bonfire! As though they hadn't seen enough things burning.—Maggie,—the dog died?

MRS. ANTROBUS:

Oh, yes. Long ago. There are no dogs left in Excelsior.—You're back again! All these years. I gave up counting on letters. The few that arrived were anywhere from six months to a year late.

ANTROBUS:

Yes, the ocean's full of letters, along with the other things.

MRS. ANTROBUS:

George, sit down, you're tired.

ANTROBUS:

No, you sit down. I'm tired but I'm restless.

Suddenly, as she comes forward:

Maggie! I've lost it. I've lost it.

MRS. ANTROBUS:

What, George? What have you lost?

ANTROBUS:

The most important thing of all: The desire to begin again, to start building.

MRS. ANTROBUS:

Sitting in the chair right of the table.

Well, it will come back.

ANTROBUS:

At the window.

I've lost it. This minute I feel like all those people dancing around the bonfire—just relief. Just the desire to settle down; to slip into the old grooves and keep the neighbors from walking over my lawn.—Hm. But during the war,—in the middle of all that blood and dirt and hot and cold-every day and night, I'd have moments, Maggie, when I *saw* the things that we could do when it was over. When you're at war you think about a better life; when you're at peace you think about a more comfortable one. I've lost it. I feel sick and tired.

MRS. ANTROBUS:

Listen! The baby's crying.

I hear Gladys talking. Probably she's quieting Henry again.

George, while Gladys and I were living here—like moles, like rats, and when we were at our wits' end to save the baby's life— the only thought we clung to was that you were going to bring something good out of this suffering. In the night, in the dark, we'd whisper about it, starving and sick.—Oh, George, you'll have to get it back again. Think! What else kept us alive all these years? Even now, it's not comfort we want. We can suffer whatever's necessary; only give us back that promise.

Enter SABINA *with a lighted lamp. She is dressed as in Act 1.*

SABINA:
Mrs. Antrobus . . .

MRS. ANTROBUS:
Yes, Sabina?

SABINA:
Will you need me?

MRS. ANTROBUS:
No, Sabina, you can go to bed.

SABINA:
Mrs. Antrobus, if it's all right with you, I'd like to go to the bonfire and celebrate seeing the war's over. And, Mrs. Antrobus, they've opened the Gem Movie Theatre and they're giving away a hand-painted soup tureen to every lady, and I thought one of us ought to go.

ANTROBUS:
Well, Sabina, I haven't any money. I haven't seen any money for quite a while.

SABINA:

Oh, you don't need money. They're taking anything you can give them. And I have some . . . some . . . Mrs. Antrobus, promise you won't tell anyone. It's a little against the law. But I'll give you some, too.

ANTROBUS:

What is it?

SABINA:

I'll give you some, too. Yesterday I picked up a lot of . . . of beef-cubes!

MRS. ANTROBUS *turns and says calmly:*

MRS. ANTROBUS:

But, Sabina, you know you ought to give that in to the Center downtown. They know who needs them most.

SABINA:

Outburst.

Mrs. Antrobus, I didn't make this war. I didn't ask for it. And, in my opinion, after anybody's gone through what we've gone through, they have a right to grab what they can find. You're a very nice man, Mr. Antrobus, but you'd have got on better in the world if you'd realized that dog-eat-dog was the rule in the beginning and always will be. And most of all now.

In tears.

Oh, the world's an awful place, and you know it is. I used to think something could be done about it; but I know better now. I hate it. I hate it.

She comes forward slowly and brings six cubes from the bag.

All right. All right. You can have them.

ANTROBUS:

Thank you, Sabina.

SABINA:

Can I have . . . can I have one to go to the movies?

ANTROBUS *in silence gives her one.*

Thank you.

ANTROBUS:

Good night, Sabina.

SABINA:

Mr. Antrobus, don't mind what I say. I'm just an ordinary girl, you know what I mean, I'm just an ordinary girl. But you're a bright man, you're a very bright man, and of course you invented the alphabet and the wheel, and, my God, a lot of things . . . and if you've got any other plans, my God, don't let me upset them. Only every now and then I've got to go to the movies. I mean my nerves can't stand it. But if you have any ideas about improving the crazy old world, I'm really with you. I really am. Because it's . . . it's . . . Good night.

She goes out. ANTROBUS *starts laughing softly with exhilaration.*

ANTROBUS:

Now I remember what three things always went together when I was able to see things most clearly: three things. Three things:

He points to where SABINA *has gone out.*

The voice of the people in their confusion and their need. And the thought of you and the children and this house. And ... Maggie! I didn't dare ask you: my books! They haven't been lost, have they?

MRS. ANTROBUS:

No. There are some of them right here. Kind of tattered.

ANTROBUS:

Yes.—Remember, Maggie, we almost lost them once before? And when we finally did collect a few torn copies out of old cellars they ran in everyone's head like a fever. They as good as rebuilt the world.

Pauses, book in hand, and looks up.

Oh, I've never forgotten for long at a time that living is struggle. I know that every good and excellent thing in the world stands moment by moment on the razor-edge of danger and must be fought for—whether it's a field, or a home, or a country. All I ask is the chance to build new worlds and God has always given us that. And has given us

Opening the book

voices to guide us; and the memory of our mistakes to warn us. Maggie, you and I will remember in peacetime all the resolves that were so clear to us in the days of war. We've come a long ways. We've learned. We're learning. And the steps of our journey are marked for us here.

He stands by the table turning the leaves of a book.

Sometimes out there in the war,—standing all night on a hill— I'd try and remember some of the words in these books. Parts of them and phrases would come back to me. And after a while I used to give names to the hours of the night.

He sits, hunting for a passage in the book.

Nine o'clock I used to call Spinoza. Where is it: "After experience had taught me—"

The back wall has disappeared, revealing the platform. FRED BAILEY *carrying his numeral has started from left to right.* MRS. ANTROBUS *sits by the table sewing.*

BAILEY:

"After experience had taught me that the common occurrences of daily life are vain and futile; and I saw that all the objects of my desire and fear were in themselves nothing good nor bad save insofar as the mind was affected by them; I at length determined to search out whether there was something truly good and communicable to man."

Almost without break HESTER, *carrying a large Roman numeral ten, starts crossing the platform.* GLADYS *appears at the kitchen door and moves towards her mother's chair.*

HESTER:

"Then tell me, O Critias, how will a man choose the ruler that shall rule over him? Will he not choose a man who has first established order in himself, knowing that any decision that has its spring from anger or pride or vanity can be multiplied a thousand fold in its effects upon the citizens?"

HESTER *disappears and* IVY, *as eleven o'clock starts speaking.*

IVY:

"This good estate of the mind possessing its object in energy we call divine. This we mortals have occasionally and it is this energy which is pleasantest and best. But God has it always. It is wonderful in us; but in Him how much more wonderful."

As MR. TREMAYNE *starts to speak,* HENRY *appears at the edge of the scene, brooding and unreconciled, but present.*

TREMAYNE:

"In the beginning, God created the Heavens and the earth; And the Earth was waste and void; And the darkness was upon the face of the deep. And the Lord said let there be light and there was light."

Sudden black-out and silence, except for the last strokes of the midnight bell. Then just as suddenly the lights go up, and SABINA *is standing at the window, as at the opening of the play.*

SABINA:

Oh, oh, oh. Six o'clock and the master not home yet. Pray God nothing serious has happened to him crossing the Hudson River. But I wouldn't be surprised. The whole world's at sixes and sevens, and why the house hasn't fallen down about our ears long ago is a miracle to me.

She comes down to the footlights.

This is where you came in. We have to go on for ages and ages yet.

You go home.

The end of this play isn't written yet.

Mr. and Mrs. Antrobus! Their heads are full of plans and they're as confident as the first day they began,—and they told me to tell you: good night.

The Matchmaker

A Farce in Four Acts

The Merchant of Yonkers *was produced by Herman Shumlin* and directed by Max Reinhardt. The production was designed by Boris Aronson. The cast included Jane Cowl, June Walker, Nydia Westman, Minna Phillips, Percy Waram, Tom Ewell, John Call, Joseph Sweeney, Philip Coolidge, and Edward Nannery. It was first performed on December 12, 1938, at the Colonial Theatre, Boston. The New York engagement opened at the Guild Theatre on December 28, 1938.

The Matchmaker was produced for the Edinburgh Festival by Tennent Productions. It was directed by Dr. Tyrone Guthrie, and the production was designed by Tanya Moiseiwitsch. The first performance was at the Royal Lyceum Theatre, Edinburgh, on August 23, 1954.

The same production opened at the Theatre Royal, Haymarket, London, on November 4, 1954. Without changes in the principal roles—with the exception of that of Mr. Vandergelder, which was played successively by Sam Levene, Eddie Mayehoff, and Loring Smith—the play was performed at the Locust Street Theatre, Philadelphia, on October 27, 1955.

The cast of the play from Edinburgh to New York, with the exceptions noted, included:

HORACE VANDERGELDER	Loring Smith
CORNELIUS HACKL	Arthur Hill
BARNABY TUCKER	Robert Morse (following Alec McCowen)
MALACHI STACK	Patrick McAlinney
AMBROSE KEMPER	Alexander Davion (following Lee Montague)
WAITERS	William Lanteau (following and followed by Timothy Findley) and John Milligan
CABMAN	Peter Bayliss
DOLLY LEVI	Ruth Gordon
IRENE MOLLOY	Eileen Herlie
MINNIE FAY	Rosamund Greenwood
ERMENGARDE	Prunella Scales
GERTRUDE	Charity Grace (following Henzie Raeburn)
FLORA VAN HUYSEN	Esme Church
COOK	Christine Thomas (following Daphne Newton)

This play is a rewritten version of *The Merchant of Yonkers,* which was directed in 1938 by Max Reinhardt and is again dedicated to Max Reinhardt with deep admiration and indebtedness

CHARACTERS

HORACE VANDERGELDER	*A merchant of Yonkers, New York*
CORNELIUS HACKL	
BARNABY TUCKER	*Clerks in his store*
MALACHI STACK	
AMBROSE KEMPER	*An artist*
JOE SCANLON	*A barber*
RUDOLPH	*Waiters*
AUGUST	
A CABMAN	
MRS. DOLLY LEVI	*Friends of Vandergelder's*
MISS FLORA VAN HUYSEN	*late wife*
MRS. IRENE MOLLOY	*A milliner*
MINNIE FAY	*Her assistant*
ERMENGARD	*Vandergelder's niece*
GERTRUDE	*Vandergelder's housekeeper*
MISS VAN HUYSEN'S COOK	

TIME: The early 80's.
Act I. Vandergelder's house in Yonkers, New York.
Act II. Mrs. Molloy's hat shop, New York.
Act III. The Harmonia Gardens Restaurant
on the Battery, New York.
Act IV. Miss Van Huysen's house, New York.

This play is based upon a comedy by Johann Nestroy, *Einen Jux will es sich Machen* (Vienna, 1842), which was in turn based upon an English original, *A Day Well Spent* (London, 1835) by John Oxenford.

—∞—

Act I

Living room of Mr. Vandergelder's house, over his hay, feed and provision store in Yonkers, fifteen miles north of New York City. Articles from the store have overflowed into this room; it has not been cleaned for a long time and is in some disorder, but it is not sordid or gloomy.

There are three entrances. One at the center back leads into the principal rooms of the house. One on the back right (all the directions are from the point of view of the actors) opens on steps which descend to the street door. One on the left leads to Ermengarde's room.

In the center of the room is a trap door; below it is a ladder descending to the store below.

Behind the trap door and to the left of it is a tall accountant's desk; to the left of it is an old-fashioned stove with a stovepipe going up into the ceiling. Before the desk is a tall stool. On the right of the stage is a table with some chairs about it.

Mr. Vandergelder's Gladstone bag, packed for a journey, is beside the desk.

It is early morning.

VANDERGELDER, sixty, choleric, vain and sly, wears a soiled dressing gown. He is seated with a towel about his neck, in a chair beside the desk, being shaved by JOE SCANLON.

VANDERGELDER is smoking a cigar and holding a hand mirror. AMBROSE KEMPER is angrily striding about the room.

VANDERGELDER:

Loudly.

I tell you for the hundredth time you will never marry my niece.

AMBROSE:

Thirty; dressed as an "artist."

And I tell you for the thousandth time that I will marry your niece; and right soon, too.

VANDERGELDER:

Never!

AMBROSE:

Your niece is of age, Mr. Vandergelder. Your niece has consented to marry me. This is a free country, Mr. Vandergelder— not a private kingdom of your own.

VANDERGELDER:

There are no free countries for fools, Mr. Kemper. Thank you for the honor of your visit—good morning.

JOE:

Fifty; lanky, mass of gray hair falling into his eyes.

Mr. Vandergelder, will you please sit still one minute? If I cut your throat it'll be practically unintentional.

VANDERGELDER:

Ermengarde is not for you, nor for anybody else who can't support her.

AMBROSE:

I tell you I can support her. I make a very good living.

VANDERGELDER:

No, sir! A living is made, Mr. Kemper, by selling something that everybody needs at least once a year. Yes, sir! And a million is made by producing something that everybody needs every day. You artists produce something that nobody needs at any time. You may sell a picture once in a while, but you'll make no living. Joe, go over there and stamp three times. I want to talk to Cornelius.

JOE *crosses to trap door and stamps three times.*

AMBROSE:

Not only can I support her now, but I have considerable expectations.

VANDERGELDER:

Expectations! We merchants don't do business with them. I don't keep accounts with people who promise somehow to pay something someday, and I don't allow my niece to marry such people.

AMBROSE:

Very well, from now on you might as well know that I regard any way we can find to get married is right and fair. Ermengarde is of age, and there's no law . . .

VANDERGELDER *rises and crosses toward Ambrose.* JOE SCANLON *follows him complainingly and tries to find a chance to cut his hair even while he is standing.*

VANDERGELDER:

Law? Let me tell you something, Mr. Kemper: most of the people in the world are fools. The law is there to prevent crime; we men of sense are there to prevent foolishness. It's I, and not the law, that will prevent Ermengarde from marrying you, and I've taken some steps already. I've sent her away to get this nonsense out of her head.

AMBROSE:

Ermengarde's . . . not here?

VANDERGELDER:

She's gone—east, west, north, south. I thank you for the honor of your visit.

Enter GERTRUDE—*eighty; deaf; half blind; and very pleased with herself.*

GERTRUDE:

Everything's ready, Mr. Vandergelder. Ermengarde and I have just finished packing the trunk.

VANDERGELDER:

Hold your tongue!

JOE *is shaving Vandergelder's throat, so he can only wave his hands vainly.*

GERTRUDE:

Yes, Mr. Vandergelder, Ermengarde's ready to leave. Her trunk's all marked. Care Miss Van Huysen, 8 Jackson Street, New York.

VANDERGELDER:

Breaking away from Joe.

Hell and damnation! Didn't I tell you it was a secret?

AMBROSE:

Picks up hat and coat—kisses Gertrude.

Care Miss Van Huysen, 8 Jackson Street, New York. Thank you very much. Good morning, Mr. Vandergelder.

Exit AMBROSE, *to the street.*

VANDERGELDER:

It won't help you, Mr. Kemper—

To Gertrude.

Deaf! And blind! At least you can do me the favor of being dumb!

GERTRUDE:

Chk—chk! Such a temper! Lord save us!

CORNELIUS *puts his head up through the trap door. He is thirty-three; mock-deferential—he wears a green apron and is in his shirt-sleeves.*

CORNELIUS:

Yes, Mr. Vandergelder?

VANDERGELDER:

Go in and get my niece's trunk and carry it over to the station. Wait! Gertrude, has Mrs. Levi arrived yet?

CORNELIUS *comes up the trap door, steps into the room and closes the trap door behind him.*

GERTRUDE:

Don't shout. I can hear perfectly well. Everything's clearly marked.

Exit left.

VANDERGELDER:

Have the buggy brought round to the front of the store in half an hour.

CORNELIUS:

Yes, Mr. Vandergelder.

VANDERGELDER:

This morning I'm joining my lodge parade and this afternoon I'm going to New York. Before I go, I have something important to say to you and Barnaby. Good news. Fact is— I'm going to promote you. How old are you?

CORNELIUS:

Thirty-three, Mr. Vandergelder.

VANDERGELDER:

What?

CORNELIUS:

Thirty-three.

VANDERGELDER:

That all? That's a foolish age to be at. I thought you were forty.

CORNELIUS:

Thirty-three.

VANDERGELDER:

A man's not worth a cent until he's forty. We just pay 'em wages to make mistakes—don't we, Joe?

JOE:

You almost lost an ear on it, Mr. Vandergelder.

VANDERGELDER:

I was thinking of promoting you to chief clerk.

CORNELIUS:

What am I now, Mr. Vandergelder?

VANDERGELDER:

You're an impertinent fool, that's what you are. Now, if you behave yourself, I'll promote you from impertinent fool to chief clerk, with a raise in your wages. And Barnaby may be promoted from idiot apprentice to incompetent clerk.

CORNELIUS:

Thank you, Mr. Vandergelder.

VANDERGELDER:

However, I want to see you again before I go. Go in and get my niece's trunk.

CORNELIUS:

Yes, Mr. Vandergelder.

Exit CORNELIUS, *left.*

VANDERGELDER:

Joe—the world's getting crazier every minute. Like my father used to say: the horses'll be taking over the world soon.

JOE:

Presenting mirror.

I did what I could, Mr. Vandergelder, what with you flying in and out of the chair.

He wipes last of the soap from Vandergelder's face.

VANDERGELDER:

Fine, fine. Joe, you do a fine job, the same fine job you've done me for twenty years. Joe . . . I've got special reasons for looking my best today . . . isn't there something a little extry you could do, something a little special? I'll pay you right up to fifty cents—see what I mean? Do some of those things you do to the young fellas. Touch me up; smarten me up a bit.

JOE:

All I know is fifteen cents' worth, like usual, Mr. Vandergelder; and that includes everything that's decent to do to a man.

VANDERGELDER:

Now hold your horses, Joe—all I meant was . . .

JOE:

I've shaved you for twenty years and you never asked me no such question before.

VANDERGELDER:

Hold your horses, I say, Joe! I'm going to tell you a secret. But I don't want you telling it to that riffraff down to the barber-shop what I'm going to tell you now. All I ask of you is a little extry because I'm thinking of getting married again; and this very afternoon I'm going to New York to call on my intended, a very refined lady.

JOE:

Your gettin' married is none of my business, Mr. Vandergelder. I done everything to you I know, and the charge is fifteen cents like it always was, and . . .

CORNELIUS *crosses, left to right, and exit, carrying a trunk on his shoulder.* ERMENGARDE *and* GERTRUDE *enter from left.*

I don't dye no hair, not even for fifty cents I don't!

VANDERGELDER:
Joe Scanlon, get out!

JOE:
And lastly, it looks to me like you're pretty rash to judge which is fools and which isn't fools, Mr. Vandergelder. People that's et onions is bad judges of who's et onions and who ain't. Good morning, ladies; good morning, Mr. Vandergelder.

Exit JOE.

VANDERGELDER:
Well, what do you want?

ERMENGARDE:
Twenty-four; pretty, sentimental.

Uncle! You said you wanted to talk to us.

VANDERGELDER:
Oh yes. Gertrude, go and get my parade regalia—the uniform for my lodge parade.

GERTRUDE:
What? Oh yes. Lord have mercy!

Exit GERTRUDE, *back center.*

VANDERGELDER:
I had a talk with that artist of yours. He's a fool.

ERMENGARDE *starts to cry.*

Weeping! Weeping! You can go down and weep for a while in New York where it won't be noticed.

He sits on desk chair, puts tie round neck and calls her over to tie it for him.

Ermengarde! I told him that when you were old enough to marry you'd marry someone who could support you. I've done you a good turn. You'll come and thank me when you're fifty.

ERMENGARDE:

But Uncle, I love him!

VANDERGELDER:

I tell you you don't.

ERMENGARDE:

But I *do!*

VANDERGELDER:

And I tell you you don't. Leave those things to me.

ERMENGARDE:

If I don't marry Ambrose I know I'll die.

VANDERGELDER:

What of?

ERMENGARDE:

A broken heart.

VANDERGELDER:

Never heard of it. Mrs. Levi is coming in a moment to take you to New York. You are going to stay two or three weeks with Miss Van Huysen, an old friend of your mother's.

GERTRUDE *re-enters with coat, sash and sword. Enter from the street, right,* MALACHI STACK.

You're not to receive any letters except from me. I'm coming to New York myself today and I'll call on you tomorrow.

To Malachi.

Who are you?

MALACHI:

Fifty. Sardonic. Apparently innocent smile; pretense of humility.

Malachi Stack, your honor. I heard you wanted an apprentice in the hay, feed, provision and hardware business.

VANDERGELDER:

An apprentice at your age?

MALACHI:

Yes, your honor; I bring a lot of experience to it.

VANDERGELDER:

Have you any letters of recommendation?

MALACHI:

Extending a sheaf of soiled papers.

Yes, indeed, your honor! First-class recommendation.

VANDERGELDER:

Ermengarde! Are you ready to start?

ERMENGARDE:

Yes.

VANDERGELDER:

Well, go and get ready some more. Ermengarde! Let me know the minute Mrs. Levi gets here.

ERMENGARDE:

Yes, Uncle Horace.

ERMENGARDE *and* GERTRUDE *exit.*

VANDERGELDER *examines the letters, putting them down one by one.*

VANDERGELDER:

I don't want an able seaman. Nor a typesetter. And I don't want a hospital cook.

MALACHI:

No, your honor, but it's all experience. Excuse me!

Selects a letter.

This one is from your former partner, Joshua Van Tuyl, in Albany.

He puts letters from table back into pocket.

VANDERGELDER:

". . . for the most part honest and reliable . . . occasionally willing and diligent." There seems to be a certain amount of hesitation about these recommendations.

MALACHI:

Businessmen aren't writers, your honor. There's only one businessman in a thousand that can write a good letter of recommendation, your honor. Mr. Van Tuyl sends his best wishes and wants to know if you can use me in the provision and hardware business.

VANDERGELDER:

Not so fast, not so fast! What's this "your honor" you use so much?

MALACHI:

Mr. Van Tuyl says you're President of the Hudson River Provision Dealers' Recreational, Musical and Burial Society.

VANDERGELDER:

I am; but there's no "your honor" that goes with it. Why did you come to Yonkers?

MALACHI:

I heard that you'd had an apprentice that was a good-for-nothing, and that you were at your wit's end for another.

VANDERGELDER:

Wit's end, wit's end! There's no dearth of good-for-nothing apprentices.

MALACHI:

That's right, Mr. Vandergelder. It's employers there's a dearth of. Seems like you hear of a new one dying every day.

VANDERGELDER:

What's that? Hold your tongue. I see you've been a barber, and a valet too. Why have you changed your place so often?

MALACHI:

Changed my place, Mr. Vandergelder? When a man's interested in experience . . .

VANDERGELDER:

Do you drink?

MALACHI:

No, thanks. I've just had breakfast.

VANDERGELDER:

I didn't ask you whether—Idiot! I asked you if you were a drunkard.

MALACHI:

No, sir! No! Why, looking at it from all sides I don't even like liquor.

VANDERGELDER:

Well, if you keep on looking at it from all sides, out you go. Remember that. Here.

Gives him remaining letters.

With all your faults, I'm going to give you a try.

MALACHI:

You'll never regret it, Mr. Vandergelder. You'll never regret it.

VANDERGELDER:

Now today I want to use you in New York. I judge you know your way around New York?

MALACHI:

Do I know New York? Mr. Vandergelder, I know every hole and corner in New York.

VANDERGELDER:

Here's a dollar. A train leaves in a minute. Take that bag to the Central Hotel on Water Street, have them save me a room. Wait for me. I'll be there about four o'clock.

MALACHI:

Yes, Mr. Vandergelder.

Picks up the bag, starts out, then comes back.

Oh, but first, I'd like to meet the other clerks I'm to work with.

VANDERGELDER:

You haven't time. Hurry now. The station's across the street.

MALACHI:

Yes, sir.

Away—then back once more.

You'll see, sir, you'll never regret it. . . .

VANDERGELDER:

I regret it already. Go on. Off with you.

Exit MALACHI, *right.*

The following speech is addressed to the audience. During it
MR. VANDERGELDER *takes off his dressing gown, puts on his*
scarlet sash, his sword and his bright-colored coat. He is
already wearing light blue trousers with a red stripe down
the sides.

VANDERGELDER:

Ninety-nine per cent of the people in the world are fools and
the rest of us are in great danger of contagion. But I wasn't
always free of foolishness as I am now. I was once young, which
was foolish; I fell in love, which was foolish; and I got married,
which was foolish; and for a while I was poor, which was more
foolish than all the other things put together. Then my wife
died, which was foolish of her; I grew older, which was sensible
of me; then I became a rich man, which is as sensible as it is rare.
Since you see I'm a man of sense, I guess you were surprised to
hear that I'm planning to get married again. Well, I've two reasons for it. In the first place, I like my house run with order,
comfort and economy. That's a woman's work; but even a
woman can't do it well if she's merely being paid for it. In order
to run a house well, a woman must have the feeling that she
owns it. Marriage is a bribe to make a housekeeper think she's

a householder. Did you ever watch an ant carry a burden twice its size? What excitement! What patience! What will! Well, that's what I think of when I see a woman running a house. What giant passions in those little bodies—what quarrels with the butcher for the best cut—what fury at discovering a moth in a cupboard! Believe me!—if women could harness their natures to something bigger than a house and a baby carriage— tck! tck!—they'd change the world. And the second reason, ladies and gentlemen? Well, I see by your faces you've guessed it already. There's nothing like mixing with women to bring out all the foolishness in a man of sense. And that's a risk I'm willing to take. I've just turned sixty, and I've just laid side by side the last dollar of my first half million. So if I should lose my head a little, I still have enough money to buy it back. After many years' caution and hard work, I have a right to a little risk and adventure, and I'm thinking of getting married. Yes, like all you other fools, I'm willing to risk a little security for a certain amount of adventure. Think it over.

Exit back center.

AMBROSE *enters from the street, crosses left, and whistles softly.* ERMENGARDE *enters from left.*

ERMENGARDE:
Ambrose! If my uncle saw you!

AMBROSE:
Sh! Get your hat.

ERMENGARDE:
My hat!

AMBROSE:

Quick! Your trunk's at the station. Now quick! We're running away.

ERMENGARDE:

Running away!

AMBROSE:

Sh!

ERMENGARDE:

Where?

AMBROSE:

To New York. To get married.

ERMENGARDE:

Oh, Ambrose, I can't do that. Ambrose dear—it wouldn't be proper!

AMBROSE:

Listen. I'm taking you to my friend's house. His wife will take care of you.

ERMENGARDE:

But, Ambrose, a girl can't go on a train with a man. I can see you don't know anything about girls.

AMBROSE:

But I'm telling you we're going to get married!

ERMENGARDE:

Married! But what would *Uncle* say?

AMBROSE:

We don't care what Uncle'd say—we're eloping.

ERMENGARDE:

Ambrose Kemper! How can you use such an awful word!

AMBROSE:

Ermengarde, you have the soul of a field mouse.

ERMENGARDE:

Crying.

Ambrose, why do you say such cruel things to me?

Enter MRS. LEVI, *from the street, right. She stands listening.*

AMBROSE:

For the last time I beg you—get your hat and coat. The train leaves in a few minutes. Ermengarde, we'll get married tomorrow. . . .

ERMENGARDE:

Oh, Ambrose! I see you don't understand anything about weddings. Ambrose, don't you *respect* me?. . .

MRS. LEVI:

Uncertain age; mass of sandy hair; impoverished elegance; large, shrewd but generous nature, an assumption of worldly cynicism conceals a tireless amused enjoyment of life. She carries a handbag and a small brown paper bag.

Good morning, darling girl—how are you?

They kiss.

ERMENGARDE:

Oh, good morning, Mrs. Levi.

MRS. LEVI:

And who is this gentleman who is so devoted to you?

ERMENGARDE:

This is Mr. Kemper, Mrs. Levi. Ambrose, this is . . . Mrs. Levi . . . she's an old friend. . . .

MRS. LEVI:

Mrs. Levi, born Gallagher. Very happy to meet you, Mr. Kemper.

AMBROSE:

Good morning, Mrs. Levi.

MRS. LEVI:

Mr. Kemper, *the artist!* Delighted! Mr. Kemper, may I say something very frankly?

AMBROSE:

Yes, Mrs. Levi.

MRS. LEVI:

This thing you were planning to do is a very great mistake.

ERMENGARDE:

Oh, Mrs. Levi, please explain to Ambrose—of *course!* I want to marry him, but to *elope!* . . . How . . .

MRS. LEVI:

Now, my dear girl, you go in and keep one eye on your uncle. I wish to talk to Mr. Kemper for a moment. You give us a warning when you hear your Uncle Horace coming. . . .

ERMENGARDE:

Ye-es, Mrs. Levi.

Exit ERMENGARDE, *back center.*

MRS. LEVI:

Mr. Kemper, I was this dear girl's mother's oldest friend. Believe me, I am on your side. I hope you two will be married very soon, and I think I can be of real service to you. Mr. Kemper, I always go right to the point.

AMBROSE:

What is the point, Mrs. Levi?

MRS. LEVI:

Mr. Vandergelder is a very rich man, Mr. Kemper, and Ermengarde is his only relative.

AMBROSE:

But I am not interested in Mr. Vandergelder's money. I have enough to support a wife and family.

MRS. LEVI:

Enough? How much is enough when one is thinking about children and the future? The future is the most expensive luxury in the world, Mr. Kemper.

AMBROSE:

Mrs. Levi, what is the point.

MRS. LEVI:

Believe me, Mr. Vandergelder wishes to get rid of Ermengarde, and if you follow my suggestions he will even permit her to marry you. You see, Mr. Vandergelder is planning to get married himself.

AMBROSE:

What? That monster!

MRS. LEVI:

Mr. Kemper!

AMBROSE:

Married! To you, Mrs. Levi?

MRS. LEVI:

Taken aback.

Oh, no, no . . . NO! I am merely arranging it. I am helping him find a suitable bride.

AMBROSE:

For Mr. Vandergelder there are no suitable brides.

MRS. LEVI:

I think we can safely say that Mr. Vandergelder will be married to someone by the end of next week.

AMBROSE:

What are you suggesting, Mrs. Levi?

MRS. LEVI:

I am taking Ermengarde to New York on the next train. I shall not take her to Miss Van Huysen's, as is planned; I shall take her to my house. I wish you to call for her at my house at five thirty. Here is my card.

AMBROSE:

"Mrs. Dolly Gallagher Levi. Varicose veins reduced."

MRS. LEVI:

Trying to take back card.

I beg your pardon . . .

AMBROSE:

Holding card.

I beg *your* pardon. "Consultations free."

MRS. LEVI:

I meant to give you my other card. Here.

AMBROSE:

"Mrs. Dolly Gallagher Levi. Aurora Hosiery. Instruction in the guitar and mandolin." You do all these things, Mrs. Levi?

MRS. LEVI:

Two and two make four, Mr. Kemper—always did. So you will come to my house at five thirty. At about six I shall take you both with me to the Harmonia Gardens Restaurant on the Battery; Mr. Vandergelder will be there and everything will be arranged.

AMBROSE:

How?

MRS. LEVI:

Oh, I don't know. One thing will lead to another.

AMBROSE:

How do I know that I can trust you, Mrs. Levi? You could easily make our situation worse.

MRS. LEVI:

Mr. Kemper, your situation could not possibly be worse.

AMBROSE:

I wish I knew what you get out of this, Mrs. Levi.

MRS. LEVI:

That is a very proper question. I get two things: profit and pleasure.

AMBROSE:

How?

MRS. LEVI:

Mr. Kemper, I am a woman who arranges things. At present I am arranging Mr. Vandergelder's domestic affairs. Out of it I get—shall we call it: little pickings? I need little pickings, Mr. Kemper, and especially just now, when I haven't got my train fare back to New York. You see: I am frank with you.

AMBROSE:

That's your profit, Mrs. Levi; but where do you get your pleasure?

MRS. LEVI:

My pleasure? Mr. Kemper, when you artists paint a hillside or a river you change everything a little, you make thousands of little changes, don't you? Nature is never completely satisfactory and must be corrected. Well, I'm like you artists. Life as it is is never quite interesting enough for me—I'm bored, Mr. Kemper, with life as it is—and so I do things. I put my hand in here, and I put my hand in there, and I watch and I listen—and often I'm very much amused.

AMBROSE:

Rises.

Not in my affairs, Mrs. Levi.

MRS. LEVI:

Wait, I haven't finished. There's another thing. I'm very interested in this household here—in Mr. Vandergelder and all that idle, frozen money of his. I don't like the thought of it lying in great piles, useless, motionless, in the bank, Mr. Kemper. Money should circulate like rain water. It should be flowing down among the people, through dressmakers and restaurants and cabmen, setting up a little business here, and furnishing a good time there. Do you see what I mean?

AMBROSE:

Yes, I do.

MRS. LEVI:

New York should be a very happy city, Mr. Kemper, but it isn't. My late husband came from Vienna; now there's a city that understands this. I want New York to be more like Vienna and less like a collection of nervous and tired ants. And if you and Ermengarde get a good deal of Mr. Vandergelder's money, I want you to see that it starts flowing in and around a lot of people's lives. And for that reason I want you to come with me to the Harmonia Gardens Restaurant tonight.

Enter ERMENGARDE.

ERMENGARDE:

Mrs. Levi, Uncle Horace is coming.

MRS. LEVI:

Mr. Kemper, I think you'd better be going. . . .

AMBROSE *crosses to trap door and disappears down the ladder, closing trap as he goes.*

Darling girl, Mr. Kemper and I have had a very good talk.

You'll see: Mr. Vandergelder and I will be dancing at your wedding very soon—

Enter VANDERGELDER *at back. He has now added a splendid plumed hat to his costume and is carrying a standard or small flag bearing the initials of his lodge.*

Oh, Mr. Vandergelder, how handsome you look! You take my breath away. Yes, my dear girl, I'll see you soon.

Exit ERMENGARDE *back center.*

Oh, Mr. Vandergelder, I wish Irene Molloy could see you now. But then! I don't know what's come over you lately. You seem to be growing younger every day.

VANDERGELDER:

Allowing for exaggeration, Mrs. Levi. If a man eats careful there's no reason why he should look old.

MRS. LEVI:

You never said a truer word.

VANDERGELDER:

I'll never see fifty-five again.

MRS. LEVI:

Fifty-five! Why, I can see at a glance that you're the sort that will be stamping about at a hundred—and eating five meals a day, like my Uncle Harry. At fifty-five my Uncle Harry was a mere boy. I'm a judge of hands, Mr. Vandergelder—show me your hand.

Looks at it.

Lord in heaven! What a life line!

VANDERGELDER:

Where?

MRS. LEVI:

From *here* to *here*. It runs right off your hand. I don't know where it goes. They'll have to hit you on the head with a mallet. They'll have to stifle you with a sofa pillow. You'll bury us all! However, to return to our business—Mr. Vandergelder, I suppose you've changed your mind again. I suppose you've given up all idea of getting married.

VANDERGELDER:

Complacently.

Not at all, Mrs. Levi. I have news for you.

MRS. LEVI:

News?

VANDERGELDER:

Mrs. Levi, I've practically decided to ask Mrs. Molloy to be my wife.

MRS. LEVI:

Taken aback.

You have?

VANDERGELDER:

Yes, I have.

MRS. LEVI:

Oh, you have! Well, I guess that's just about the best news I ever heard. So there's nothing more for me to do but wish you every happiness under the sun and say good-by.

Crosses as if to leave.

VANDERGELDER:
Stopping her.

Well—Mrs. Levi—Surely I thought—

MRS. LEVI:
Well, I did have a little suggestion to make—but I won't. You're going to marry Irene Molloy, and that closes the matter.

VANDERGELDER:
What suggestion was that, Mrs. Levi?

MRS. LEVI:
Well—I *had* found *another* girl for you.

VANDERGELDER:
Another?

MRS. LEVI:
The most wonderful girl, the ideal wife.

VANDERGELDER:
Another, eh? What's her name?

MRS. LEVI:
Her name?

VANDERGELDER:
Yes!

MRS. LEVI:
Groping for it.

Err . . . er . . . her *name?*—Ernestina—Simple. *Miss* Ernestina Simple. But now of course all that's too late. After all, you're engaged—you're practically engaged to marry Irene Molloy.

VANDERGELDER:

Oh, I ain't engaged to Mrs. Molloy!

MRS. LEVI:

Nonsense! You can't break poor Irene's heart now and change to another girl . . . When a man at your time of life calls four times on an attractive widow like that—and sends her a pot of geraniums—that's practically an engagement!

VANDERGELDER:

That ain't an engagement!

MRS. LEVI:

And yet—! If only you were free! I've found this treasure of a girl. Every moment I felt like a traitor to Irene Molloy—but let me tell you: I couldn't help it. I told this girl all about you, just as though you were a free man. Isn't that dreadful? The fact is: she has fallen in love with you already.

VANDERGELDER:

Ernestina?

MRS. LEVI:

Ernestina Simple.

VANDERGELDER:

Ernestina Simple.

MRS. LEVI:

Of course she's a very different idea from Mrs. Molloy, Ernestina is. Like her name—simple, domestic, practical.

VANDERGELDER:

Can she cook?

MRS. LEVI:

Cook, Mr. Vandergelder? I've had two meals from her hands, and—as I live—I don't know what I've done that God should reward me with such meals.

[The following passage—adapted from a scene in Molière's L'Avare—has been cut in recent performances:

MRS. LEVI:

Continues.

Her duck! Her steak!

VANDERGELDER:

Eh! Eh! In this house we don't eat duck and steak every day, Mrs. Levi.

MRS. LEVI:

But didn't I tell you?—that's the wonderful part about it. Her duck—what was it? Pigeon! I'm alive to tell you. I don't know how she does it. It's a secret that's come down in her family. The greatest chefs would give their right hands to know it. And the steaks? Shoulder of beef—four cents a pound. Dogs wouldn't eat. But when Ernestina passes her hands over it—!!

VANDERGELDER:

Allowing for exaggeration, Mrs. Levi.

MRS. LEVI:

No exaggeration.*]*

I'm the best cook in the world myself, and I *know* what's good.

VANDERGELDER:

Hm. How old is she, Mrs. Levi?

MRS. LEVI:

Nineteen, well—say twenty.

VANDERGELDER:

Twenty, Mrs. Levi? Girls of twenty are apt to favor young fellows of their own age.

MRS. LEVI:

But you don't listen to me. And you don't know the girl. Mr. Vandergelder, she has a positive horror of flighty, brainless young men. A fine head of gray hair, she says, is worth twenty shined up with goose grease. No, sir. "I like a man that's *settled*"—in so many words she said it.

VANDERGELDER:

That's . . . that's not usual, Mrs. Levi.

MRS. LEVI:

Usual? I'm not wearing myself to the bone hunting up *usual* girls to interest you, Mr. Vandergelder. Usual, indeed. Listen to me. Do you know the sort of pictures she has on her wall? Is it any of these young Romeos and Lochinvars? No!—it's Moses on the Mountain—that's what she's got. If you want to make her happy, you give her a picture of Methuselah surrounded by his grandchildren. That's my advice to you.

[*Following passage—also based on Molière—has generally been cut in performance:*

VANDERGELDER:

I hope . . . hm . . . that she has some means, Mrs. Levi. I have a large household to run.

MRS. LEVI:

Ernestina? She'll bring you five thousand dollars a year.

VANDERGELDER:

Eh! Eh!

MRS. LEVI:

Listen to me, Mr. Vandergelder. You're a man of sense, I hope. A man that can reckon. In the first place, she's an orphan. She's been brought up with a great saving of food. What does she eat herself? Apples and lettuce. It's what she's been used to eat and what she likes best. She saves you two thousand a year right there. Secondly, she makes her own clothes—out of old table-cloths and window curtains. And she's the best-dressed woman in Brooklyn this minute. She saves you a thousand dollars right there. Thirdly, her health is of iron—

VANDERGELDER:

But, Mrs. Levi, that's not money in the pocket.

MRS. LEVI:

We're talking about marriage, aren't we, Mr. Vandergelder? The money she saves while she's in Brooklyn is none of your affair—but if she were your wife that would be *money*. Yes, sir, that's money.]

VANDERGELDER:

What's her family?

MRS. LEVI:

Her father?—God be good to him! He was the best—what am I trying to say?—the best undertaker in Brooklyn, respected, esteemed. He knew all the best people—knew them well, even before they died. So—well, that's the way it is.

Lowering her voice, intimately.

Now let me tell you a little more of her appearance. Can you hear me: as I say, a beautiful girl, beautiful, I've seen her go down the street—you know what I mean?—the young men get dizzy. They have to lean against lampposts. And she? Modest, eyes on the ground—I'm not going to tell you any more. . . . Couldn't you come to New York today?

VANDERGELDER:

I was thinking of coming to New York this afternoon. . . .

MRS. LEVI:

You were? Well now, I wonder if something could be arranged—oh, she's so eager to see you! Let me see . . .

VANDERGELDER:

Could I . . . Mrs. Levi, could I give you a little dinner, maybe?

MRS. LEVI:

Really, come to think of it, I don't see where I could get the time. I'm so busy over that wretched lawsuit of mine. Yes. If I win it, I don't mind telling you, I'll be what's called a very rich woman. I'll own half of Long Island, that's a fact. But just now I'm at my wit's end for a little help, just enough money to finish it off. My wit's end!

She looks in her bandbag.

In order not to hear this, VANDERGELDER *has a series of coughs, sneezes and minor convulsions.*

But perhaps I could arrange a little dinner; I'll see. Yes, for that lawsuit all I need is fifty dollars, and Staten Island's as good as mine. I've been trotting all over New York for you, trying to find you a suitable wife.

VANDERGELDER:

Fifty dollars!!

MRS. LEVI:

Two whole months I've been . . .

VANDERGELDER:

Fifty dollars, Mrs. Levi . . . is no joke.

Producing purse.

I don't know where money's gone to these days. It's in hiding. . . . There's twenty . . . well, there's twenty-five. I can't spare no more, not now I can't.

MRS. LEVI:

Well, this will help—will help somewhat. Now let me tell you what we'll do. I'll bring Ernestina to that restaurant on the Battery. You know it: the Harmonia Gardens. It's good, but it's not flashy. Now, Mr. Vandergelder, I think it'd be nice if just this once you'd order a real nice dinner. I guess you can afford it.

VANDERGELDER:

Well, just this once.

MRS. LEVI:

A chicken wouldn't hurt.

VANDERGELDER:

Chicken!!—Well, just this once.

MRS. LEVI:

And a little wine.

VANDERGELDER:

Wine? Well, just this once.

MRS. LEVI:

Now about Mrs. Molloy—what do you think? Shall we call that subject closed?

VANDERGELDER:

No, not at all, Mrs. Levi, I want to have dinner with Miss . . . with Miss . . .

MRS. LEVI:

Simple.

VANDERGELDER:

With Miss Simple; but first I want to make another call on Mrs. Molloy.

MRS. LEVI:

Dear, dear, dear! And Miss Simple? What races you make me run! Very well; I'll meet you on one of those benches in front of Mrs. Molloy's hat store at four thirty, as usual.

Trap door rises, and CORNELIUS' *head appears.*

CORNELIUS:

The buggy's here, ready for the parade, Mr. Vandergelder.

VANDERGELDER:

Call Barnaby. I want to talk to both of you.

CORNELIUS:

Yes, Mr. Vandergelder.

Exit CORNELIUS *down trap door. Leaves trap open.*

MRS. LEVI:

Now do put your thoughts in order, Mr. Vandergelder. I can't keep upsetting and disturbing the finest women in New York City unless you mean business.

VANDERGELDER:

Oh, I mean business all right!

MRS. LEVI:

I hope so. Because, you know, you're playing a very dangerous game.

VANDERGELDER:

Dangerous?—Dangerous, Mrs. Levi?

MRS. LEVI:

Of course, it's dangerous—and there's a name for it! You're tampering with these women's affections, aren't you? And the only way you can save yourself now is to be married to *someone* by the end of next week. So think that over!

Exit center back.

Enter CORNELIUS *and* BARNABY, *by the trap door.*

VANDERGELDER:

This morning I'm joining my lodge parade, and this afternoon I'm going to New York. When I come back, there are going to be some changes in the house here. I'll tell you what the change is, but I don't want you discussing it amongst yourselves: you're going to have a mistress.

BARNABY:

Seventeen; round-faced, wide-eyed innocence; wearing a green apron.

I'm too young, Mr. Vandergelder!!

VANDERGELDER:

Not yours! Death and damnation! Not yours, idiot—*mine!*

Then, realizing:

Hey! Hold your tongue until you're spoken to! I'm thinking of getting married.

CORNELIUS:

Crosses, hand outstretched.

Many congratulations, Mr. Vandergelder, and my compliments to the lady.

VANDERGELDER:

That's none of your business. Now go back to the store.

The BOYS *start down the ladder,* BARNABY *first.*

Have you got any questions you want to ask before I go?

CORNELIUS:

Mr. Vandergelder—er—Mr. Vandergelder, does the chief clerk get one evening off every week?

VANDERGELDER:

So that's the way you begin being chief clerk, is it? When I was your age I got up at five; I didn't close the shop until ten at night, and then I put in a good hour at the account books. The world's going to pieces. You elegant ladies lie in bed until six and at nine o'clock at night you rush to close the door so fast the line of customers bark their noses. No, sir—you'll attend to the store as usual, and on Friday and Saturday nights you'll remain open until ten—now hear what I say! This is the first time I've been away from the store overnight. When I come back I want to hear that you've run the place perfectly in my absence. If I hear of any foolishness, I'll discharge you. An evening free! Do you suppose that *I* had evenings free?

At the top of his complacency.

If I'd had evenings free I wouldn't be what I am now!

He marches out, right.

BARNABY:
Watching him go.

The horses nearly ran away when they saw him. What's the matter, Cornelius?

CORNELIUS:
Sits in dejected thought.

Chief clerk! Promoted from chief clerk to chief clerk.

BARNABY:
Don't you like it?

CORNELIUS:
Chief clerk!—and if I'm good, in ten years I'll be promoted to chief clerk again. Thirty-three years old and I still don't get an evening free? When am I going to begin to live?

BARNABY:
Well—ah . . . you can begin to live on Sundays, Cornelius.

CORNELIUS:
That's not living. Twice to church, and old Wolf-trap's eyes on the back of my head the whole time. And as for holidays! What did we do last Christmas? All those canned tomatoes went bad

and exploded. We had to clean up the mess all afternoon. Was that living?

BARNABY:

Holding his nose at the memory of the bad smell.

No!!!

CORNELIUS:

Rising with sudden resolution.

Barnaby, how much money have you got—where you can get at it?

BARNABY:

Oh—three dollars. Why, Cornelius?

CORNELIUS:

You and I are going to New York.

BARNABY:

Cornelius!!! We can't! Close the store?

CORNELIUS:

Some more rotten-tomato cans are going to explode.

BARNABY:

Holy cabooses! How do you know?

CORNELIUS:

I know they're rotten. All you have to do is to light a match under them. They'll make such a smell that customers can't come into the place for twenty-four hours. That'll get us an evening free. We're going to New York too, Barnaby, we're going to live! I'm going to have enough adventures to last me until I'm *partner*. So go and get your Sunday clothes on.

BARNABY:

Wha-a-a-t?

CORNELIUS:

Yes, I mean it. We're going to have a good meal; and we're going to be in danger; and we're going to get almost arrested; and we're going to spend all our money.

BARNABY:

Holy cabooses!!

CORNELIUS:

And one more thing: we're not coming back to Yonkers until we've kissed a girl.

BARNABY:

Kissed a girl! Cornelius, you can't do that. You don't know any girls.

CORNELIUS:

I'm thirty-three. I've got to begin sometime.

BARNABY:

I'm only seventeen, Cornelius. It isn't so urgent for me.

CORNELIUS:

Don't start backing down now—if the worst comes to the worst and we get discharged from here we can always join the Army.

BARNABY:

Uh—did I hear you say that you'd be old Wolf-trap's partner?

CORNELIUS:

How can I help it? He's growing old. If you go to bed at nine and open the store at six, you get promoted upward whether you like it or not.

BARNABY:

My! Partner.

CORNELIUS:

Oh, there's no way of getting away from it. You and I will be Vandergelders.

BARNABY:

I? Oh, no—I may rise a little, but I'll never be a Vandergelder.

CORNELIUS:

Listen—everybody thinks when he gets rich he'll be a different kind of rich person from the rich people he sees around him; later on he finds out there's only one kind of rich person, and he's it.

BARNABY:

Oh, but I'll—

CORNELIUS:

No. The best of all would be a person who has all the good things a poor person has, and all the good meals a rich person has, but that's never been known. No, you and I are going to be Vandergelders; all the more reason, then, for us to try and get some living and some adventure into us now—will you come, Barnaby?

BARNABY:

In a struggle with his fears, a whirlwind of words.

But Wolf-trap—KRR-pt, Gertrude-KRR-pt—

With a sudden cry of agreement.

Yes, Cornelius!

Enter MRS. LEVI, ERMENGARDE *and* GERTRUDE *from back center. The* BOYS *start down the ladder,* CORNELIUS *last.*

MRS. LEVI:

Mr. Hackl, is the trunk waiting at the station?

CORNELIUS:

Yes, Mrs. Levi.

Closes the trap door.

MRS. LEVI:

Take a last look, Ermengarde.

ERMENGARDE:

What?

MRS. LEVI:

Take a last look at your girlhood home, dear. I remember when I left my home. I gave a whinny like a young colt, and off I went.

ERMENGARDE *and* GERTRUDE *exit.*

ERMENGARDE:

As they go.

Oh, Gertrude, do you think I ought to get married this way? A young girl has to be so careful!

MRS. LEVI *is alone. She addresses the audience.*

MRS. LEVI:

You know, I think I'm going to have this room with *blue* wallpaper,—yes, in blue!

Hurries out after the others.

BARNABY *comes up trap door, looks off right, then lies on floor, gazing down through the trap door.*

BARNABY:

All clear up here, Cornelius! Cornelius—hold the candle steady a minute—the bottom row's all right—but try the top now . . . they're swelled up like they are ready to bust!

BANG.

Holy CABOOSES!

BANG, BANG.

Cornelius! I can smell it up here!

Rises and dances about, holding his nose.

CORNELIUS:

Rushing up the trap door.

Get into your Sunday clothes, Barnaby. We're going to New York!

As they run out . . . there is a big explosion. A shower of tomato cans comes up from below, as—

THE
CURTAIN
FALLS

—⟨∽⟩—

Act II

Mrs. Molloy's hat shop, New York City.

    There are two entrances. One door at the extreme right of the back wall, to Mrs. Molloy's workroom; one at the back left corner, to the street. The whole left wall is taken up with the show windows, filled with hats. It is separated from the shop by a low brass rail, hung with net; during the act both MRS. MOLLOY *and* BARNABY *stoop under the rail and go into the shop window. By the street door stands a large cheval glass. In the middle of the back wall is a large wardrobe or clothes cupboard, filled with ladies' coats, large enough for* CORNELIUS *to hide in. At the left, beginning at the back wall, between the wardrobe and the workroom door, a long counter extends toward the audience, almost to the footlights. In the center of the room is a large round table with a low-hanging red cloth. There are a small gilt chair by the wardrobe and two chairs in front of the counter. Over the street door and the workroom door are bells which ring when the doors are opened.*

    As the curtain rises, MRS. MOLLOY *is in the window, standing on a box, reaching up to put hats on the stand.* MINNIE FAY *is sewing by the counter.* MRS. MOLLOY *has a pair of felt over-shoes, to be removed later.*

MRS. MOLLOY:

Minnie, you're a fool. Of course I shall marry Horace Vandergelder.

MINNIE:

Oh, Mrs. Molloy! I didn't ask you. I wouldn't dream of asking you such a personal question.

MRS. MOLLOY:

Well, it's what you meant, isn't it? And there's your answer. I shall certainly marry Horace Vandergelder if he asks me.

Crawls under window rail, into the room, singing loudly.

MINNIE:

I know it's none of my business . . .

MRS. MOLLOY:

Speak up, Minnie, I can't hear you.

MINNIE:

. . . but do you . . . do you . . . ?

MRS. MOLLOY:

Having crossed the room, is busy at the counter.

Minnie, you're a fool. Say it: Do I love him? Of course, I don't love him. But I have two good reasons for marrying him just the same. Minnie, put something on that hat. It's not ugly enough.

Throws hat over counter.

MINNIE:

Catching and taking hat to table.

Not ugly enough!

MRS. MOLLOY:

I couldn't sell it. Put a . . . put a sponge on it.

MINNIE:

Why, Mrs. Molloy, you're in such a *mood* today.

MRS. MOLLOY:

In the first place I shall marry Mr. Vandergelder to get away from the millinery business. I've hated it from the first day I had anything to do with it. Minnie, I hate hats.

Sings loudly again.

MINNIE:

Why, what's the matter with the millinery business?

MRS. MOLLOY:

Crossing to window with two hats.

I can no longer stand being suspected of being a wicked woman, while I have nothing to show for it. I can't stand it.

She crawls under rail into window.

MINNIE:

Why, no one would dream of suspecting you—

MRS. MOLLOY:

On her knees, she looks over the rail.

Minnie, you're a fool. All millineresses are suspected of being wicked women. Why, half the time all those women come into the shop merely to look at me.

MINNIE:

Oh!

MRS. MOLLOY:

They enjoy the suspicion. But they aren't certain. If they were *certain* I was a wicked woman, they wouldn't put foot in this place again. Do I go to restaurants? No, it would be bad for business. Do I go to balls, or theaters, or operas? No, it would be bad for business. The only men I ever meet are feather merchants.

Crawls out of window, but gazes intently into the street.

What are those two young men doing out there on that park bench? Take my word for it, Minnie, either I marry Horace Vandergelder, or I break out of this place like a fire engine. I'll go to every theater and ball and opera in New York City.

Returns to counter, singing again.

MINNIE:

But Mr. Vandergelder's not . . .

MRS. MOLLOY:

Speak up, Minnie, I can't hear you.

MINNIE:

. . . I don't think he's attractive.

MRS. MOLLOY:

But what I think he is—and it's very important—I think he'd make a good fighter.

MINNIE:

Mrs. Molloy!

MRS. MOLLOY:

Take my word for it, Minnie: the best part of married life is the fights. The rest is merely so-so.

MINNIE:

Fingers in ears.

I won't listen.

MRS. MOLLOY:

Peter Molloy—God rest him!—was a fine arguing man. I pity the woman whose husband slams the door and walks out of the house at the beginning of an argument. Peter Molloy would stand up and fight for hours on end. He'd even throw things, Minnie, and there's no pleasure to equal that. When I felt tired I'd start a good bloodwarming fight and it'd take ten years off my age; now Horace Vandergelder would put up a good fight; I know it. I've a mind to marry him.

MINNIE:

I think they're just awful, the things you're saying today.

MRS. MOLLOY:

Well, I'm enjoying them myself, too.

MINNIE:

At the window.

Mrs. Molloy, those two men out in the street—

MRS. MOLLOY:

What?

MINNIE:

Those men. It looks as if they meant to come in here.

MRS. MOLLOY:

Well now, it's time some men came into this place. I give you the younger one, Minnie.

MINNIE:

Aren't you terrible!

MRS. MOLLOY *sits on center table, while* MINNIE *takes off her felt overshoes.*

MRS. MOLLOY:

Wait till I get my hands on that older one! Mark my words, Minnie, we'll get an adventure out of this yet. Adventure, adventure! Why does everybody have adventures except me, Minnie? Because I have no spirit, I have no gumption. Minnie, they're coming in here. Let's go into the workroom and make them wait for us for a minute.

MINNIE:

Oh, but Mrs. Molloy . . . my work!. . .

MRS. MOLLOY:

Running to workroom.

Hurry up, be quick now, Minnie!

They go out to workroom.

BARNABY *and* CORNELIUS *run in from street, leaving front door open. They are dressed in the stiff discomfort of their Sunday clothes.* CORNELIUS *wears a bowler hat,* BARNABY *a straw hat too large for him.*

BARNABY:

No one's here.

CORNELIUS:

Some women were here a minute ago. I saw them.

They jump back to the street door and peer down the street.

That's Wolf-trap all right!

Coming back.

Well, we've got to hide here until he passes by.

BARNABY:

He's sitting down on that bench. It may be quite a while.

CORNELIUS:

When these women come in, we'll have to make conversation until he's gone away. We'll pretend we're buying a hat. How much money have you got now?

BARNABY:

Counting his money.

Forty cents for the train—seventy cents for dinner—twenty cents to see the whale—and a dollar I lost—I have seventy cents.

CORNELIUS:

And I have a dollar seventy-five. I wish I knew how much hats cost!

BARNABY:

Is this an adventure, Cornelius?

CORNELIUS:

No, but it may be.

BARNABY:

I think it is. There we wander around New York all day and nothing happens; and then we come to the quietest street in the whole city and suddenly Mr. Vandergelder turns the corner.

Going to door.

I think that's an adventure. I think . . . Cornelius! That Mrs. Levi is there now. She's sitting down on the bench with him.

CORNELIUS:

What do you know about that! We know only one person in all New York City, and there she is!

BARNABY:

Even if our adventure came along now I'd be too tired to enjoy it. Cornelius, why isn't this an adventure?

CORNELIUS:

Don't be asking that. When you're in an adventure, you'll know it all right.

BARNABY:

Maybe I wouldn't. Cornelius, let's arrange a signal for you to give me when an adventure's really going on. For instance, Cornelius, you say . . . uh . . . uh . . . *pudding;* you say *pudding* to me if it's an adventure we're in.

CORNELIUS:

I wonder where the lady who runs this store is? What's her name again?

BARNABY:

"Mrs. Molloy, hats for ladies."

CORNELIUS:

Oh yes. I must think over what I'm going to say when she comes in.

To counter.

"Good afternoon, Mrs. Molloy, wonderful weather we're having. We've been looking everywhere for some beautiful hats."

BARNABY:

That's fine, Cornelius!

CORNELIUS:

"Good afternoon, Mrs. Molloy; wonderful weather . . . " We'll make her think we're very rich.

One hand in trouser pocket, the other on back of chair.

"Good afternoon, Mrs. Molloy . . . " You keep one eye on the door the whole time. "We've been looking everywhere for . . . "

Enter MRS. MOLLOY *from the workroom.*

MRS. MOLLOY:

Behind the counter.

Oh, I'm sorry. Have I kept you waiting? Good afternoon, gentlemen.

CORNELIUS:

Hat off.

Here, Cornelius Hackl.

BARNABY:

Hat off.

Here, Barnaby Tucker.

MRS. MOLLOY:

I'm very happy to meet you. Perhaps I can help you. Won't you sit down?

CORNELIUS:

Thank you, we will.

The BOYS *place their hats on the table, then sit down at the counter facing Mrs. Molloy.*

You see, Mrs. Molloy, we're looking for hats. We've looked everywhere. Do you know what we heard? Go to Mrs. Molloy's, they said. So we came here. Only place we *could* go . . .

MRS. MOLLOY:

Well now, that's *very* complimentary.

CORNELIUS:

. . . and we were right. Everybody was right.

MRS. MOLLOY:

You wish to choose some hats for a friend?

CORNELIUS:

Yes, exactly.

Kicks Barnaby.

BARNABY:

Yes, exactly.

CORNELIUS:

We were thinking of five or six, weren't we, Barnaby?

BARNABY:

Er-five.

CORNELIUS:

You see, Mrs. Molloy, money's no object with us. None at all.

MRS. MOLLOY:

Why, Mr. Hackl . . .

CORNELIUS:

Rises and goes toward street door.

. . . I beg your pardon, what an interesting street! Something happening every minute. Passers-by, and . . .

BARNABY *runs to join him.*

MRS. MOLLOY:

You're from out of town, Mr. Hackl?

CORNELIUS:

Coming back.

Yes, ma'am—Barnaby, just keep your eye on the street, will you? You won't see that in Yonkers every day.

BARNABY *remains kneeling at street door.*

BARNABY:

Oh yes, I will.

CORNELIUS:

Not all of it.

MRS. MOLLOY:

Now this friend of yours—couldn't she come in with you someday and choose her hats herself?

CORNELIUS:

Sits at counter.

No. Oh, no. It's a surprise for her.

MRS. MOLLOY:

Indeed? That may be a little difficult, Mr. Hackl. It's not entirely customary.—Your friend's very interested in the street, Mr. Hackl.

CORNELIUS:

Oh yes. Yes. He has reason to be.

MRS. MOLLOY:

You said you were from out of town?

CORNELIUS:

Yes, we're from Yonkers.

MRS. MOLLOY:

Yonkers?

CORNELIUS:

Yonkers . . . yes, Yonkers.

He gazes rapt into her eyes.

You should know Yonkers, Mrs. Molloy. Hudson River; Palisades; drives; some say it's the most beautiful town in the world; that's what they say.

MRS. MOLLOY:

Is that so!

CORNELIUS:

Rises.

Mrs. Molloy, if you ever had a Sunday free, I'd . . . we'd like to show you Yonkers. Y'know, it's very historic, too.

MRS. MOLLOY:

That's very kind of you. Well, perhaps . . . now about those hats.

Takes two hats from under counter, and crosses to back center of the room.

CORNELIUS:

Following.

Is there . . . Have you a . . . Maybe Mr. Molloy would like to see Yonkers too?

MRS. MOLLOY:

Oh, I'm a widow, Mr. Hackl.

CORNELIUS:

Joyfully.

You are!

With sudden gravity.

Oh, that's too bad. Mr. Molloy would have enjoyed Yonkers.

MRS. MOLLOY:

Very likely. Now about these hats. Is your friend dark or light?

CORNELIUS:

Don't think about that for a minute. Any hat you'd like would be perfectly all right with her.

MRS. MOLLOY:

Really!

She puts one on.

Do you like this one?

CORNELIUS:

In awe-struck admiration.

Barnaby!

In sudden anger.

Barnaby! Look!

BARNABY *turns; unimpressed, he laughs vaguely, and turns to door again.*

Mrs. Molloy, that's the most beautiful hat I ever saw.

BARNABY *now crawls under the rail into the window.*

MRS. MOLLOY:

Your friend is acting very strangely, Mr. Hackl.

CORNELIUS:

Barnaby, stop acting strangely. When the street's quiet and empty, come back and talk to us. What was I saying? Oh yes: Mrs. Molloy, you should know Yonkers.

MRS. MOLLOY:

Hat off.

The fact is, I have a friend in Yonkers. Perhaps you know him. It's always so foolish to ask in cases like that, isn't it?

They both laugh over this with increasing congeniality.

MRS. MOLLOY *goes to counter with hats from table.*
CORNELIUS *follows.*

It's a Mr. Vandergelder.

CORNELIUS:
Stops abruptly.

What was that you said?

MRS. MOLLOY:
Then you do know him?

CORNELIUS:
Horace Vandergelder?

MRS. MOLLOY:
Yes, that's right.

CORNELIUS:
Know him!

Look to Barnaby.

Why, no. No!

BARNABY:
No! No!

CORNELIUS:
Starting to glide about the room, in search of a hiding place.

I beg your pardon, Mrs. Molloy—what an attractive shop you have!

Smiling fixedly at her he moves to the workshop door.

And where does this door lead to?

Opens it, and is alarmed by the bell which rings above it.

MRS. MOLLOY:
Why, Mr. Hackl, that's my workroom.

CORNELIUS:
Everything here is so interesting.

Looks under counter.

Every corner. Every door, Mrs. Molloy. Barnaby, notice the interesting doors and cupboards.

He opens the cupboard door.

Deeply interesting. Coats for ladies.

Laughs.

Barnaby, make a note of the table. Precious piece of furniture, with a low-hanging cloth, I see.

Stretches his leg under table.

MRS. MOLLOY:
Taking a hat from box left of wardrobe.

Perhaps your friend might like some of this new Italian straw. Mr. Vandergelder's a substantial man and very well liked, they tell me.

CORNELIUS:
A lovely man, Mrs. Molloy.

MRS. MOLLOY:
Oh yes—charming, charming!

CORNELIUS:

Smiling sweetly.

Has only one fault, as far as I know; he's hard as nails; but apart from that, as you say, a charming nature, ma'am.

MRS. MOLLOY:

And a large circle of friends—?

CORNELIUS:

Yes, indeed, yes indeed—five or six.

BARNABY:

Five!

CORNELIUS:

He comes and calls on you here from time to time, I suppose.

MRS. MOLLOY:

Turns from mirror where she has been putting a hat on.

This summer we'll be wearing ribbons down our back. Yes, as a matter of fact I am expecting a call from him this afternoon.

Hat off.

BARNABY:

·I think . . . Cornelius! I think . . . !!

MRS. MOLLOY:

Now to show you some more hats—

BARNABY:

Look out!

He takes a flying leap over the rail and flings himself under the table.

CORNELIUS:

Begging your pardon, Mrs. Molloy.

He jumps into the cupboard.

MRS. MOLLOY:

Gentlemen! Mr. Hackl! Come right out of there this minute!

CORNELIUS:

Sticking his head out of the wardrobe door.

Help us just this once, Mrs. Molloy! We'll explain later!

MRS. MOLLOY:

Mr. Hackl!

BARNABY:

We're as innocent as can be, Mrs. Molloy.

MRS. MOLLOY:

But really! Gentlemen! I can't have this! *What are you doing?*

BARNABY:

Cornelius! Cornelius! Pudding?

CORNELIUS:

A shout.

Pudding!

They disappear. Enter from the street MRS. LEVI, *followed by* MR. VANDERGELDER. VANDERGELDER *is dressed in a too-bright checked suit, and wears a green derby—or bowler—hat. He is carrying a large ornate box of chocolates in one hand, and a cane in the other.*

MRS. LEVI:

Irene, my darling child, how *are* you? Heaven be good to us, how well you look!

They kiss.

MRS. MOLLOY:

But what a surprise! And Mr. Vandergelder in New York—what a pleasure!

VANDERGELDER:

Swaying back and forth on his heels complacently.

Good afternoon, Mrs. Molloy.

They shake hands. MRS. MOLLOY *brings chair from counter for him. He sits at left of table.*

MRS. LEVI:

Yes, Mr. Vandergelder's in New York. Yonkers lies up there— *decimated* today. Irene, we thought we'd pay you a very short call. Now you'll tell us if it's inconvenient, won't you?

MRS. MOLLOY:

Placing a chair for Mrs. Levi at right of table.

Inconvenient, Dolly! The idea! Why, it's sweet of you to come.

She notices the boys' hats on the table—sticks a spray of flowers into crown of Cornelius' bowler and winds a piece of chiffon round Barnaby's panama.

VANDERGELDER:

We waited outside a moment.

MRS. LEVI:

Mr. Vandergelder thought he saw two customers coming in—two men.

MRS. MOLLOY:

Men! Men, Mr. Vandergelder? Why, what will you be saying next?

MRS. LEVI:

Then we'll sit down for a minute or two. . . .

MRS. MOLLOY:

Wishing to get them out of the shop into the workroom.

Before you sit down—

She pushes them both.

Before you sit down, there's something I want to show you. I want to show Mr. Vandergelder my workroom, too.

MRS. LEVI:

I've seen the workroom a hundred times. I'll stay right here and try on some of these hats.

MRS. MOLLOY:

No, Dolly, you come too. I have something for you. Come along, everybody.

Exit MRS. LEVI *to workroom.*

Mr. Vandergelder, I want your advice. You don't know how helpless a woman in business is. Oh, I feel I need advice every minute from a fine business head like yours.

Exit VANDERGELDER *to workroom.* MRS. MOLLOY *shouts this line and then slams the workroom door.*

Now I shut the door!!

Exit MRS. MOLLOY.

CORNELIUS *puts his head out of the wardrobe door and gradually comes out into the room, leaving door open.*

CORNELIUS:

Hsst!

BARNABY:

Pokes his head out from under the table.

Maybe she wants us to go, Cornelius?

CORNELIUS:

Certainly I won't go. Mrs. Molloy would think we were just thoughtless fellows. No, all I want is to stretch a minute.

BARNABY:

What are you going to do when he's gone, Cornelius? Are we just going to run away?

CORNELIUS:

Well . . . I don't know yet. I like Mrs. Molloy a lot. I wouldn't like her to think badly of me. I think I'll buy a hat. We can walk home to Yonkers, even if it takes us all night. I wonder how much hats cost. Barnaby, give me all the money you've got.

As he leans over to take the money, he sneezes. Both return to their hiding places in alarm; then emerge again.

My, all those perfumes in that cupboard tickle my nose! But I like it in there . . . it's a woman's world, and very different.

BARNABY:

I like it where I am, too; only I'd like it better if I had a pillow.

CORNELIUS:

Taking coat from wardrobe.

Here, take one of these coats. I'll roll it up for you so it won't get mussed. Ladies don't like to have their coats mussed.

BARNABY:

That's fine. Now I can just lie here and hear Mr. Vandergelder talk.

CORNELIUS *goes slowly above table towards cheval mirror, repeating Mrs. Molloy's line dreamily:*

CORNELIUS:

This summer we'll be wearing ribbons down our back. . . .

BARNABY:

Can I take off my shoes, Cornelius?

CORNELIUS *does not reply. He comes to the footlights and addresses the audience, in completely simple naïve sincerity:*

CORNELIUS:

Isn't the world full of wonderful things. There we sit cooped up in Yonkers for years and years and all the time wonderful people like Mrs. Molloy are walking around in New York and we don't know them at all. I don't know whether—from where you're sitting—you can see—well, for instance, the way

He points to the edge of his right eye.

her eye and forehead and cheek come together, up here. Can you? And the kind of fireworks that shoot out of her eyes all the

time. I tell you right now: a fine woman is the greatest work of
God. You can talk all you like about Niagara Falls and the Pyra-
mids; they aren't in it at all. Of course, up there at Yonkers they
came into the store all the time, and bought this and that, and
I said, "Yes, ma'am," and "That'll be seventy-five cents,
ma'am"; and I *watched* them. But today I've talked to one,
equal to equal, equal to equal, and to the finest one that ever
existed, in my opinion. They're so different from men! Everything that they say and do is so different that you feel like laughing all the time.

He laughs.

Golly, they're different from men. And they're awfully mysterious, too. You never can be really sure what's going on in their
heads. They have a kind of wall around them all the time—of
pride and a sort of play-acting: I bet you could know a woman
a hundred years without ever being really sure whether she
liked you or not. This minute I'm in danger. I'm in danger of
losing my job and my future and everything that people think
is important; but I don't care. Even if I have to dig ditches for
the rest of my life, I'll be a ditch digger who once had a wonderful day.

Barnaby!

BARNABY:
Oh, you woke me up!

CORNELIUS:
Kneels.

Barnaby, we can't go back to Yonkers yet and you know why.

BARNABY:

Why not?

CORNELIUS:

We've had a good meal. We've had an adventure. We've been in danger of getting arrested. There's only one more thing we've got to do before we go back to be successes in Yonkers.

BARNABY:

Cornelius! You're never going to kiss Mrs. Molloy!

CORNELIUS:

Maybe.

BARNABY:

But she'll scream.

CORNELIUS:

Barnaby, you don't know anything at all. You might as well know right now that everybody except us goes through life kissing right and left all the time.

BARNABY:

Pauses for reflection: humbly:

Well, thanks for telling me, Cornelius. I often wondered.

Enter MRS. LEVI *from workroom.*

MRS. LEVI:

Just a minute, Irene. I must find my handkerchief.

CORNELIUS, *caught by the arrival of Mrs. Levi, drops to his hands and knees, and starts very slowly to crawl back to the wardrobe, as though the slowness rendered him invisible.* MRS. LEVI, *leaning over the counter, watches him. From the cupboard he puts his head out of it and looks pleadingly at her.*

Why, Mr. Hackl, I thought you were up in Yonkers.

CORNELIUS:

I almost always am, Mrs. Levi. Oh, Mrs. Levi, don't tell Mr. Vandergelder! I'll explain everything later.

BARNABY:

Puts head out.

We're terribly innocent, Mrs. Levi.

MRS. LEVI:

Why, who's that?

BARNABY:

Barnaby Tucker—just paying a call.

MRS. LEVI:

Looking under counter and even shaking out her skirts.

Well, who else is here?

CORNELIUS:

Just the two of us, Mrs. Levi, that's all.

MRS. LEVI:

Old friends of Mrs. Molloy's, is that it?

CORNELIUS:

We never knew her before a few minutes ago, but we like her a lot—don't we, Barnaby? In fact, I think she's . . . I think she's the finest person in the world. I'm ready to tell that to anybody.

MRS. LEVI:

And does she think *you're* the finest person in the world?

CORNELIUS:

Oh, no. I don't suppose she even notices that I'm alive.

MRS. LEVI:

Well, I think she must notice that you're alive in that cupboard, Mr. Hackl. Well, if I were you, I'd get back into it right away. Somebody could be coming in any minute.

CORNELIUS *disappears. She sits unconcernedly in chair right.*
Enter MRS. MOLLOY.

MRS. MOLLOY:

Leaving door open and looking about in concealed alarm.

Can I help you, Dolly?

MRS. LEVI:

No, no, no. I was just blowing my nose.

Enter VANDERGELDER *from workroom.*

VANDERGELDER:

Mrs. Molloy, I've got some advice to give you about your business.

MRS. MOLLOY *comes to the center of the room and puts*
Barnaby's hat on floor in window, then Cornelius' hat on the
counter.

MRS. LEVI:

Oh, advice from Mr. Vandergelder! The whole city should hear this.

VANDERGELDER:

Standing in the workroom door, pompously:

In the first place, the aim of business is to make profit.

MRS. MOLLOY:

Is that so?

MRS. LEVI:

I never heard it put so clearly before. Did you hear it?

VANDERGELDER:

Crossing the room to the left.

You pay those girls of yours too much. You pay them as much as men. Girls like that enjoy their work. Wages, Mrs. Molloy, are paid to make people do work they don't want to do.

MRS. LEVI:

Mr. Vandergelder thinks so ably. And that's exactly the way his business is run up in Yonkers.

VANDERGELDER:

Patting her hand.

Mrs. Molloy, I'd like for you to come up to Yonkers.

MRS. MOLLOY:

That would be very nice.

He hands her the box of chocolates.

Oh, thank you. As a matter of fact, I know someone from Yonkers, someone else.

VANDERGELDER:

Hangs hat on the cheval mirror.

Oh? Who's that?

MRS. MOLLOY *puts chocolates on table and brings gilt chair forward and sits center at table facing the audience.*

MRS. MOLLOY:

Someone quite well-to-do, I believe, though a little free and easy in his behavior. Mr. Vandergelder, do you know Mr. Cornelius Hackl in Yonkers?

VANDERGELDER:

I know him like I know my own boot. He's my head clerk.

MRS. MOLLOY:

Is that so?

VANDERGELDER:

He's been in my store for ten years.

MRS. MOLLOY:

Well, I never!

VANDERGELDER:

Where would you have known him?

MRS. MOLLOY *is in silent confusion. She looks for help to Mrs. Levi, seated at right end of table.*

MRS. LEVI:

Groping for means to help Mrs. Molloy.

Err . . . blah . . . err . . . bl . . . er . . . Oh, just one of those chance meetings, I suppose.

MRS. MOLLOY:

Yes, oh yes! One of those chance meetings.

VANDERGELDER:

What? Chance meetings? Cornelius Hackl has no right to chance meetings. Where was it?

MRS. MOLLOY:

Really, Mr. Vandergelder, it's very unlike you to question me in such a way. I think Mr. Hackl is better known than you think he is.

VANDERGELDER:

Nonsense.

MRS. MOLLOY:

He's in New York often, and he's very well liked.

MRS. LEVI:

Having found her idea, with decision.

Well, the truth might as well come out now as later. Mr. Vandergelder, Irene is quite right. Your head clerk is often in New York. Goes everywhere; has an army of friends. Everybody knows Cornelius Hackl.

VANDERGELDER:

Laughs blandly and sits in chair at left of table.

He never comes to New York. He works all day in my store and at nine o'clock at night he goes to sleep in the bran room.

MRS. LEVI:

So you think. But it's not true.

VANDERGELDER:

Dolly Gallagher, you're crazy.

MRS. LEVI:

Listen to me. You keep your nose so deep in your account books you don't know what goes on. Yes, by day, Cornelius Hackl is your faithful trusted clerk—that's true; but by night!

Well, he leads a double life, that's all! He's here at the opera; at the great restaurants; in all the fashionable homes . . . why, he's at the Harmonia Gardens Restaurant three nights a week. The fact is, he's the wittiest, gayest, naughtiest, most delightful man in New York. Well, he's just *the* famous Cornelius Hackl!

VANDERGELDER:
Sure of himself.

It ain't the same man. If I ever thought Cornelius Hackl came to New York, I'd discharge him.

MRS. LEVI:
Who took the horses out of Jenny Lind's carriage and pulled her through the streets?

MRS. MOLLOY:
Who?

MRS. LEVI:
Cornelius Hackl! Who dressed up as a waiter at the Fifth Avenue Hotel the other night and took an oyster and dropped it right down Mrs . . .

Rises.

No, it's too wicked to tell you!

MRS. MOLLOY:
Oh yes, Dolly, tell it! Go on!

MRS. LEVI:
No. But it *was* Cornelius Hackl.

VANDERGELDER:
Loud.

It ain't the same man. Where'd he get the money?

MRS. LEVI:

But he's very rich.

VANDERGELDER:

Rises.

Rich! I keep his money in my own safe. He has a hundred and forty-six dollars and thirty-five cents.

MRS. LEVI:

Oh, Mr. Vandergelder, you're killing me! Do come to your senses. He's one of *the* Hackls.

MRS. MOLLOY *sits at chair right of table where Mrs. Levi has been sitting.*

VANDERGELDER:

The Hackls?

MRS. LEVI:

They built the Raritan Canal.

VANDERGELDER:

Then why should he work in my store?

MRS. LEVI:

Well, I'll tell you.

Sits at the center of the table, facing the audience.

VANDERGELDER:

Striding about.

I don't want to hear! I've got a headache! I'm going home. *It ain't the same man!!* He sleeps in my bran room. You can't get away from facts. I just made him my chief clerk.

MRS. LEVI:

If you had any sense you'd make him partner.

Rises, crosses to Mrs. Molloy.

Now Irene, I can see you were as taken with him as everybody else is.

MRS. MOLLOY:

Why, I only met him once, very hastily.

MRS. LEVI:

Yes, but I can see that you were taken with him. Now don't you be thinking of marrying him!

MRS. MOLLOY:

Her hands on her cheeks.

Dolly! What are you saying! Oh!

MRS. LEVI:

Maybe it'd be fine. But think it over carefully. He breaks hearts like hickory nuts.

VANDERGELDER:

Who?

MRS. LEVI:

Cornelius Hackl!

VANDERGELDER:

Mrs. Molloy, how often has he called on you?

MRS. MOLLOY:

Oh, I'm telling the truth. I've only seen him once in my life. Dolly Levi's been exaggerating so. I don't know where to look!

Enter MINNIE *from workroom and crosses to window.*

MINNIE:

Excuse me, Mrs. Molloy. I must get together that order for Mrs. Parkinson.

MRS. MOLLOY:

Yes, we must get that off before closing.

MINNIE:

I want to send it off by the errand girl.

Having taken a hat from the window.

Oh, I almost forgot the coat.

She starts for the wardrobe.

MRS. MOLLOY:

Running to the wardrobe to prevent her.

Oh, oh! I'll do that, Minnie!

But she is too late. MINNIE *opens the right-hand cupboard door and falls back in terror, and screams:*

MINNIE:

Oh, Mrs. Molloy! Help! There's a man!

MRS. MOLLOY *with the following speech pushes her back to the workroom door.* MINNIE *walks with one arm pointing at the cupboard. At the end of each of Mrs. Molloy's sentences she repeats—at the same pitch and degree—the words: "There's a man!"*

MRS. MOLLOY:

Slamming cupboard door.

Minnie, you imagined it. You're tired, dear. You go back in the workroom and lie down. Minnie, you're a fool; hold your tongue!

MINNIE:

There's a man!

Exit MINNIE *to workroom.*

MRS. MOLLOY *returns to the front of the stage.*

VANDERGELDER *raises his stick threateningly.*

VANDERGELDER:

If there's a man there, we'll get him out. Whoever you are, come out of there!

Strikes table with his stick.

MRS. LEVI:

Goes masterfully to the cupboard—sweeps her umbrella around among the coats and closes each door as she does so.

Nonsense! There's no man there. See! Miss Fay's nerves have been playing tricks on her. Come now, let's sit down again. What were you saying, Mr. Vandergelder?

They sit, MRS. MOLLOY *right,* MRS. LEVI *center,* VANDERGELDER *left.*

A sneeze is heard from the cupboard. They all rise, look towards cupboard, then sit again.

Well now . . .

Another tremendous sneeze.

With a gesture that says, "I can do no more":

God bless you!

They all rise. MRS. MOLLOY *stands with her back to the cupboard.*

MRS. MOLLOY:
To VANDERGELDER:

Yes, there is a man in there. I'll explain it all to you another time. Thank you very much for coming to see me. Good afternoon, Dolly. Good afternoon, Mr. Vandergelder.

VANDERGELDER:
You're protecting a man in there!

MRS. MOLLOY:
With back to cupboard.

There's a very simple explanation, but for the present, good afternoon.

BARNABY *now sneezes twice, lifting the table each time.*
VANDERGELDER, *right of table, jerks off the tablecloth.*
BARNABY *pulls cloth under table and rolls himself up in it.*
MRS. MOLLOY *picks up the box of chocolates, which has rolled on to the floor.*

MRS. LEVI:
Lord, the whole room's *crawling* with men! I'll never get over it.

VANDERGELDER:
The world is going to pieces! I can't believe my own eyes!

MRS. LEVI:

Come, Mr. Vandergelder. Ernestina Simple is waiting for us.

VANDERGELDER:

Finds his hat and puts it on.

Mrs. Molloy, I shan't trouble you again, and *vice versa.*

MRS. MOLLOY *is standing transfixed in front of cupboard, clasping the box of chocolates.* VANDERGELDER *snatches the box from her and goes out.*

MRS. LEVI:

Crosses to her.

Irene, when I think of all the interesting things you have in this room!

Kisses her.

Make the most of it, dear.

Raps cupboard.

Good-by!

Raps on table with umbrella.

Good-by!

Exit MRS. LEVI.

MRS. MOLLOY *opens door of cupboard.* CORNELIUS *steps out.*

MRS. MOLLOY:

So that was one of your practical jokes, Mr. Hackl?

CORNELIUS:

No, no, Mrs. Molloy!

MRS. MOLLOY:

Come out from under that, Barnaby Tucker, you trouble-maker!

She snatches the cloth and spreads it back on table. MINNIE *enters.*

There's nothing to be afraid of, Minnie, I know all about these gentlemen.

CORNELIUS:

Mrs. Molloy, we realize that what happened here—

MRS. MOLLOY:

You think because you're rich you can make up for all the harm you do, is that it?

CORNELIUS:

No, no!

BARNABY:

On the floor putting shoes on.

No, no!

MRS. MOLLOY:

Minnie, this is the famous Cornelius Hackl who goes round New York tying people into knots; and that's Barnaby Tucker, another troublemaker.

BARNABY:

How d'you do?

MRS. MOLLOY:

Minnie, choose yourself any hat and coat in the store. We're going out to dinner. If this Mr. Hackl is so rich and gay and charming, he's going to be rich and gay and charming to us. He dines three nights a week at the Harmonia Gardens Restaurant, does he? Well, he's taking us there now.

MINNIE:

Mrs. Molloy, are you sure it's safe?

MRS. MOLLOY:

Minnie, hold your tongue. We're in a position to put these men into jail if they so much as squeak.

CORNELIUS:

Jail, Mrs. Molloy?

MRS. MOLLOY:

Jail, Mr. Hackl. Officer Cogarty does everything I tell him to do. Minnie, you and I have been respectable for years; now we're in disgrace, we might as well make the most of it. Come into the workroom with me; I know some ways we can perk up our appearances. Gentlemen, we'll be back in a minute.

CORNELIUS:

Uh—Mrs. Molloy, I hear there's an awfully good restaurant at the railway station.

MRS. MOLLOY:
High indignation.

Railway station? Railway station? Certainly not! No, sir! You're going to give us a good dinner in the heart of the fashionable world. Go on in, Minnie! Don't you boys forget that you've made us lose our reputations, and now the fashionable world's the only place we *can* eat.

MRS. MOLLOY *exits to workroom.*

BARNABY:

She's angry at us, Cornelius. Maybe we'd better run away now.

CORNELIUS:

No, I'm going to go through with this if it kills me. Barnaby, for a woman like that a man could consent to go back to Yonkers and be a success.

BARNABY:

All I know is no woman's going to make a success out of me.

CORNELIUS:

Jail or no jail, we're going to take those ladies out to dinner. So grit your teeth.

Enter MRS. MOLLOY *and* MINNIE *from workroom dressed for the street.*

MRS. MOLLOY:

Gentlemen, the cabs are at the corner, so forward march!

She takes a hat—which will be Barnaby's at the end of Act III—and gives it to MINNIE.

CORNELIUS:

Yes, ma'am.

BARNABY *stands shaking his empty pockets warningly.*

Oh, Mrs. Molloy . . . is it far to the restaurant? Couldn't we walk?

MRS. MOLLOY:

Pauses a moment, then:

Minnie, take off your things. We're not going.

OTHERS:

Mrs. Molloy!

MRS. MOLLOY:

Mr. Hackl, I don't go anywhere I'm not wanted. Good night. I'm not very happy to have met you.

She crosses the stage as though going to the workroom door.

OTHERS:

Mrs. Molloy!

MRS. MOLLOY:

I suppose you think we're not fashionable enough for you? Well, I won't be a burden to you. Good night, Mr. Tucker.

The others follow her behind counter: CORNELIUS, BARNABY, *then* MINNIE.

CORNELIUS:

We want you to come with us more than anything in the world, Mrs. Molloy.

MRS. MOLLOY turns and pushes the three back. They are now near the center of the stage, to the right of the table, MRS. MOLLOY *facing the audience.*

MRS. MOLLOY:

No, you don't! Look at you! Look at the pair of them, Minnie! Scowling, both of them!

CORNELIUS:

Please, Mrs. Molloy!

MRS. MOLLOY:

Then smile.

To Barnaby.

Go on, smile! No, that's not enough. Minnie, you come with me and we'll get our own supper.

CORNELIUS:

Smile, Barnaby, you lout!

BARNABY:

My face can't smile any stronger than that.

MRS. MOLLOY:

Then do something! Show some interest. Do something lively: sing!

CORNELIUS:

I can't sing, really I can't.

MRS. MOLLOY:

We're wasting our time, Minnie. They don't want us.

CORNELIUS:

Barnaby, what can you sing? Mrs. Molloy, all we know are sad songs.

MRS. MOLLOY:

That doesn't matter. If you want us to go out with you, you've got to sing something.

All this has been very rapid; the boys turn up to counter, put their heads together, confer and abruptly turn, stand stiffly and sing "Tenting tonight; tenting tonight; tenting on the old camp ground." The four of them now repeat the refrain, softly harmonizing.

At the end of the song, after a pause, MRS. MOLLOY, *moved, says:*

MRS. MOLLOY:

We'll come!

The boys shout joyfully.

You boys go ahead.

CORNELIUS *gets his hat from counter; as he puts it on he discovers the flowers on it.* BARNABY *gets his hat from window. They go out whistling.*

MINNIE *turns and puts her hat on at the mirror.*

Minnie, get the front door key—I'll lock the workroom.

MRS. MOLLOY *goes to workroom.*

MINNIE *takes key from hook left of wardrobe and goes to Mrs. Molloy, at the workroom door. She turns her around.*

MINNIE:

Why, Mrs. Molloy, you're crying!

MRS. MOLLOY *flings her arms round Minnie.*

MRS. MOLLOY:

Oh, Minnie, the world is full of wonderful things. Watch me, dear, and tell me if my petticoat's showing.

She crosses to door, followed by MINNIE, *as—*

THE
CURTAIN
FALLS

—m—

Act III

Veranda at the Harmonia Gardens Restaurant on the Battery, New York.

This room is informal and rustic. The main restaurant is indicated to be off stage back right.

There are three entrances: swinging double doors at the center of the back wall leading to the kitchen; one on the right wall (perhaps up a few steps and flanked by potted palms) to the street; one on the left wall to the staircase leading to the rooms above.

On the stage are two tables, left and right, each with four chairs. It is now afternoon and they are not yet set for dinner.

Against the back wall is a large folding screen. Also against the back wall are hat and coat racks.

As the curtain rises, VANDERGELDER is standing, giving orders to RUDOLPH, a waiter. MALACHI STACK sits at table left.

VANDERGELDER:

Now, hear what I say. I don't want you to make any mistakes. I want a table for three.

RUDOLPH:

Tall "snob" waiter, alternating between cold superiority and rage. German accent.

For three.

VANDERGELDER:

There'll be two ladies and myself.

MALACHI:

It's a bad combination, Mr. Vandergelder. You'll regret it.

VANDERGELDER:

And I want a chicken.

MALACHI:

A chicken! You'll regret it.

VANDERGELDER:

Hold your tongue. Write it down: chicken.

RUDOLPH:

Yes, sir. Chicken Esterhazy? Chicken cacciatore? Chicken à la crème—?

VANDERGELDER:

Exploding.

A chicken! A chicken like everybody else has. And with the chicken I want a bottle of wine.

RUDOLPH:

Moselle? Chablis? Vouvray?

MALACHI:

He doesn't understand you, Mr. Vandergelder. You'd better speak louder.

VANDERGELDER:

Spelling.

W-I-N-E.

RUDOLPH:

Wine.

VANDERGELDER:

Wine! And I want this table removed. We'll eat at that table alone.

Exit RUDOLPH *through service door at back.*

MALACHI:

There are some people coming in here now, Mr. Vandergelder.

VANDERGELDER *goes to back right to look at the newcomers.*

VANDERGELDER:

What! Thunder and damnation! It's my niece Ermengarde! What's she doing here?!—Wait till I get my hands on her.

MALACHI:

Running up to him.

Mr. Vandergelder! You must keep your temper!

VANDERGELDER:

And there's that rascal artist with her. Why, it's a plot. I'll throw them in jail.

MALACHI:

Mr. Vandergelder! They're old enough to come to New York. You can't throw people into jail for coming to New York.

VANDERGELDER:

And there's Mrs. Levi! What's she doing with them? It's a plot. It's a conspiracy! What's she saying to the cabman? Go up and hear what she's saying.

MALACHI:

Listening at entrance, right.

She's telling the cabman to wait, Mr. Vandergelder. She's telling the young people to come in and have a good dinner, Mr. Vandergelder.

VANDERGELDER:

I'll put an end to this.

MALACHI:

Now, Mr. Vandergelder, if you lose your temper, you'll make matters worse. Mr. Vandergelder, come here and take my advice.

VANDERGELDER:

Stop pulling my coat. What's your advice?

MALACHI:

Hide, Mr. Vandergelder. Hide behind this screen, and listen to what they're saying.

VANDERGELDER:

Being pulled behind the screen.

Stop pulling at me.

They hide behind the screen as MRS. LEVI, ERMENGARDE and AMBROSE enter from the right. AMBROSE is carrying Ermengarde's luggage.

ERMENGARDE:

But I don't want to eat in a restaurant. It's not proper.

MRS. LEVI:

Now, Ermengarde, dear, there's nothing wicked about eating in a restaurant. There's nothing wicked, even, about being in New York. Clergymen just make those things up to fill out their sermons.

ERMENGARDE:

Oh, I wish I were in Yonkers, where *nothing* ever happens!

MRS. LEVI:

Ermengarde, you're hungry. That's what's troubling you.

ERMENGARDE:

Anyway, after dinner you must promise to take me to Aunt Flora's. She's been waiting for me all day and she must be half dead of fright.

MRS. LEVI:

All right but of course, you know at Miss Van Huysen's you'll be back in your uncle's hands.

AMBROSE:

Hands raised to heaven.

I can't stand it.

MRS. LEVI:

To Ambrose.

Just keep telling yourself how pretty she is. Pretty girls have very little opportunity to improve their other advantages.

AMBROSE:

Listen, Ermengarde! You don't want to go back to your uncle
Stop and think! That old man with one foot in the grave!

MRS. LEVI:

And the other three in the cash box.

AMBROSE:

Smelling of oats—

MRS. LEVI:

And axle grease.

MALACHI:

That's not true. It's only partly true.

VANDERGELDER:

Loudly.

Hold your tongue! I'm going to teach them a lesson.

MALACHI:

Whisper.

Keep your temper, Mr. Vandergelder. Listen to what they say.

MRS. LEVI:

*Hears this; throws a quick glance toward the screen; her whole
manner changes.*

Oh dear, what was I saying? The Lord be praised, how glad I
am that I found you two dreadful children just as you were
about to break poor dear Mr. Vandergelder's heart.

AMBROSE:

He's got no heart to break!

MRS. LEVI:

Vainly signaling.

Mr. Vandergelder's a much kinder man than you think.

AMBROSE:

Kinder? He's a wolf.

MRS. LEVI:

Remember that he leads a very lonely life. Now you're going to have dinner upstairs. There are some private rooms up there,—just meant for shy timid girls like Ermengarde. Come with me.

She pushes the young people out left, AMBROSE *carrying the luggage.*

VANDERGELDER:

Coming forward.

I'll show them!

He sits at table right.

MALACHI:

Everybody should eavesdrop once in a while, I always say. There's nothing like eavesdropping to show you that the world outside your head is different from the world inside your head.

VANDERGELDER:

Producing a pencil and paper.

I want to write a note. Go and call that cabman in here. I want to talk to him.

MALACHI:

No one asks advice of a cabman, Mr. Vandergelder. They see so much of life that they have no ideas left.

VANDERGELDER:

Do as I tell you.

MALACHI:

Yes, sir. Advice of a cabman!

Exit right.

VANDERGELDER *writes his letter.*

VANDERGELDER:

"My dear Miss Van Huysen"—

To audience:

Everybody's dear in a letter. It's enough to make you give up writing 'em. "My dear Miss Van Huysen. This is Ermengarde and that rascal Ambrose Kemper. They are trying to run away. Keep them in your house until I come."

MALACHI *returns with an enormous* CABMAN *in a high hat and a long coat. He carries a whip.*

CABMAN:

Entering.

What's he want?

VANDERGELDER:

I want to talk to you.

CABMAN:

I'm engaged. I'm waiting for my parties.

VANDERGELDER:
Folding letter and writing address.

I know you are. Do you want to earn five dollars?

CABMAN:
Eh?

VANDERGELDER:
I asked you, do you want to earn five dollars?

CABMAN:
I don't know. I never tried.

VANDERGELDER:
When those parties of yours come downstairs, I want you to drive them to this address. Never mind what they say, drive them to this address. Ring the bell: give this letter to the lady of the house: see that they get in the door and keep them there.

CABMAN:
I can't make people go into a house if they don't want to.

VANDERGELDER:
Producing purse.

Can you for ten dollars?

CABMAN:
Even for ten dollars, I can't do it alone.

VANDERGELDER:
This fellow here will help you.

MALACHI:
Sitting at table left.

Now I'm pushing people into houses.

VANDERGELDER:

There's the address: Miss Flora Van Huysen, 8 Jackson Street.

CABMAN:

Even if I get them in the door I can't be sure they'll stay there.

VANDERGELDER:

For fifteen dollars you can.

MALACHI:

Murder begins at twenty-five.

VANDERGELDER:

Hold your tongue!

To cabman.

The lady of the house will help you. All you have to do is to sit in the front hall and see that the man doesn't run off with the girl. I'll be at Miss Van Huysen's in an hour or two and I'll pay you then.

CABMAN:

If they call the police, I can't do anything.

VANDERGELDER:

It's perfectly honest business. Perfectly honest.

MALACHI:

Every man's the best judge of his own honesty.

VANDERGELDER:

The young lady is my niece.

The CABMAN *laughs, skeptically.*

The young lady is my niece!!

The CABMAN *looks at Malachi and shrugs.*

She's trying to run away with a good-for-nothing and we're preventing it.

CABMAN:

Oh, I know them, sir. They'll win in the end. Rivers don't run uphill.

MALACHI:

What did I tell you, Mr. Vandergelder? Advice of a cabman.

VANDERGELDER:
Hits table with his stick.

Stack! I'll be back in half an hour. See that the table's set for three. See that nobody else eats here. Then go and join the cabman on the box.

MALACHI:
Yes, sir.

Exit VANDERGELDER *right*

CABMAN:
Who's your friend?

MALACHI:
Friend!! That's not a friend; that's an employer I'm trying out for a few days.

CABMAN:
You won't like him.

MALACHI:

I can see you're in business for yourself because you talk about liking employers. No one's ever liked an employer since business began.

CABMAN:

AW—!

MALACHI:

No, sir. I suppose you think *your horse* likes you?

CABMAN:

My old Clementine? She'd give her right feet for me.

MALACHI:

That's what all employers think. You imagine it. The streets of New York are full of cab horses winking at one another. Let's go in the kitchen and get some whiskey. I can't push people into houses when I'm sober. No, I've had about fifty employers in my life, but this is the most employer of them all. He talks to everybody as though he were paying them.

CABMAN:

I had an employer once. He watched me from eight in the morning until six at night—just sat there and watched me. Oh, dear! Even my mother didn't think I was as interesting as that.

CABMAN *exits through service door.*

MALACHI:
Following him off.

Yes, being employed is like being loved: you know that somebody's thinking about you the whole time.

Exits.

Enter right, MRS. MOLLOY, MINNIE, BARNABY *and*
CORNELIUS.

MRS. MOLLOY:

See! Here's the place I meant! Isn't it fine? Minnie, take off
your things; we'll be here for hours.

CORNELIUS:
Stopping at door.

Mrs. Molloy, are you sure you'll like it here? I think I feel a
draught.

MRS. MOLLOY:

Indeed, I do like it. We're going to have a fine dinner right in
this room; it's private, and it's elegant. Now we're all going
to forget our troubles and call each other by our first names.
Cornelius! Call the waiter.

CORNELIUS:

Wait—wait—I can't make a sound. I must have caught a cold
on that ride. Wai—No! It won't come.

MRS. MOLLOY:

I don't believe you. Barnaby, you call him.

BARNABY:
Boldly.

Waiter! Waiter!

CORNELIUS *threatens him.* BARNABY *runs left.*

MINNIE:

I never thought I'd be in such a place in my whole life. Mrs.
Molloy, is this what they call a "café"?

MRS. MOLLOY:

Sits at table left, facing audience.

Yes, this a café. Sit down, Minnie. Cornelius, Mrs. Levi gave us to understand that every waiter in New York knew you.

CORNELIUS:

They will.

BARNABY *sits at chair left;* MINNIE *in chair back to audience.*

Enter RUDOLPH *from service door.*

RUDOLPH:

Good evening, ladies and gentlemen.

CORNELIUS:

Shaking his hand.

How are you, Fritz? How are you, my friend?

RUDOLPH:

I am Rudolph.

CORNELIUS:

Of course. Rudolph, of course. Well, Rudolph, these ladies want a little something to eat—you know what I mean? Just if you can find the time—we know how busy you are.

MRS. MOLLOY:

Cornelius, there's no need to be so familiar with the waiter.

Takes menu from RUDOLPH.

CORNELIUS:

Oh, yes, there is.

MRS. MOLLOY:

Passing menu across.

Minnie, what do you want to eat?

MINNIE:

Just anything, Irene.

MRS. MOLLOY:

No, speak up, Minnie. What do you want?

MINNIE:

No, really, I have no appetite at all.

Swings round in her chair and studies the menu, horrified at the prices.

Oh . . . Oh . . . I'd like some sardines on toast and a glass of milk.

CORNELIUS:

Takes menu from her.

Great grindstones! What a sensible girl. Barnaby, shake Minnie's hand. She's the most sensible girl in the world. Rudolph, bring us gentlemen two glasses of beer, a loaf of bread and some cheese.

MRS. MOLLOY:

Takes menu.

I never heard such nonsense. Cornelius, we've come here for a good dinner and a good time. Minnie, have you ever eaten pheasant?

MINNIE:

Pheasant? No-o-o-o!

MRS. MOLLOY:

Rudolph, have you any pheasant?

RUDOLPH:

Yes, ma'am. Just in from New Jersey today.

MRS. MOLLOY:

Even the pheasants are leaving New Jersey.

She laughs loudly, pushing CORNELIUS, *then* RUDOLPH; *not from menu.*

Now, Rudolph, write this down: mock turtle soup; pheasant; mashed chestnuts; green salad; and some nice red wine.

RUDOLPH *repeats each item after her.*

CORNELIUS:

Losing all his fears, boldly.

All right, Barnaby, you watch me.

He reads from the bill of fare.

Rudolph, write this down: Neapolitan ice cream; hothouse peaches; champagne . . .

ALL:

Champagne!

BARNABY *spins round in his chair.*

CORNELIUS:

Holds up a finger.

. . . and a German band. Have you got a German band?

MRS. MOLLOY:

No, Cornelius, I won't let you be extravagant. Champagne, but no band. Now, Rudolph, be quick about this. We're hungry.

Exit RUDOLPH *to kitchen.* MRS. MOLLOY *crosses to right.*

Minnie, come upstairs. I have an idea about your hair. I think it'd be nice in two wee horns—

MINNIE:

Hurrying after her, turns and looks at the boys.

Oh! Horns!

They go out right.

There is a long pause. CORNELIUS *sits staring after them.*

BARNABY:

Cornelius, in the Army, you have to peel potatoes all the time.

CORNELIUS:

Not turning.

Oh, that doesn't matter. By the time we get out of jail we can move right over to the Old Men's Home.

Another waiter, AUGUST, *enters from service door bearing a bottle of champagne in cooler, and five glasses.* MRS. MOLLOY *re-enters right, followed by* MINNIE, *and stops* AUGUST.

MRS. MOLLOY:

Waiter! What's that? What's that you have?

AUGUST:

Young waiter; baby face; is continually bursting into tears.

It's some champagne, ma'am.

MRS. MOLLOY:

Cornelius; it's our champagne.

ALL *gather round August.*

AUGUST:

No, no. It's for His Honor the Mayor of New York and he's very impatient.

MRS. MOLLOY:

Shame on him! The Mayor of New York has more important things to be impatient about. Cornelius, open it.

CORNELIUS *takes the bottle, opens it and fills the glasses.*

AUGUST:

Ma'am, he'll kill me.

MRS. MOLLOY:

Well, have a glass first and die happy.

AUGUST:

Sits at table right, weeping.

He'll kill me.

RUDOLPH *lays the cloth on the table, left.*

MRS. MOLLOY:

I go to a public restaurant for the first time in ten years and all the waiters burst into tears. There, take that and stop crying, love.

She takes a glass to August and pats his head, then comes back.

Barnaby, make a toast!

BARNABY:

Center of the group, with naïve sincerity.

I? . . . uh . . . To all the ladies in the world . . . may I get to know more of them . . . and . . . may I get to know them better.

There is a hushed pause.

CORNELIUS:

Softly.

To the ladies!

MRS. MOLLOY:

That's *very* sweet and *very* refined. Minnie, for that I'm going to give Barnaby a kiss.

MINNIE:

Oh!

MRS. MOLLOY:

Hold your tongue, Minnie. I'm old enough to be his mother, and—

Indicating a height three feet from the floor.

a dear wee mother I would have been too. Barnaby, this is for you from all the ladies in the world.

She kisses him. BARNABY *is at first silent and dazed, then:*

BARNABY:

Now I can go back to Yonkers, Cornelius. Pudding. Pudding. Pudding!

He spins round and falls on his knees.

MRS. MOLLOY:

Look at Barnaby. He's not strong enough for a kiss. His head can't stand it.

Exit AUGUST, *right service door, with tray and cooler. The sound of "Les Patineurs" waltz comes from off left.*
CORNELIUS *sits in chair facing audience, top of table.*
MINNIE *at left.* BARNABY *at right and* MRS. MOLLOY *back to audience.*

Minnie, I'm enjoying myself. To think that this goes on in hundreds of places every night, while I sit at home darning my stockings.

MRS. MOLLOY *rises and dances, alone, slowly about the stage.*

Cornelius, dance with me.

CORNELIUS:

Rises.

Irene, the Hackls don't dance. We're Presbyterian.

MRS. MOLLOY:

Minnie, you dance with me.

MINNIE *joins her.* CORNELIUS *sits again.*

MINNIE:

Lovely music.

MRS. MOLLOY:

Why, Minnie, you dance beautifully.

MINNIE:

We girls dance in the workroom when you're not looking, Irene.

MRS. MOLLOY:

You thought I'd be angry! Oh dear, no one in the world understands anyone else in the world.

The girls separate. MINNIE *dances off to her place at the table.* MRS. MOLLOY *sits thoughtfully at table right. The music fades away.*

Cornelius! Jenny Lind and all those other ladies—do you see them all the time?

CORNELIUS:

Rises and joins her at table right.

Irene, I've put them right out of my head. I'm interested in . . .

RUDOLPH *has entered by the service door. He now flings a tablecloth between them on table.*

MRS. MOLLOY:

Rudolph, what are you doing?

RUDOLPH:

A table's been reserved here. Special orders.

MRS. MOLLOY:

Stop right where you are. That party can eat inside. This veranda's ours.

RUDOLPH:

I'm very sorry. This veranda is open to anybody who wants it. Ah, there comes the man who brought the order.

Enter MALACHI *from the kitchen, drunk.*

MRS. MOLLOY:

To Malachi.

Take your table away from here. We got here first, Cornelius, throw him out.

MALACHI:

Ma'am, my employer reserved this room at four o'clock this afternoon. You can go and eat in the restaurant. My employer said it was very important that he have a table alone.

MRS. MOLLOY:

No, sir. We got here first and we're going to stay here— alone, too.

MINNIE *and* BARNABY *come forward.*

RUDOLPH:

Ladies and gentlemen!

MRS. MOLLOY:

Shut up, you!

To Malachi.

You're an impertinent, idiotic kill-joy.

MALACHI:

Very pleased.

That's an insult!

MRS. MOLLOY:

All the facts about you are insults.

To Cornelius.

Cornelius, do something. Knock it over! The table.

CORNELIUS:

Knock it over.

After a shocked struggle with himself CORNELIUS *calmly overturns the table.* AUGUST *rights the table and picks up cutlery, weeping copiously.*

RUDOLPH:

In cold fury.

I'm sorry, but this room can't be reserved for anyone. If you want to eat alone, you must go upstairs. I'm sorry, but that's the rule.

MRS. MOLLOY:

We're having a nice dinner alone and we're going to stay here. Cornelius, knock it over.

CORNELIUS *overturns the table again. The girls squeal with pleasure. The waiter* AUGUST *again scrambles for the silver.*

MALACHI:

Wait till you see my employer!

RUDOLPH:

Bringing screen down.

Ladies and gentlemen! I tell you what we'll do. There's a big screen here. We'll put the screen up between the tables. August, come and help me.

MRS. MOLLOY:

I won't eat behind a screen. I won't. Minnie, make a noise. We're not animals in a menagerie. Cornelius, no screen. Minnie, there's a fight. I feel ten years younger. No screen! No screen!

During the struggle with the screen all talk at once.

MALACHI:

Loud and clear and pointing to entrance right.

Now you'll learn something. There comes my employer now, getting out of that cab.

CORNELIUS:

Coming to him, taking off his coat.

Where? I'll knock him down too.

BARNABY *has gone up to right entrance. He turns and shouts clearly:*

BARNABY:

Cornelius, it's Wolf-trap. Yes, it is!

CORNELIUS:

Wolf-trap! Listen, everybody. I think the screen's a good idea. Have you got any more screens, Rudolph? We could use three or four.

He pulls the screen forward again.

MRS. MOLLOY:

Quiet down, Cornelius, and stop changing your mind. Hurry up, Rudolph, we're ready for the soup.

During the following scene RUDOLPH *serves the meal at the table left, as unobtrusively as possible.*

The stage is now divided in half. The quartet's table is at the left. Enter VANDERGELDER *from the right. Now wears overcoat and carries the box of chocolates.*

VANDERGELDER:

Stack! What's the meaning of this? I told you I wanted a table alone. What's that?

VANDERGELDER *hits the screen twice with his stick.* MRS. MOLLOY *hits back twice with a spoon. The four young people sit:* BARNABY *facing audience;* MRS. MOLLOY *right,* MINNIE *left, and* CORNELIUS *back to audience.*

MALACHI:

Mr. Vandergelder, I did what I could. Mr. Vandergelder, you wouldn't believe what wild savages the people of New York are. There's a woman over there, Mr. Vandergelder—civilization hasn't touched her.

VANDERGELDER:

Everything's wrong. You can't even manage a thing like that. Help me off with my coat. Don't kill me. Don't kill me.

During the struggle with the overcoat MR. VANDERGELDER'S *purse flies out of his pocket and falls by the screen.* VANDERGELDER *goes to the coat tree and hangs his coat up.*

MRS. MOLLOY:

Speak up! I can't hear you.

CORNELIUS:

My voice again. Barnaby, how's your throat? Can you speak?

BARNABY:

Can't make a sound.

MRS. MOLLOY:

Oh, all right. Bring your heads together, and we'll whisper.

VANDERGELDER:

Who are those people over there?

MALACHI:

Some city sparks and their girls, Mr. Vandergelder. What goes on in big cities, Mr. Vandergelder—best not think of it.

VANDERGELDER:

Has that couple come down from upstairs yet? I hope they haven't gone off without your seeing them.

MALACHI:

No, sir. Myself and the cabman have kept our eyes on everything.

VANDERGELDER:

Sits at right of table right, profile to the audience.

I'll sit here and wait for my guests. You go out to the cab.

MALACHI:

Yes, sir.

VANDERGELDER *unfurls newspaper and starts to read.*

MALACHI *sees the purse on the floor and picks it up.*

Eh? What's that? A purse. Did you drop something. Mr. Vandergelder?

VANDERGELDER:

No. Don't bother me any more. Do as I tell you.

MALACHI:

Stopping over. Coming center.

A purse. That fellow over there must have let it fall during the misunderstanding about the screen. No, I won't look inside. Twenty-dollar bills, dozens of them. I'll go over and give it to him.

Starts towards Cornelius, then turns and says to audience:

You're surprised? You're surprised to see me getting rid of this money so quickly, eh? I'll explain it to you. There was a time in my life when my chief interest was picking up money that didn't belong to me. The law is there to protect property, but— sure, the law doesn't care whether a property owner deserves his property or not, and the law has to be corrected. There are several thousands of people in this country engaged in correcting the law. For a while, I too was engaged in the redistribution of superfluities. A man works all his life and leaves a million to his widow. She sits in hotels and eats great meals and plays cards all afternoon and evening, with ten diamonds on her fingers. Call in the robbers! Call in the robbers! Or a man leaves it to his son who stands leaning against bars all night boring a bartender. Call in the robbers! Stealing's a weakness. There are some people who say you shouldn't have any weaknesses at all—no vices. But if a man has no vices, he's in great danger of making vices out of his virtues, and there's a spectacle. We've all seen them: men who were monsters of philanthropy and women who were dragons of purity. We've seen people who told the truth, though the Heavens fall,—and the Heavens fell. No, no—nurse one vice in your bosom. Give it the attention it deserves and let your virtues spring up modestly around it. Then you'll have the miser who's no liar; and the drunkard who's the benefactor of a whole city. Well, after I'd had that weakness of stealing for a while, I found another: I took to whisky—whisky took to me. And then I discovered an important rule that I'm going to pass on to you: Never support two weaknesses at the same time. It's your combination sinners—your lecherous liars and your miserly drunkards—who dishonor the vices and bring them into bad repute. So now you see why I want to get rid of this money: I want to keep my mind free to do the credit to whisky that it deserves. And my last word to you, ladies and gentlemen, is this: one vice at a time.

Goes over to Cornelius.

Can I speak to you for a minute?

CORNELIUS:
Rises.

You certainly can. We all want to apologize to you about that screen—that little misunderstanding.

They all rise, with exclamations of apology.

What's your name, sir?

MALACHI:
Stack, sir. Malachi Stack. If the ladies will excuse you, I'd like to speak to you for a minute.

Draws CORNELIUS *down to front of stage.*

Listen, boy, have you lost . . . ? Come here . . .

Leads him further down, out of Vandergelder's hearing.

Have you lost something?

CORNELIUS:
Mr. Stack, in this one day I've lost everything I own.

MALACHI:

There it is.

Gives him purse.

Don't mention it.

CORNELIUS:

Why, Mr. Stack . . . you know what it is? It's a miracle.

Looks toward the ceiling.

MALACHI:

Don't mention it.

CORNELIUS:

Barnaby, come here a minute. I want you to shake hands with Mr. Stack.

BARNABY, *napkin tucked into his collar, joins them.*

Mr. Stack's just found the purse I lost, Barnaby. You know— the purse full of money.

BARNABY:

Shaking his hand vigorously.

You're a wonderful man, Mr. Stack.

MALACHI:

Oh, it's nothing—nothing.

CORNELIUS:

I'm certainly glad I went to church all these years. You're a good person to know, Mr. Stack. In a way. Mr. Stack, where do you work?

MALACHI:

Well, I've just begun. I work for a Mr. Vandergelder in Yonkers.

CORNELIUS *is thunderstruck. He glances at Barnaby and turns to Malachi with awe. All three are swaying slightly, back and forth.*

CORNELIUS:

You do? It's a miracle.

He points to the ceiling.

Mr. Stack, I know you don't need it—but can I give you something for . . . for the good work?

MALACHI:

Putting out his hand.

Don't mention it. It's nothing.

Starts to go left.

CORNELIUS:

Take that.

Hands him a note.

MALACHI:

Taking note.

Don't mention it.

CORNELIUS:

And that.

Another note.

MALACHI:

Takes it and moves away.

I'd better be going.

CORNELIUS:

Oh, here. And that.

MALACHI:

Hands third note back.

No . . . I might get to like them.

Exit left.

CORNELIUS *bounds exultantly back to table.*

CORNELIUS:

Irene, I feel a lot better about everything. Irene, I feel so well that I'm going to tell the truth.

MRS. MOLLOY:

I'd forgotten that, Minnie. Men get drunk so differently from women. All right, what is the truth?

CORNELIUS:

If I tell the truth, will you let me . . . will you let me put my arm around your waist?

MINNIE *screams and flings her napkin over her face.*

MRS. MOLLOY:

Hold your tongue, Minnie. All right, you can put your arm around my waist just to show it can be done in a gentlemanly way; but I might as well warn you: a corset is a corset.

CORNELIUS:

His arm around her; softly.

You're a wonderful person, Mrs. Molloy.

MRS. MOLLOY:

Thank you.

She removes his hand from around her waist.

All right, now that's enough. What is the truth?

CORNELIUS:

Irene, I'm not rich as Mrs. Levi said I was.

MRS. MOLLOY:

Not rich!

ELIUS:

I almost never came to New York. And I'm not like she said I was,—bad. And I think you ought to know that at this very minute Mr. Vandergelder's sitting on the other side of that screen.

MRS. MOLLOY:

What!! Well, he's not going to spoil any party of mine. So *that's* why we've been whispering? Let's forget all about Mr. Vandergelder and have some more wine.

They start to sing softly: "The Sidewalks of New York."

Enter MRS. LEVI, *from the street, in an elaborate dress.* VANDERGELDER *rises.*

MRS. LEVI:

Good evening, Mr. Vandergelder.

VANDERGELDER:

Where's—where's Miss Simple?

MRS. LEVI:

Mr. Vandergelder, I'll never trust a woman again as long as I live.

VANDERGELDER:

Well? What is it?

MRS. LEVI:

She ran away this afternoon and got married!

VANDERGELDER:

She did?

MRS. LEVI:

Married, Mr. Vandergelder, to a young boy of fifty.

VANDERGELDER:

She did?

MRS. LEVI:

Oh, I'm as disappointed as you are. I-can't-eat-a-thing-what-have-you-ordered?

VANDERGELDER:

I ordered what you told me to, a chicken.

Enter AUGUST. *He goes to Vandergelder's table.*

MRS. LEVI:

I don't think I could face a chicken. Oh, waiter. How do you do? What's your name?

AUGUST:

August, ma'am.

MRS. LEVI:

August, this is Mr. Vandergelder of Yonkers—Yonkers' most influential citizen, in fact. I want you to see that he's served with the best you have and served promptly. And there'll only be the two of us.

MRS. LEVI *gives one set of cutlery to* AUGUST.
VANDERGELDER *puts chocolate box under table.*

Mr. Vandergelder's been through some trying experiences today—what with men hidden all over Mrs. Molloy's store— like Indians in ambush.

VANDERGELDER:

Between his teeth.

Mrs. Levi, you don't have to tell him everything about me.

The quartet commences singing again very softly.

MRS. LEVI:

Mr. Vandergelder, if you're thinking about getting married, you might as well learn right now you have to let women be women. Now, August, we want excellent service.

AUGUST:

Yes, ma'am.

Exits to kitchen.

VANDERGELDER:

You've managed things very badly. When I plan a thing it takes place.

MRS. LEVI *rises.*

Where are you going?

MRS. LEVI:

Oh, I'd just like to see who's on the other side of that screen.

MRS. LEVI *crosses to the other side of the stage and sees the quartet. They are frightened and fall silent.*

CORNELIUS:

Rising.

Good evening, Mrs. Levi.

MRS. LEVI *takes no notice, but, taking up the refrain where they left off, returns to her place at the table right.*

VANDERGELDER:

Well, who was it?

MRS. LEVI:

Oh, just some city sparks entertaining their girls, I guess.

VANDERGELDER:

Always wanting to know everything; always curious about everything; always putting your nose into other people's affairs. Anybody who lived with you would get as nervous as a cat.

MRS. LEVI:

What? What's that you're saying?

VANDERGELDER:

I said anybody who lived with you would—

MRS. LEVI:

Horace Vandergelder, get that idea right out of your head this minute. I'm surprised that you even mentioned such a thing. Understand once and for all that I have no intention of marrying you.

VANDERGELDER:

I didn't mean that.

MRS. LEVI:

You've been hinting around at such a thing for some time, but from now on put such ideas right out of your head.

VANDERGELDER:

Stop talking that way. That's not what I meant at all.

MRS. LEVI:

I hope not. I should hope not. Horace Vandergelder, you go your way

Points a finger.

and I'll go mine.

Points again in same direction.

I'm not some Irene Molloy, whose head can be turned by a pot of geraniums. Why, the idea of your even suggesting such a thing.

VANDERGELDER:

Mrs. Levi, you misunderstood me.

MRS. LEVI:

I certainly hope I did. If I had any intention of marrying again it would be to a far more pleasure-loving man than you. Why I'd marry Cornelius Hackl before I'd marry you.

CORNELIUS *raises his head in alarm. The others stop eating and listen.*

However, we won't discuss it any more.

Enter AUGUST *with a tray.*

Here's August with our food. I'll serve it, August.

AUGUST:

Yes, ma'am.

Exit AUGUST.

MRS. LEVI:

Here's some white meat for you, and some giblets, very tender
and very good for you. No, as I said before, you go your way
and I'll go mine.—Start right in on the wine. I think you'll feel
better at once. However, since you brought the matter up,
there's one more thing I think I ought to say.

VANDERGELDER:

Rising in rage.

I didn't bring the matter up at all.

MRS. LEVI:

We'll have forgotten all about it in a moment, but—sit down,
sit down, we'll close the matter forever in just a moment, but
there's one more thing I ought to say:

VANDERGELDER *sits down.*

It's true, I'm a woman who likes to know everything that's
going on; who likes to manage things, you're perfectly right
about that. But I wouldn't like to manage anything as disor-
derly as your household, as out of control, as untidy. You'll have
to do that yourself, God helping you.

VANDERGELDER:

It's not out of control.

MRS. LEVI:

Very well, let's not say another word about it. Take some more of that squash, it's good. No, Horace, a complaining, quarrelsome, friendless soul like you is no sort of companion for me. You go your way

Peppers her own plate.

and I'll go mine.

Peppers his plate.

VANDERGELDER:

Stop saying that.

MRS. LEVI:

I won't say another word.

VANDERGELDER:

Besides . . . I'm not those things you said I am.

MRS. LEVI:

What?—Well, I guess you're friendless, aren't you? Ermengarde told me this morning you'd even quarreled with your barber—a man who's held a razor to your throat for twenty years! Seems to me that that's sinking pretty low.

VANDERGELDER:

Well, . . . but . . . my clerks, they . . .

MRS. LEVI:

They like you? Cornelius Hackl and that Barnaby? Behind your back they call you Wolf-trap.

Quietly the quartet at the other table have moved up to the screens—bringing chairs for Mrs. Molloy and Minnie. Wine glasses in hand, they overhear this conversation.

VANDERGELDER:

Blanching.

They don't.

MRS. LEVI:

No, Horace. It looks to me as though I were the last person in the world that liked you, and even I'm just so-so. No, for the rest of my life I intend to have a good time. You'll be able to find some housekeeper who can prepare you three meals for a dollar a day—it can be done, you know, if you like cold baked beans. You'll spend your last days listening at keyholes, for fear someone's cheating you. Take some more of that.

VANDERGELDER:

Dolly, you're a damned exasperating woman.

MRS. LEVI:

There! You see? That's the difference between us. I'd be nagging you all day to get some spirit into you. You could be a perfectly charming, witty, amiable man, if you wanted to.

VANDERGELDER:

Rising, bellowing.

I don't want to be charming.

MRS. LEVI:

But you are. Look at you now. You can't hide it.

VANDERGELDER:

Sits.

Listening at keyholes! Dolly, you have no right to say such things to me.

MRS. LEVI:

At your age you ought to enjoy hearing the honest truth.

VANDERGELDER:

My age! My age! You're always talking about my age.

MRS. LEVI:

I don't know what your age is, but I do know that up at Yonkers with bad food and bad temper you'll double it in six months. Let's talk of something else; but before we leave the subject there's one more thing I *am* going to say.

VANDERGELDER:

Don't!

MRS. LEVI:

Sometimes, just sometimes, I think I'd be tempted to marry you out of sheer pity; and if the confusion in your house gets any worse I may *have* to.

VANDERGELDER:

I haven't asked you to marry me.

MRS. LEVI:

Well, *please don't*.

VANDERGELDER:

And my house is not in confusion.

MRS. LEVI:

What? With your niece upstairs in the restaurant right now?

VANDERGELDER:

I've fixed that better than you know.

MRS. LEVI:

And your clerks skipping around New York behind your back?

VANDERGELDER:

They're in Yonkers where they always are.

MRS. LEVI:

Nonsense!

VANDERGELDER:

What do you mean, nonsense?

MRS. LEVI:

Cornelius Hackl's the other side of that screen this very minute.

VANDERGELDER:

It ain't the same man!

MRS. LEVI:

All right. Go on. Push it, knock it down. Go and see.

VANDERGELDER:

Goes to screen, pauses in doubt, then returns to his chair again.

I don't believe it.

MRS. LEVI:

All right. All right. Eat your chicken. Of course, Horace, if your affairs went from bad to worse and you became actually miserable, I might feel that it was my duty to come up to Yonkers and be of some assistance to you. After all, I was your wife's oldest friend.

VANDERGELDER:

I don't know how you ever got any such notion. Now understand, once and for all, I have *no intention of marrying anybody.* Now, I'm tired and I don't want to talk.

CORNELIUS *crosses to extreme left,* MRS. MOLLOY *following him.*

MRS. LEVI:

I won't say another word, either.

CORNELIUS:

Irene, I think we'd better go. You take this money and pay the bill. Oh, don't worry, it's not mine.

MRS. MOLLOY:

No, no, I'll tell you what we'll do. You boys put on our coats and veils, and if he comes stamping over here, he'll think you're girls.

CORNELIUS:

What! Those things!

MRS. MOLLOY:

Yes. Come on.

She and MINNIE *take the clothes from the stand.*

VANDERGELDER:

Rises.

I've got a headache. I've had a bad day. I'm going to Flora Van Huysen's, and then I'm going back to my hotel.

Reaches for his purse.

So, here's the money to pay for the dinner.

Searching another pocket.

Here's the money to pay for the . . .

Going through all his pockets.

Here's the money . . . I've lost my purse!!

MRS. LEVI:

Impossible! I can't imagine you without your purse.

VANDERGELDER:

It's been stolen.

Searching overcoat.

Or I left it in the cab. What am I going to do? I'm new at the hotel; they don't know me. I've never been here before. . . . Stop eating the chicken, I can't pay for it!

MRS. LEVI:
Laughing gaily.

Horace, I'll be able to find some money. Sit down and calm yourself.

VANDERGELDER:

Dolly Gallagher, I gave you twenty-five dollars this morning.

MRS. LEVI:

I haven't a cent. I gave it to my lawyer. We can borrow it from Ambrose Kemper, upstairs.

VANDERGELDER:

I wouldn't take it.

MRS. LEVI:

Cornelius Hackl will lend it to us.

VANDERGELDER:

He's in Yonkers.—Waiter!

CORNELIUS *comes forward dressed in Mrs. Molloy's coat, thrown over his shoulder like a cape.*

MRS. LEVI *is enjoying herself immensely.* VANDERGELDER
again goes to back wall to examine the pockets of his overcoat.

MRS. MOLLOY:

Cornelius, is that Mr. Vandergelder's purse?

CORNELIUS:

I didn't know it myself. I thought it was money just wander-
ing around loose that didn't belong to anybody.

MRS. MOLLOY:

Goodness! That's what politicians think!

VANDERGELDER:

Waiter!

A band off left starts playing a polka. BARNABY *comes
forward dressed in Minnie's hat, coat and veil.*

MINNIE:

Irene, doesn't Barnaby make a lovely girl? He just ought to
stay that way.

MRS. LEVI *and* VANDERGELDER *move their table upstage
while searching for the purse.*

MRS. MOLLOY:

Why should we have our evening spoiled? Cornelius, I can
teach you to dance in a few minutes. Oh, he won't recognize
you.

MINNIE:

Barnaby, it's the easiest thing in the world.

They move their table up against the back wall.

MRS. LEVI:

Horace, you danced with me at your wedding and you danced with me at mine. Do you remember?

VANDERGELDER:

No. Yes.

MRS. LEVI:

Horace, you were a good dancer then. Don't confess to me that you're too old to dance.

VANDERGELDER:

Not too old. I just don't want to dance.

MRS. LEVI:

Listen to that music. Horace, do you remember the dances in the firehouse at Yonkers on Saturday nights? You gave me a fan. Come, come on!

VANDERGELDER *and* MRS. LEVI *start to dance.* CORNELIUS, *dancing with* MRS. MOLLOY, *bumps into Vandergelder, back to back.* VANDERGELDER, *turning, fails at first to recognize him, then does and roars:*

VANDERGELDER:

You're discharged! Not a word! You're fired! Where's that idiot, Barnaby Tucker? He's fired, too.

The four young people, laughing, start rushing out the door to the street. VANDERGELDER, *pointing at Mrs. Molloy, shouts:*

You're discharged!

MOLLOY:

Pointing at him.

You're discharged!

Exit.

VANDERGELDER:

You're discharged!

Enter from left, AMBROSE *and* ERMENGARDE.
To Ermengarde.

I'll lock you up for the rest of your life, young lady.

ERMENGARDE:

Uncle!

She faints in AMBROSE'S *arms.*

VANDERGELDER:

To Ambrose.

I'll have you arrested. Get out of my sight. I never want to see
you again.

AMBROSE:

Carrying ERMENGARDE *across to exit right.*

You can't do anything to me, Mr. Vandergelder.

Exit AMBROSE *and* ERMENGARDE.

MRS. LEVI:

Who has been laughing heartily, follows the distraught
VANDERGELDER *about the stage as he continues to hunt for
his purse.*

Well, there's your life, Mr. Vandergelder! Without niece—without clerks—without bride—and without your purse. *Will you marry me now?*

VANDERGELDER:

No!

To get away from her, he dashes into the kitchen.
MRS. LEVI, *still laughing, exclaims to the audience:*

MRS. LEVI:

Damn!!

And rushes off right.

THE
CURTAIN
FALLS

—∞—

Act IV

Miss Flora Van Huysen's house.

    This is a prosperous spinster's living room and is filled with knickknacks, all in bright colors, and hung with family portraits, bird cages, shawls, etc.

    There is only one entrance—a large double door in the center of the back wall. Beyond it one sees the hall which leads left to the street door and right to the kitchen and the rest of the house. On the left are big windows hung with lace curtains on heavy draperies. Front left is Miss Van Huysen's sofa, covered with bright-colored cushions, and behind it a table. On the right is another smaller sofa. MISS VAN HUYSEN is lying on the sofa. The COOK is at the window, left. MISS VAN HUYSEN, fifty, florid, stout and sentimental, is sniffing at smelling salts. COOK (enormous) holds a china mixing bowl.

COOK:

No, ma'am. I could swear I heard a cab drawing up to the door.

MISS VAN H.:

You imagined it. Imagination. Everything in life . . . like that
. . . disappointment . . . illusion. Our plans . . . our hopes . . .
what becomes of them? Nothing. The story of my life.

She sings for a moment.

COOK:

Pray God nothing's happened to the dear girl. Is it a long
journey from Yonkers?

MISS VAN H.:

No; but long enough for a thousand things to happen.

COOK:

Well, we've been waiting all day. Don't you think we ought
to call the police about it?

MISS VAN H.:

The police! If it's God's will, the police can't prevent it. Oh,
in three days, in a week, in a year, we'll know what's happened. . . . And if anything *has* happened to Ermengarde, it'll
be a lesson to *him*—that's what it'll be.

COOK:

To who?

MISS VAN H.:

To that cruel uncle of hers, of course,—to Horace Vandergelder, and to everyone else who tries to separate young
lovers. Young lovers have enough to contend with as it is. Who
should know that better than I? No one. The story of my life.

Sings for a moment, then:

There! Now I hear a cab. Quick!

COOK:

No. No, ma'am. I don't see anything.

MISS VAN H.:

There! What did I tell you? Everything's imagination—illusion.

COOK:

But surely, if they'd changed their plans Mr. Vandergelder would have sent you a message.

MISS VAN H.:

Oh, I know what's the matter. That poor child probably thought she was coming to another prison—to another tyrant. If she'd known that I was her friend, and a friend of all young lovers, she'd be here by now. Oh, yes, she would. Her life shall not be crossed with obstacles and disappointments as . . . Cook, a minute ago my smelling salts were on this table. Now they've completely disappeared.

COOK:

Why, there they are, ma'am, right there in your hand.

MISS VAN H.:

Goodness! How did they get there? I won't inquire. Stranger things have happened!

COOK:

I suppose Mr. Vandergelder was sending her down with someone?

MISS VAN H.:

Two can go astray as easily as . . .

She sneezes.

COOK:

God bless you!

Runs to window.

Now, here's a carriage stopping.

The doorbell rings.

MISS VAN H.:

Well, open the door, Cook.

COOK *exits.*

It's probably some mistake . . .

Sneezes again.

God bless you!

Sounds of altercation off in hall.

It almost sounds as though I heard voices.

CORNELIUS:

Off.

I don't want to come in. This is a free country, I tell you.

CABMAN:

Off.

Forward march!

MALACHI:

Off.

In you go. We have orders.

CORNELIUS:

Off.

You can't make a person go where he doesn't want to go.

Enter MALACHI, *followed by* COOK. *The* CABMAN *bundles* BARNABY *and* CORNELIUS *into the room, but they fight their way back into the hall.* CORNELIUS *has lost Mrs. Molloy's coat, but* BARNABY *is wearing Minnie's clothes.*

MALACHI:

Begging your pardon, ma'am, are you Miss Van Huysen?

MISS VAN H.:

Yes, I am, unfortunately. What's all this noise about?

MALACHI:

There are two people here that Mr. Vandergelder said must be brought to this house and kept here until he comes. And here's his letter to you.

MISS VAN H.:

No one has any right to tell me whom I'm to keep in my house if they don't want to stay.

MALACHI:

You're right, ma'am. Everybody's always talking about people breaking into houses, ma'am; but there are more people in the world who want to break out of houses, that's what I always say.—Bring them in, Joe.

Enter CORNELIUS *and* BARNABY *being pushed by the* CABMAN.

CORNELIUS:

This young lady and I have no business here. We jumped into a cab and asked to be driven to the station and these men brought us to the house and forced us to come inside. There's been a mistake.

CABMAN:

Is your name Miss Van Huysen?

MISS VAN H.:

Everybody's asking me if my name's Miss Van Huysen. I think that's a matter I can decide for myself. Now will you all be quiet while I read this letter?... "This is Ermengarde and that rascal Ambrose Kemper..." Now I know who you two are, anyway. "They are trying to run away..." Story of my life. "Keep them in your house until I come." Mr. Kemper, you have nothing to fear.

To Cabman.

Who are you?

CABMAN:

I'm Joe. I stay here until the old man comes. He owes me fifteen dollars.

MALACHI:

That's right, Miss Van Huysen, we must stay here to see they don't escape.

MISS VAN H.:
To Barnaby

My dear child, take off your things. We'll all have some coffee.

To Malachi and cabman.

You two go out and wait in the hall. I'll send coffee out to you.
Cook, take them.

COOK *pushes* MALACHI *and* CABMAN *into the hall.*

CORNELIUS:

Ma'am, we're not the people you're expecting, and there's
no reason . . .

MISS VAN H.:

Mr. Kemper, I'm not the tyrant you think I am. . . . You don't
have to be afraid of me. . . . I know you're trying to run away
with this innocent girl. . . . All my life I have suffered from the
interference of others. You shall not suffer as I did. So put yourself entirely in my hands.

She lifts Barnaby's veil.

Ermengarde!

Kisses him on both cheeks.

Where's your luggage?

BARNABY:

It's—uh—uh—it's . . .

CORNELIUS:

Oh, I'll find it in the morning. It's been mislaid.

MISS VAN H.:

Mislaid! How like life! Well, Ermengarde; you shall put on
some of my clothes.

BARNABY:

Oh, I know I wouldn't be happy, really.

MISS VAN H.:

She's a shy little thing, isn't she? Timid little darling! . . . Cook! Put some gingerbread in the oven and get the coffee ready . . .

COOK:

Yes, ma'am.

Exits to kitchen.

MISS VAN H.:

. . . while I go and draw a good hot bath for Ermengarde.

CORNELIUS:

Oh, oh—Miss Van Huysen . . .

MISS VAN H.:

Believe me, Ermengarde, your troubles are at an end. You two will be married tomorrow.

To Barnaby.

My dear, you look just like I did at your age, and your sufferings have been as mine. While you're bathing, I'll come and tell you the story of my life.

BARNABY:

Oh, I don't want to take a bath. I always catch cold.

MISS VAN H.:

No, dear, you won't catch cold. I'll slap you all over. I'll be back in a minute.

Exit.

CORNELIUS:

Looking out of window.

Barnaby, do you think we could jump down from this window?

BARNABY:

Yes—we'd kill ourselves.

CORNELIUS:

We'll just have to stay here and watch for something to happen. Barnaby, the situation's desperate.

BARNABY:

It began getting desperate about half-past four and it's been getting worse ever since. Now I have to take a bath and get slapped all over.

Enter MISS VAN HUYSEN *from kitchen.*

MISS VAN H.:

Ermengarde, you've still got those wet things on. Your bath's nearly ready. Mr. Kemper, you come into the kitchen and put your feet in the oven.

The doorbell rings. Enter COOK.

What's that? It's the doorbell. I expect it's your uncle.

COOK:

There's the doorbell.

At window.

It's *another* man and a girl in a cab!

MISS VAN H.:

Well, go and let them in, Cook. Now, come with me, you two. Come, Ermengarde.

Exit COOK. MISS VAN HUYSEN *drags* CORNELIUS *and the protesting* BARNABY *off into the kitchen.*

COOK:

Off.

No, that's impossible. Come in, anyway.

Enter ERMENGARDE, *followed by* AMBROSE, *carrying the two pieces of luggage.*

There's some mistake. I'll tell Miss Van Huysen, but there's some mistake.

ERMENGARDE:

But, I tell you, I *am* Mr. Vandergelder's niece; I'm Ermengarde.

COOK:

Beg your pardon, Miss, but you *can't* be Miss Ermengarde.

ERMENGARDE:

But—but—here I *am*. And that's my baggage.

COOK:

Well, I'll tell Miss Van Huysen who you *think* you are, but she won't like it.

Exits.

AMBROSE:

You'll be all right now, Ermengarde. I'd better go before she sees me.

ERMENGARDE:

Oh, no. You must stay. I feel so strange here.

AMBROSE:

I know, but Mr. Vandergelder will be here in a minute. . . .

ERMENGARDE:

Ambrose, you can't go. You can't leave me in this crazy house with those drunken men in the hall. Ambrose . . . Ambrose, let's say you're someone else that my uncle sent down to take care of me. Let's say you're—you're Cornelius Hackl!

AMBROSE:

Who's Cornelius Hackl?

ERMENGARDE:

You know. He's chief clerk in Uncle's store.

AMBROSE:

I don't want to be Cornelius Hackl. No, no, Ermengarde, come away with me now. I'll take you to my friend's house. Or I'll take you to Mrs. Levi's house.

ERMENGARDE:

Why, it was Mrs. Levi who threw us right at Uncle Horace's face. Oh, I wish I were back in Yonkers where nothing ever happens.

Enter MISS VAN HUYSEN.

MISS VAN H.:

What's all this I hear? Who do you say you are?

ERMENGARDE:

Aunt Flora . . . don't you remember me? I'm Ermengarde.

MISS VAN H.:

And you're Mr. Vandergelder's niece?

ERMENGARDE:

Yes, I am.

MISS VAN H.:

Well, that's very strange indeed, because he has just sent me another niece named Ermengarde. She came with a letter from him, explaining everything. Have you got a letter from him?

ERMENGARDE:

No . . .

MISS VAN H.:

Really!—And who is this?

ERMENGARDE:

This is Cornelius Hackl, Aunt Flora.

MISS VAN H.:

Never heard of him.

ERMENGARDE:

He's chief clerk in Uncle's store.

MISS VAN H.:

Never heard of him. The other Ermengarde came with the man she's in love with, and that *proves* it. She came with Mr. Ambrose Kemper.

AMBROSE:

Shouts.

Ambrose Kemper!

MISS VAN H.:

Yes, Mr. Hackl, and Mr. Ambrose Kemper is in the kitchen there now *with his feet in the oven.*

ERMENGARDE *starts to cry.* MISS VAN HUYSEN *takes her to the sofa. They both sit.*

Dear child, what is your trouble?

ERMENGARDE:

Oh, dear. I don't know what to do.

MISS VAN H.:
In a low voice.

Are you in love with this man?

ERMENGARDE:

Yes, I am.

MISS VAN H.:

I could see it—and are people trying to separate you?

ERMENGARDE:

Yes, they are.

MISS VAN H.:

I could see it—who? Horace Vandergelder?

ERMENGARDE:

Yes.

MISS VAN H.:

That's enough for me. I'll put a stop to Horace Vandergelder's goings on.

MISS VAN HUYSEN *draws* AMBROSE *down to sit on her other side.*

Mr. Hackl, think of me as your friend. Come in the kitchen
and get warm. . . .

She rises and starts to go out.

We can decide later who everybody is. My dear, would you
like a good hot bath?

ERMENGARDE:
Yes, I would.

MISS VAN H.:
Well, when Ermengarde comes out you can go in.

Enter CORNELIUS *from the kitchen.*

CORNELIUS:
Oh, Miss Van Huysen . . .

ERMENGARDE:
Why, Mr. Hack—!!

CORNELIUS:
Sliding up to her, urgently.

Not yet! I'll explain. I'll explain everything.

MISS VAN H.:
Mr. Kemper!—Mr. Kemper! This is Mr. Cornelius Hackl.

To Ambrose.

Mr. Hackl, this is Mr. Ambrose Kemper.

Pause, while the men glare at one another.

Perhaps you two know one another?

AMBROSE:
No!

CORNELIUS:

No, we don't.

AMBROSE:

Hotly.

Miss Van Huysen, I know that man is not Ambrose Kemper.

CORNELIUS:

Ditto.

And he's not Cornelius Hackl.

MISS VAN H.:

My dear young men, what does it matter what your names are? The important thing is that you are you.

To Ambrose.

You are alive and breathing, aren't you, Mr. Hackl?

Pinches Ambrose's left arm.

AMBROSE:

Ouch, Miss Van Huysen.

MISS VAN H.:

This dear child imagines she is Horace Vandergelder's niece Ermengarde.

ERMENGARDE:

But I am.

MISS VAN H.:

The important thing is that you're all in love. Everything else is illusion.

She pinches Cornelius' arm.

CORNELIUS:

Ouch! Miss Van Huysen!

MISS VAN H.:

Comes down and addresses the audience.

Everybody keeps asking me if I'm Miss Van Huys . . .

She seems suddenly to be stricken with doubt as to who she is; her face shows bewildered alarm. She pinches herself on the upper arm and is abruptly and happily relieved.

Now, you two gentlemen sit down and have a nice chat while this dear child has a good hot bath.

The doorbell rings ERMENGARDE *exit,* MISS VAN HUYSEN *about to follow her, but stops. Enter* COOK.

COOK:

There's the doorbell again.

MISS VAN H.:

Well, answer it.

She and ERMENGARDE *exit to kitchen.*

COOK:

At window, very happy about all these guests.

It's a cab and three ladies. I never saw such a night.

Exit to front door.

MISS VAN H.:

Gentlemen, you can rest easy. I'll see that Mr. Vandergelder lets his nieces marry you both.

Enter MRS. LEVI.

MRS. LEVI:

Flora, how are you?

MISS VAN H.:

Dolly Gallagher! What brings you here?

MRS. LEVI:

Great Heavens, Flora, what are those two drunken men doing in your hall?

MISS VAN H.:

I don't know. Horace Vandergelder sent them to me.

MRS. LEVI:

Well, I've brought you two girls in much the same condition. Otherwise they're the finest girls in the world.

She goes up to the door and leads in MRS. MOLLOY. MINNIE *follows.*

I want you to meet Irene Molloy and Minnie Fay.

MISS VAN H.:

Delighted to know you.

MRS. LEVI:

Oh, I see you two gentlemen are here, too. Mr. Hackl, I was about to look for you

Pointing about the room.

somewhere here.

CORNELIUS:

No, Mrs. Levi. I'm ready to face anything now.

MRS. LEVI:

Mr. Vandergelder will be here in a minute. He's downstairs trying to pay for a cab without any money.

MRS. MOLLOY:

Holding Vandergelder's purse.

Oh, I'll help him.

MRS. LEVI:

Yes, will you, dear? You had to pay the restaurant bills. You must have hundreds of dollars there it seems.

MRS. MOLLOY:

This is his own purse he lost. I can't give it back to him without seeming . . .

MRS. LEVI:

I'll give it back to him.—There, you help him with this now.

She gives Mrs. Molloy a bill and puts the purse airily under her arm.

VANDERGELDER:

Off.

Will somebody please pay for this cab?

MRS. MOLLOY *exits to front door.*

MRS. MOLLOY:

Off stage.

I'll take care of that, Mr. Vandergelder.

As MR. VANDERGELDER *enters,* MALACHI *and the* CABMAN *follow him in.* VANDERGELDER *carries overcoat, stick and box of chocolates.*

CABMAN:

Fifteen dollars, Mr. Vandergelder.

MALACHI:

Hello, Mr. Vandergelder.

VANDERGELDER:

To Malachi.

You're discharged!

To Cabman.

You too!

MALACHI *and* CABMAN *go out and wait in the ball.*

So I've caught up with you at last!

To Ambrose.

I never want to see you again!

To Cornelius.

You're discharged! Get out of the house, both of you.

He strikes sofa with his stick; a second after, MISS VAN HUYSEN *strikes him on the shoulder with a folded newspaper or magazine.*

MISS VAN H.:

Forcefully.

Now then you. Stop ordering people out of my house. You can shout and carry on in Yonkers, but when you're in my house you'll behave yourself.

VANDERGELDER:

They're both dishonest scoundrels.

MISS VAN H.:

Take your hat off. Gentlemen, you stay right where you are.

CORNELIUS:

Mr. Vandergelder, I can explain—

MISS VAN H.:

There aren't going to be any explanations. Horace, stop scowling at Mr. Kemper and forgive him.

VANDERGELDER:

That's not Kemper, that's a dishonest rogue named Cornelius Hackl.

MISS VAN H.:

You're crazy.

Points to Ambrose.

That's Cornelius Hackl.

VANDERGELDER:

I guess I know my own chief clerk.

MISS VAN H.:

I don't care what their names are. You shake hands with them both, or out you go.

VANDERGELDER:

Shake hands with those dogs and scoundrels!

MRS. LEVI:

Mr. Vandergelder, you've had a hard day. You don't want to go out in the rain now. Just for form's sake, you shake hands with them. You can start quarreling with them tomorrow.

VANDERGELDER:

Gives CORNELIUS *one finger to shake.*

There! Don't regard that as a handshake.

He turns to AMBROSE, *who mockingly offers him one finger.*

Hey! I never want to see you again.

MRS. MOLLOY *enters from front door.*

MRS. MOLLOY:

Miss Van Huysen.

MISS VAN H.:

Yes, dear?

MRS. MOLLOY:

Do I smell coffee?

MISS VAN H.:

Yes, dear.

MRS. MOLLOY:

Can I have some, good and black?

MISS VAN H.:

Come along, everybody. We'll all go into the kitchen and have some coffee.

As they all go:

Horace, you'll be interested to know there are two Ermengardes in there. . . .

VANDERGELDER:

Two!!

Last to go is MINNIE, *who revolves about the room dreamily waltzing, a finger on her forehead.* MRS. LEVI *has been standing at one side. She now comes forward, in thoughtful mood.* MINNIE *continues her waltz round the left sofa and out to the kitchen.*

MRS. LEVI, *left alone, comes to front, addressing an imaginary Ephraim.*

MRS. LEVI:

Ephraim Levi, I'm going to get married again. Ephraim, I'm marrying Horace Vandergelder for his money. I'm going to send his money out doing all the things you taught me. Oh, it won't be a marriage in the sense that we had one—but I shall certainly make him happy, and Ephraim—I'm tired. I'm tired of living from hand to mouth, and I'm asking your permission, Ephraim—will you give me away?

Now addressing the audience, she holds up the purse.

Money! Money!—it's like the sun we walk under; it can kill or cure.—Mr. Vandergelder's money! Vandergelder's never tired of saying most of the people in the world are fools, and in a way he's right, isn't he? Himself, Irene, Cornelius, myself! But there comes a moment in everybody's life when he must decide whether he'll live among human beings or not—a fool among fools or a fool alone.

As for me, I've decided to live among them.

I wasn't always so. After my husband's death I retired into myself. Yes, in the evenings, I'd put out the cat, and I'd lock the door, and I'd make myself a little rum toddy; and before I went to bed I'd say a little prayer, thanking God that I was independent—that no one else's life was mixed up with mine. And when ten o'clock sounded from Trinity Church tower, I fell off to sleep and I was a perfectly contented woman. And one night, after two years of this, an oak leaf fell out of my Bible. I had placed it there on the day my husband asked me to marry him; a perfectly good oak leaf—but without color and without life. And suddenly I realized that for a long time I had not shed one tear; nor had I been filled with the wonderful hope that something or other would turn out well. I saw that I was like that oak leaf, and on that night I decided to rejoin the human race.

Yes, we're all fools and we're all in danger of destroying the world with our folly. But the surest way to keep us out of harm is to give us the four or five human pleasures that are our right in the world,—and that takes a little *money!*

The difference between a little money and no money at all is enormous—and can shatter the world. And the difference between a little money and an enormous amount of money is very slight—and that, also, can shatter the world.

Money, I've always felt, money—pardon my expression—is like manure; it's not worth a thing unless it's spread about encouraging young things to grow.

Anyway,—that's the opinion of the second Mrs. Vandergelder.

VANDERGELDER *enters with two cups of coffee. With his back, he closes both doors.*

VANDERGELDER:
Miss Van Huysen asked me to bring you this.

MRS. LEVI:
Thank you both. Sit down and rest yourself. What's been going on in the kitchen?

VANDERGELDER:

A lot of foolishness. Everybody falling in love with everybody. I forgave 'em; Ermengarde and that artist.

MRS. LEVI:

I knew you would.

VANDERGELDER:

I made Cornelius Hackl my partner.

MRS. LEVI:

You won't regret it.

VANDERGELDER:

Dolly, you said some mighty unpleasant things to me in the restaurant tonight . . . all that about my house . . . and everything.

MRS. LEVI:

Let's not say another word about it.

VANDERGELDER:

Dolly, you have a lot of faults—

MRS. LEVI:

Oh, I know what you mean.

VANDERGELDER:

You're bossy, scheming, inquisitive . . .

MRS. LEVI:

Go on.

VANDERGELDER:

But you're a wonderful woman. Dolly, marry me.

MRS. LEVI:

Horace!

Rises.

Stop right there.

VANDERGELDER:

I know I've been a fool about Mrs. Molloy, and that other woman. But, Dolly, forgive me and marry me.

He goes on his knees.

MRS. LEVI:

Horace, I don't dare. No. I don't dare.

VANDERGELDER:

What do you mean?

MRS. LEVI:

You know as well as I do that you're the first citizen of Yonkers. Naturally, you'd expect your wife to keep open house, to have scores of friends in and out all the time. Any wife of yours should be used to that kind of thing.

VANDERGELDER:

After a brief struggle with himself.

Dolly, you can live any way you like.

MRS. LEVI:

Horace, you can't deny it, your wife would have to be a *somebody*. Answer me: am I a somebody?

VANDERGELDER:

You are . . . you are. Wonderful woman.

MRS. LEVI:

Oh, you're partial.

She crosses, giving a big wink at the audience, and sits on sofa right.

VANDERGELDER *follows her on his knees.*

Horace, it won't be enough for you to load your wife with money and jewels; to insist that she be a benefactress to half the town.

He rises and, still struggling with himself, coughs so as not to hear this.

No, she must be a somebody. Do you really think I have it in me to be a credit to you?

VANDERGELDER:

Dolly, everybody knows that you could do anything you wanted to do.

MRS. LEVI:

I'll try. With your help, I'll try—and by the way, I found your purse.

Holds it up.

VANDERGELDER:

Where did you—! Wonderful woman!

MRS. LEVI:

It just walked into my hand. I don't know how I do it. Sometimes I frighten myself. Horace, take it. Money walks out of my hands, too.

VANDERGELDER:

Keep it. Keep it.

MRS. LEVI:

Horace!

Half laughing, half weeping, and with an air of real affection for him.

I never thought . . . I'd ever . . . hear you say a thing like that!

BARNABY *dashes in from the kitchen in great excitement. He has discarded Minnie's clothes.*

BARNABY:

Oh! Excuse me. I didn't know anybody was here.

VANDERGELDER:

Bellowing.

Didn't know anybody was here. Idiot!

MRS. LEVI:

Putting her hand on Vandergelder's arm; amiably:

Come in, Barnaby. Come in.

VANDERGELDER *looks at her a minute; then says, imitating her tone:*

VANDERGELDER:

Come in, Barnaby. Come in.

BARNABY:

Cornelius is going to marry Mrs. Molloy!!

MRS. LEVI:

Isn't that fine! Horace!. . .

MRS. LEVI *rises, and indicates that he has an announcement to make.*

VANDERGELDER:

Barnaby, go in and tell the rest of them that Mrs. Levi has consented—

MRS. LEVI:

Finally consented!

VANDERGELDER:

Finally consented to become my wife.

BARNABY:

Holy cabooses.

Dashes back to the doorway.

Hey! Listen, everybody! Wolf-trap—I mean—Mr. Vandergelder is going to marry Mrs. Levi.

MISS VAN HUYSEN *enters followed by all the people in this act. She is now carrying the box of chocolates.*

MISS VAN H.:

Dolly, that's the best news I ever heard.

She addresses the audience.

There isn't any more coffee; there isn't any more gingerbread; but there are three couples in my house and they're all going to get married. And do you know, one of those Ermengardes wasn't a dear little girl at all—she was a boy! Well, that's what life is: disappointment, illusion.

MRS. LEVI:

To audience.

There isn't any more coffee; there isn't any more ginger-bread, and there isn't any more play—but there is one more thing we have to do. . . . Barnaby, come here.

She whispers to him, pointing to the audience. Then she says to the audience:

I think the youngest person here ought to tell us what the moral of the play is.

BARNABY *is reluctantly pushed forward to the footlights.*

BARNABY:

Oh, I think it's about . . . I think it's about adventure. The test of an adventure is that when you're in the middle of it, you say to yourself, "Oh, now I've got myself into an awful mess; I wish I were sitting quietly at home." And the sign that something's wrong with you is when you sit quietly at home wishing you were out having lots of adventure. What we would like for you is that you have just the right amount of sitting quietly at home, and just the right amount of—adventure! So that now we all want to thank you for coming tonight, and we all hope that in your lives you have just the right amount of—adventure!

THE
CURTAIN
FALLS

Our Town

—∿—

1938

After a brief disastrous run in Boston, Our Town *received* overwhelmingly positive reviews when it opened on Broadway on February 4, 1938, at the Henry Miller Theater. The *New York Times*, then as now the most influential theater-reviewing journal in the country, led the chorus by heralding the work as "one of the finest achievements of the current stage" in a rave review published on February 5, 1938. "Although Thornton Wilder is celebrated chiefly for his fiction," declared *Times* reviewer Brooks Atkinson, "it will be necessary now to reckon with him as a dramatist. . . . Mr. Wilder has transmuted the simple events of human life into universal reveries. He has given familiar facts a deeply moving, philosophical perspective." In Atkinson's opinion, the unconventional elements in the play's staging only added to its power and beauty: "[B]y stripping the play of everything that is not essential," he wrote, "Mr. Wilder has given it profound, strange, unworldly significance. . . . [I]t is a hauntingly beautiful play."

The reviewer for *Time* magazine was even more emphatic

in praising the play's use of a bare stage and omniscient Stage Manager: "[T]he whole effect gives ten times as much 'theatre' as conventional scenery could give." The anonymous reviewer contrasted Wilder's "cloistered" approach to novel-writing with his "adventurous" stance in the theater. Like several other critics, the *Time* reviewer preferred the first two acts, which concern the living folk of Grover's Corners, to the final act, which is dominated by the dead. "A good playwright when he deals with living people," the review concludes, "[Wilder] is only a bad philosopher when he deals with dead ones."

John Mason Brown, reviewing the play for the *New York Evening Post*, stated that Wilder's nonrealistic stagecraft was not, in fact, radically different from the staging techniques employed by more traditional dramas. "Both types of production depend in the last analysis upon their audiences to supply that final belief which is the mandate under which all theatrical illusion operates. The form Mr. Wilder uses is franker, that is all. It does not attempt to hide the fact it is make-believe." Brown argued further that the true strength of the form Wilder chose was its perfect harmony with the content of his play. "What he has done in *Our Town* is to strip life down to its essentials, too. There is nothing of the 'stunt' about the old-new form he has employed. His form is the inevitable one his content demands."

The one skeptic was the reviewer for *Commonweal*, who felt that Wilder's bare stage and Stage Manager ranked as a "stunt" that "make[s] . . . the play seem more important than it is."

Joseph Wood Krutch, writing for *The Nation*, touched briefly on the unconventionality of the staging, but the majority of his very favorable and thoughtful review was devoted to the "mood" aroused by the play: "Here is no easy fun poked at the age of buggies and innocence, but here also is no sentimental overvaluation. Indeed, it is amazing how little Mr. Wilder claims for his villagers. . . . If one asks what remains, what is left to feel when one feels neither condescension nor partisan warmth, the answer is simply that the mood of quiet contemplation which Mr. Wilder generates is one which would be hopelessly submerged by any suggestion of either satire or sentimentality."

Our Town was adapted for a film version in 1940 and was also made into the musical *Grover's Corners* by Harvey Schmidt and Tom Jones in 1987. Although Thornton Wilder's critical reputation remains somewhat mixed in the present day, *Our Town* continues to be one of the most frequently performed plays of the century. Its popularity is both a testament to Wilder's enduring talent and an affirmation of his belief in theater as the greatest of all art forms, the most immediate way, as he wrote, "in which a human being can share with another the sense of what it means to be human."

The Skin of Our Teeth

—⁓—

1942

The Skin of Our Teeth, *which opened on Broadway in* November 1942, was Wilder's most controversial play, inspiring fierce disagreements among critics. While some reviewers found the work refreshingly original, alive, and exciting, others condemned it as hollow, flat-footed, or just plain silly. Wilder's innovative stagecraft was one facet of the debate: some felt it worked beautifully as unconventional theater while others found it gimmicky. Reviewers were also divided in their reactions to the play's "message" of human endurance in the face of catastrophe.

The most glowing praise came from Wolcott Gibbs, writing in *The New Yorker*. Gibbs trumpeted *The Skin of Our Teeth* as "by far the most interesting and exciting play I've seen this year. . . . [A] remarkably original and literate experiment in theatre." As for the play's experimental qualities, Gibbs remarked that they posed no difficulty to understanding and enjoying the drama: "[O]nce you have come to accept the nonexistence of time and a certain amount of rudimentary symbolism, Mr. Wilder's offering is comparatively simple." Lewis Nichols, reviewing the play for the *New York Times*, also proffered praise, but more faintly: Wilder's "comedy about man," he wrote "is the best play the Forties have seen in many months, the best pure theatre." Nichols, like many other reviewers, singled out Tallulah Bankhead's performance as Sabina, calling her "magnificent—breezy, hard, practical by turns."

While Lewis Nichols described the play as a comedy, James N. Vaughan, writing in *Commonweal*, labeled it a "sermon" and a rather tedious sermon at that. Vaughan felt that the play "lacks enchantment" and that the innovative stagecraft was forced: Although "bringing the audience into the play" worked in *Our Town*, it "fails in the present play because it is too overt, too garish, too sensational in the literal sense." Stark Young voiced much the same opinion in *The New Republic*, writing that "a good many of these shakeups, overturned devices and carefully naive bits of business and stage properties are fairly threadbare, and the humor of them is academic, if not collegiate even." *The Skin of Our Teeth*, concludes Young, is "a kind of cosmic variety show . . . bantering and poking theatre conventions in the ribs."

Time magazine ran an outright pan that dismissed the play as "a cockeyed and impudent vaudeville littered with asides and swarming with premeditated anachronisms. . . . *The Skin of Our Teeth* is like a philosophy class conducted in a monkey house. In showing how man through the ages has escaped destruction by the skin of his teeth, the play tweaks his nose, barks his shins, musses his hair, gives him the hotfoot." In sum, *Time* concluded that the "play dolls up its theme rather than dramatizes it."

The controversy over *The Skin of Our Teeth* intensified

when Joseph Campbell and Henry M. Robinson published a piece in the *Saturday Review of Literature* accusing Wilder of lifting the play's central concept of telescoping time from James Joyce's *Finnegans Wake*. Though many critics rose to defend Wilder, the suspicion of plagiarism lingered. Nonetheless, the play won the Pulitzer Prize for drama. Wilder himself later admitted that his play was "deeply indebted" to *Finnegans Wake*, and most critics today feel that Wilder made legitimate, indeed imaginative, use of Joyce's difficult novel.

Controversy proved to be a boon at the box office, and *The Skin of Our Skin* ran on Broadway for 355 performances.

The Matchmaker

—⚮—

1955

Although The Matchmaker *was a smash hit on Broadway in* 1955, the play failed in its original 1938 version, entitled *The Merchant of Yonkers*. Reviews for this Max Reinhardt production, which opened on December 28, 1938, ranged from the respectful to the disdainful. The highest praise came from the *New York Times*, where Brooks Atkinson called the farce a "giddy jest . . . a gay and generally spirited tour de force against old-fashioned canvas settings," and recommended the play to "those who laugh easily at innocent trifles."

The pans for *The Merchant of Yonkers* were far more vehement than the faint accolades. George Jean Nathan, writing in *Newsweek*, called it a "depressing spectacle" based on a "tiresome old joke." Another reviewer groaned, "Never to my knowledge have two brief and supposedly merry hours stretched themselves out into such an eternity." The play closed after thirty-nine performances.

Though only slightly altered in text, the 1955 revival as *The Matchmaker* fared far better in the press. Brooks Atkinson credited director Tyrone Guthrie with mounting the play as an "old-fashioned farce, and that may be the best thing that could happen to any play of theatrical proportions." The new production was "loud, vulgar, slapdash and uproarious"—all virtues, in Atkinson's view, and the "traditional nonsense" had been transformed into "something extremely original and funny." The reviewer for *Time* was also struck by how Guthrie had cranked up the play's volume and frenzy level: "[W]hat once merely clattered now careens; what formerly sputtered now explodes. There is a brazen, often hilarious farcicality about it all." A short notice in *Life* magazine declared that Wilder had given the play "all the fun and fuss of old-fashioned farces . . . and touched it all with his own brand of tender wisdom."

Not all critics, however, were charmed by the revival. Henry Hewes, writing in *Saturday Review*, recollected the sorry fate of *The Merchant of Yonkers* and concluded that *The Matchmaker* was the same shoddy goods: The new production has "merely camouflaged tedium with noise. . . . It is indeed lamentable that so much genius has been wasted in an effort to resuscitate such an anemic trifle." The only virtue Hewes saw in the production was the actress Ruth Gordon, playing Dolly Levi, but even here it was a case of talent shamefully thrown away. Gordon's appearance in the play, he wrote, was "merely an excuse to see one of America's greatest comic actresses blast her way through a pretentiously inadequate series of scenes."

Audiences resoundingly disagreed with Henry Hewes, and *The Matchmaker* ran for 486 performances. In its next incarnation as the 1964 musical *Hello, Dolly!* starring Carol Channing, the play was a far greater success, running for nearly three thousand performances and spawning a popular film with Barbra Streisand and a long-running Broadway revival with an all-black cast headed by Pearl Bailey.

Although Thornton Wilder's critical reputation remains somewhat mixed in the present day, his plays continue to be some of the most frequently performed works of the century. Their popularity is both a testament to Wilder's enduring talent and an affirmation of his belief in theater as the greatest of all art forms, the most immediate way, as he wrote, "in which a human being can share with another the sense of what it means to be human."

Afterword

—∞—

OVERVIEW

Just as these three Broadway hits remain very much alive and well on amateur and professional stages worldwide, this volume has been in print, and successfully so, since 1957, or nearly half a century. That Wilder's own words in the 1957 edition of *Three Plays* are as ubiquitous in theater programs as are the plays on stage, in classrooms, and on bedside tables, is still another reason why you hold in your hands a "hit."

Why introduce change in this famous volume? Where changes in the front of the book are concerned, the answer was driven partly by the desire for uniformity: each of the other volumes in this new Wilder publication series carries a foreword by a contemporary artist—a writer invited to write about a fellow writer. We could have skipped *Three Plays* because, unlike all his other major works, it had a preface—Wilder's own. But that seemed unfair to the series, and we were fortunate to have playwright John Guare agree to contribute his reflections on Wilder's creativity and his dramatic legacy.

On the occasion of this volume's first appearance as a HarperCollins Perennial Classic in 2000, the editors added brief histories of each play. In this new series, you will find a more extensive overview of the history of the work. Because of the length of *Three Plays* and because *Our Town* and *The Skin of Our Teeth* have their own separate editions (to which interested readers may go for more detail), this volume contains concise overviews. Because *The Matchmaker* appears only in this volume of the series, we felt justified in giving it a more extensive overview than its two companion plays.

Ladies and gentlemen, welcome to the show.

OUR TOWN

The idea for *Our Town* first appears in Wilder's records as "M Marries N" in a list of ideas for plays in a journal entry of July 2, 1935. This precise language—possibly the oldest in the play—survives in the final version: At the end of Act II the Stage Manager, as the minister, says: "M . . . marries N . . . millions of them." In 1936, the working title of the play evolved into "Our Village," and a year later into *Our Town*. In keeping with Wilder's peripatetic habits as a writer, the gestation of the play took place on transatlantic steamers, at writing tables in hotels and hideaways in such varied places as the Caribbean island of St. Lucia; the MacDowell Colony in Peterborough, New Hampshire (an artists' and writers' retreat); Zürich, St. Moritz, Sils-Maria, Sils-Baselia, and Ascona in Switzerland; and in a cottage on Long Island in the swanky Cold Spring Harbor area. Of these locations, the Hotel Belvoir in Ruschlikon, a village outside Zürich, deserves to be remembered as the place where much of the hardest writing and shaping of the script occurred. The MacDowell Colony as well as other sites in New Hampshire served as the inspiration for the play's setting.

The play was produced and directed by Jed Harris, Wilder's friend, and a towering and controversial figure in Broadway history in the first half of the twentieth century. Harris was admired and hated, often by the same people, but he possessed the essential qualities Wilder wanted for the director of his unorthodox play: an extraordinary knowledge of drama and a passionate belief in the work. It was perhaps inevitable, as was often the case for those who worked with Harris, that the two men were not speaking by the time *Our Town* opened on Broadway.

The play's route to Broadway, winding through Princeton and Boston to New York, is a classic story of theatrical

success snatched from the jaws of near-failure. The premiere
was a single performance at the McCarter Theatre in Princeton, New Jersey, on January 22, 1938. The play drew a
ferociously negative review in *Variety* ("it will probably go
down as the season's most extravagant waste of fine talent");
but a sold-out audience, as Wilder reported, was "swept by
laughter often; astonishment; and lots of tears; long applause
at the end by an audience that did not move from its seats."
Boston, however, was a different story. Although reviews
were not as negative as has often been suggested, and audiences were deeply absorbed in the play, liberally using their
handkerchiefs, there were no sell-out houses in Boston. In
fact, business was so terrible that Harris considered with-
drawing the play for further work, or closing it altogether.
Instead, apparently influenced by the opinions of several
influential figures who came from New York to see what was
afoot at Boston's Wilbur Theater, Harris closed a week early
and opened the play temporarily at Henry Miller's Theatre
in New York on Friday, February 4. The gamble paid off.
The *Our Town* opening, with lots of tears again in evidence,
was an exciting occasion, and a line was waiting for the box
office to open the next morning.

The original Broadway reviews were mixed. Negative
comments focused on whether the play was "dramatic"
enough to be called a play or merely what Robert Benchley
in *The New Yorker* saw as "so much ersatz." John Gassner in
One Act Play Magazine dismissed it as "devoid of developed
situations" and thus much less than "a major dramatic experience," and George Jean Nathan later called it "a stunt."
Time found the third act full of disappointing "mysticism
and high-flown speculation." *The New Masses*, the Com-
munist journal whose editor, Michael Gold, had famously
trashed Wilder's fiction earlier in the decade, tipped its hat

slightly to the work while leveling a salvo: "It is an exasperating play, hideous in its basic idea and beautiful in its writing, acting and staging." (The "hideous" idea was the playwright's favorable treatment of middle-class, bourgeois values and lives.)

But elsewhere, in such papers as the *Herald-Tribune*, *World-Telegram*, *Brooklyn Daily Eagle*, and the tabloid *Sunday Mirror*, the play's staging, acting, directing, and themes evoked powerful adjectives and praise. It was "beautiful," "touching," "one of the great plays of our day," "magnificent." Robert Coleman in the *Mirror* pulled out all stops, proclaiming it "worthy of an honored place in any anthology of the American drama," a position it would achieve soon enough starting in 1940. Brooks Atkinson in the *New York Times* wrote a review of poetic intensity, hailing Wilder and Harris for a play that "transmuted the simple events of human life into universal reverie," and contained "a fragment of the immortal truth."

The original Broadway production broke no records. Atkinson recalled in 1973 that had it not received the Pulitzer Prize in May 1938, four months into the run, "it might have relapsed into the yawning obscurity of those innumerable Broadway plays that never really succeeded." To keep the production alive during the difficult hot summer months, Wilder accepted steep royalty reductions. Business improved somewhat when he played the part of the Stage Manager for two weeks in September. But as business fell off, Harris closed the New York run on November 19 after 336 performances, and took the play out on what was projected to be a lengthy national tour.

Three months and twelve cities later, on February 11, 1939, the run ended abruptly in Chicago. Thomas Coley, an original cast member, recalled the reason in a memoir:

Jed noticed that Frank Craven [who played the Stage Manager] was earning more each week than he, the producer-director. He came out to persuade Mr. Craven to reduce his percentage of the gross. They argued. Jed lost. In a rage, he closed the play, thus cutting off the nose to spite his face, and, incidentally, the noses of forty-seven actors plus the crew.

Although *Our Town* had a less than less record-breaking launch, its subsequent history, measured in amateur and stock productions, quickly earned it the "smashing success" that Frank Craven had predicted to Wilder on the eve of the first rehearsals. After April 1939, in the first twenty months of the availability of amateur rights, *Our Town* was produced no fewer than 795 times in communities across the country. This record laid the foundation for what has been the *Our Town* rule of thumb ever since, a performance at least once each night somewhere in this country. Behind these figures lies a play that has marvelous parts for young people, is not expensive to mount, is glorious to teach, and treats life, death, and love in such an immediate fashion as to leave indelible and typically nostalgic impressions on generations of students.

Our Town was also a hit from the beginning with professional stock companies. By May 1944 it had already been performed forty-three times, principally in summer theaters in New England and the mid-Atlantic states. Five of these productions featured Wilder as the Stage Manager. Since World War II, the pattern has continued, now tied to the growth of the American regional theater movement. Between 1970 and 2005, the play was performed ninety-one times in professional stock and regional theaters.

Long Wharf Theatre in Wilder's home city of New Haven, Connecticut, mounted the play's fiftieth anniversary production staring Hal Holbrook. Another landmark production occurred in 1976 at the Williamstown Theatre Festival when Geraldine Fitzgerald bowed as the first woman to play the Stage Manager. Marc Connelly played the Stage Manager when *Our Town* had its first major New York revival in 1944. There have been four revivals since, the most recent being the Westport Country Playhouse's hugely successful production starring Paul Newman in a sold-out ten-week Broadway run in the fall and winter of 2002–2003. These professional productions routinely provide the opportunity for audiences, critics, and artists to explore the play's existential depths in fresh ways. The findings can be dramatic, as witnessed playwright Lanford Wilson, writing about the fiftieth anniversary production in 1987 in the *New York Times* in language increasingly used to describe the play: "And where the hell did [Wilder] get the reputation for being soft? Let's agree never to say that again. Let's not be blinded by the homey cute surface from the fact that *Our Town*'s a deadly cynical and acidly accurate play." After 9/11, theatergoers saw in it what Richard Hamberger at the Dallas Theatre Center spoke of as a tough-minded but also reassuring "sense of continuity and community."

Our Town has also been an international success story. Since 1960 it has been produced in at least twenty-two languages in twenty-seven countries outside of Germany, and translated and almost certainly performed in many others. ("Hard" figures can be hard to come by in this chapter of *Our Town*'s history.) Germany has always been a special venue for this play, as well as for Wilder's other works. Between 1950 and 1970, *Our Town* was produced eighty times on the German-speaking stage, and although done less often now, continues to be performed and read widely in German schools. It says much about the drama's planetary appeal and vision that the cover of the new German paperback edition depicts not a typical small town but a major metropolis.

During his lifetime Wilder permitted a now-forgotten radio production of *Our Town*. The play's early televised history is also forgotten, with the exception of the 1955 ninety-minute musical version starring Frank Sinatra and featuring the Sammy Cahn–James Van Heusen song, "Love and Marriage." Video recordings are available of three recent and successful televised productions, starring Hal Holbrook, Spalding Gray, and Paul Newman, respectively. Since Wilder's death, his estate has permitted a ballet and an opera based on the play. The latter, had its world premiere in Feruary 2006 at the Indiana University Opera Theater, with music composed by Ned Rorem and the libretto by poet J. D. McClatchy.

Thanks to cable television, videocassettes, and DVDs, the *Our Town* movie released by producer Sol Lesser at a huge celebration in Boston in May 1940 continues to have a public presence. Wilder, who had credentials as a screenwriter, was nonetheless not interested in participating in the writing of the script. But to protect his increasingly valuable property, he became deeply involved in the screenplay, including the famous and subsequently controversial decision to let Emily live in the film, agreeing that she could die only in a dream. He expressed his view on the matter this way in a letter to Lesser:

> I've always thought [Emily should live]. In a movie you see the people so close up that a different relation is established. In the theatre they are halfway abstractions in an allegory; in the movie they are very concrete. So in so far as the play is a Generalized Allegory she dies—we die—they die; in so far as it's

a Concrete Happening it's not important that she die. Let her live—the idea will have been imparted anyway.

Within a few weeks of the Broadway opening, Wilder had fled to Arizona to complete *The Merchant of Yonkers*, another play-in-the-making that he had worked on in Switzerland. It is clear from letters that he was thinking hard about what he had learned about playwriting from his *Our Town* experience. He credited Jed Harris for much of that play's success, and would approach him two more times to direct new plays. Harris passed. It is also clear, however, that Wilder did not believe that Harris grasped *Our Town*'s deeper meanings. In March 1938, he wrote his sister:

> I've now decided that on one plane Our Town is a very pessimistic piece. But on a higher plane it isn't. That's where Jed fell down. If you hang the planets and the years high up above the play, you can get the Reconciliation but if you don't it's crushing. Jed gypped me on the "cosmic overtones" just where [Max] Reinhardt would be best.

Less than a year later, Reinhardt, the great Austrian director whom Wilder had idealized since boyhood, took *The Merchant of Yonkers* to Broadway—and failed dismally. To quote Wilder (and legions of others): "Theater is a funny business."

In the end, the funny business that Wilder sought to conquer in the 1930s blessed him with great artistic and monetary success. Success also throws shadows, none longer and deeper for Wilder the dramatist than *Our Town*. Incapable of resting on his laurels, he would go on to write more plays and novels, including another Pulitzer Prize–winning drama and a novel that received the National Book Award. He busied himself to the day of his death with such a host of other literary deeds that he earned among the cognoscenti a reputation as a Man of Letters rather than as only a novelist or playwright. But the *Our Town* shadow has been long and deep, and remains so.

In 1997, when Wilder's turn came to appear on a postage stamp, the artist did not hesitate to depict him against the backdrop of a New England landscape. The sun is setting and soon the village will be set against "the life of the stars." That is where Thornton Wilder rests.

THE MATCHMAKER

As Thornton Wilder explained, *The Matchmaker* is based on Johann Nestroy's 1842 Viennese satire, *Einer Jux will er sich machen* (awkwardly translated as "He Wants to Have a Fling"). Nestroy's drama was in turn inspired by the English one-act play *A Day Well Spent* by John Oxenford (1835). Drawing for inspiration on a far more famous work, Wilder also spliced into the middle of Act I of *The Matchmaker* a six-minute scene from Act II, scene v, of Molière's *L'Avare*. (Molière's Frosine, the marriage broker, interests Harpagon in a young woman whereas Wilder's Dolly praises the culinary skills of Ernestina Semple.) Thanks to this *homage*, which Wilder often recounted with glee, the roots of *The Matchmaker* can be traced back directly to Plautus and Terence, thus providing a textbook example of the creative process as Wilder expressed it in his preface to this volume: "Literature has always more resembled a torch race than a furious dispute among heirs."

Putting the play's intellectual roots aside, *The Matchmaker* is Wilder's dream come true. The play had a 486-

performance Broadway run in 1955–1956, a Wilder Broadway record (110 more performances than *Our Town*'s 336), followed by a recording-breaking five-month national tour. All this was preceded by a highly successful eight-month engagement on London's Broadway, the West End, and succeeded by three successful works based on *The Matchmaker*—two films (of the original play and of the musical) and its most famous offspring by far, the internationally acclaimed, record-breaking smash musical, *Hello, Dolly!* (1964).

All this is not to overlook the play's ongoing popularity with amateurs and professionals in this country and abroad, despite being an expensive play to produce. While it is now *de rigueur* for critics to observe that it is impossible to see *The Matchmaker* without wanting to break into song, it is also true that the musical has not eclipsed the play, although the latter was legally embargoed for years at a time to provide an open road for the films and the musical. Since 1972 when the last legal shackle was removed, *The Matchmaker* has been revived professionally some forty times in this country, and performed in eleven languages in fourteen countries. *The Matchmaker* may lack the Pulitzer Prizes held by its companion plays in this volume, but it won for Wilder many prizes of artistic and financial merit.

Surprisingly, the road to this stunning record was rocky. It included a washout—a highly visible flop on Broadway in 1939, after only thirty-nine performances, of a four-act farce entitled *The Merchant of Yonkers*, aka *The Matchmaker* in its first incarnation. The run would have been even shorter had the play not been propped up temporarily by the Theatre Guild's subscription audience.

As Wilder noted in his preface to this volume, the foundations of this hydra-headed play were built during his

youthful encounters with the undoubtedly boisterous stock
company productions he saw as a boy at the Ye Liberty Theatre in Oakland, California. He did not reveal in the preface,
however, the extent of his youthful fascination with vaudeville and stage comedy expressed in his voracious reading of
plays, his own roles in the Berkeley High School's annual
vaudeville show, and the hundreds of hours he spent hiding in back rows in other theaters in the Berkeley area. Nor
did he mention his hobby as a boy and young man: collect-
ing German theatrical statistics. Thanks to this passionate
interest, Wilder, like a stamp collector learning about the
royalty and heroes of exotic foreign lands, became intimately
acquainted with the names and production histories of the
leading theaters, directors, and actors of the period, including the famed Austrian-born director and educator Max
Reinhardt (1873–1943). Given his interests, it is no surprise
that Wilder sought Reinhardt out for the first time as early as
1923, at a theater in Philadelphia, and noted the meeting in
a letter home with prophetic understatement: "A most valuable connection when I get back to playwriting."

Almost certainly it was from his record-keeping that
young Thornton also first encountered the name of Johann
Nestroy (1801–1862), the Viennese actor and playwright
whose satires were indelibly associated with that city's stage
and argot, but whose work, until Wilder drew attention to
it in the late 1930s, was unknown in the United States. It is
more than likely that Wilder read the first influential study
of Reinhardt published in this country in English, *The Art
of Max Reinhardt* (1914), and came across in the appendix
a statistical summary of Reinhardt's productions between
1903 and 1910 (how young Wilder loved records and statistics!). There, on page 319, he would have discovered
the name of the Nestroy play Reinhardt had mounted in

1904 at the Neues Theatre in Berlin: *Einer Jux will er sich machen.*

From his earliest years, Wilder was writing drama, and it is no surprise that farcical elements appear in several of his early three-minute plays, and that Molière, one of his theatrical heroes, inspired *Queens of France*, one of the six one-act plays published in 1931 that marked Wilder's arrival as a serious dramatist (written under the "l'ombre to Molière," is the way Wilder phrased it in 1930). Nor is it surprising that his 1935 novel *Heaven's My Destination* is constructed with significant comedic-farcical elements; indeed, as he wrote in April 1934 to that novel's German translator (and one of Nestroy's fellow Austrians): "[Ferdinand] Raimund and Nestroy have become my great enthusiasm during the last two years and I should like to think that my book (though so far short of those in literary merit) should nevertheless breathe that loving saturation in the detailed atmosphere of a district that is one of the great qualities of *Einer Jux will er sich machen.* . . ." Finally, to offer one more piece of the literary context for the full-length farce he had begun to write in the summer of 1935, we have Wilder writing to his great friend, the actress Ruth Gordon, in April 1936: "I've been reading all the great 'formal' comedies in every language: Molière and Goldoni, and Lessing—just to make sure that I've expunged every lurking vestige of what Sam Behrman and George Kaufman think comedy is."

The play-in-progress was *The Merchant of Yonkers*, a farce appropriately listed in Wilder's records of this period as "Merchant of Yonkers (Nestroy-Molière)." From the beginning, it is clear that he dreamed of having Reinhardt as its director. The dream was hardly far-fetched; in the fall of 1934, the two men had had long talks in Chicago, at the end of which, as Wilder informed his family, "with one hand on my shoulder [he] asked me to write a play for him. That was all; but I walked on air."

At least one-half of *The Merchant* was written in the same period and at the same places as *Our Town*, and Wilder sent Reinhardt, now a political refugee living in Los Angeles, the first two acts on February 6, 1938, shortly after *Our Town* opened on Broadway. By early March, Wilder had fled to Tucson, Arizona, to complete the play. Here, by telegram, he learned the wonderful news that Reinhardt was "entzücht" (charmed) by what he had read. In addition to Wilder's love affair with farce, and Reinhardt's interest in the play, the playwright now had another driving reason to complete *The Merchant*. He had been surprised that *Our Town* left audiences feeling so sad, or, as he put it in a letter from Tucson to his confidante Lady Sibyl Colfax in London, that *Our Town* "raises a devastating pessimism, a repudiation of the state of being alive." More than ever Wilder wanted to show how the stage could also be employed to make audiences laugh. Not that *The Merchant* was only farce; it was humorously treated, but Wilder wrote Colfax that he was also weaving into it "trenchant sparks of social comment," his polite way of describing the play's treatment of the effects of wealth on individual behavior and on society. By mid-July the acting drafts for Act III and IV had been typed, and names of actors began to be tossed around for a play Reinhardt hoped to mount in Los Angeles, among them Mickey Rooney as Barnaby and Charles Boyer as Cornelius.

Nothing about theater is predictable. Because of a change in Reinhardt's schedule, the play's producer, Herman Shumlin, arranged with the Theatre Guild, for *The Merchant* to be born the traditional way, in the East—an out-of-town tryout, followed by a Broadway opening. After a short and frantic rehearsal period, a strategy not recommended for a theatrical form with as many tricky moving parts as farce, *The Merchant* opened in Boston in late December. It was an omen for the disaster that lay ahead that the three top choices for the key role of Dolly Levi—Edith Evans, Ina Claire, and Ruth Gordon—turned down the part. This forced the producers to settle on Jane Cowl—a headliner, but an actress whom they had initially passed over. Wilder's view of her before she was picked: "affected 'great lady' dignity unsuitable to us."

The Merchant of Yonkers premiered at Boston's Colonial Theatre on December 12, 1938. It faced a critical establishment walking on eggshells from having embarrassed itself by misjudging *Our Town* so badly less than a year earlier. So while scribes found plenty to criticize, especially the play's pace (too slow), its length (too long), and the fact that many a line still had to be learned, they were determined to find the glass at least half full. The *Boston Globe* reported it "hilariously successful in places," and The *Christian Science Monitor* saw "an imaginative warmth that is rare in the theater." The playwright's older brother, then living in Boston, would recall later that the play was far better received than *Our Town* had been.

Any hope that Wilder would have a third Broadway hit in two years (his adaptation of *A Doll's House* in 1927 and *Our Town* being the other two) died the morning after *The Merchant* opened on December 28 at Broadway's Guild Theatre. Some reviews were kind, but the burden of opinion spelled debacle. The difficulty, as John Anderson put it brutally in the *New York Journal American,* was that "When a farce isn't funny, there is nothing to be done." "Dull," "overly arch and tedious," "drugged boredom," "little dexterity or finesse," and a "depressing spectacle" appeared in print under other bylines. Jane Cowl was either panned for her performance or pitied for being associated with such a play. In addition to damning the production, several critics questioned the viability of the entire enterprise: "What in the name of God made a writer as exalted as Thornton Wilder think that it was important for him to wrench himself into the past to the extent of reviving a farce from the Vienna of 1842," wrote the unhappy Robert Benchley in *The New Yorker*.

Was *The Merchant* fatally flawed? Wilder's close friend, the feisty critic and radio commentator Alexander Woollcott, to whom Wilder had dedicated *Our Town*, was confident the play was sound. He laid its failure at Reinhardt's door, accusing him of wrecking it with "heavy handed" directing and poor casting. Even before it closed on Broadway Woollcott predicted to Wilder that the play would be successfully revived in a few years "in the American idiom." (So angry was Woollcott that he apparently nearly assaulted Reinhardt.) Students of Wilder and the play have echoed Woollcott's view ever since. Donald Haberman in his valuable work, *The Plays of Thornton Wilder: A Critical Study* stated it this way:

> Reinhardt was expert at directing Nestroy's kind of play for German audiences, but he seemed to understand neither Wilder's play nor the American crowd. His reputation depended on his creating style through elaborate stage effects and slow pace. . . . Wilder's play is not a period piece. To emphasize its time and place through visual effects is to destroy its immediacy, which is established in part by the deliberate removal of all marks of any particular culture.

Wilder never shared this view completely. He believed that events of the time—the depression and war jitters— rather than the production alone, played a significant role in the play's failure, and when the script was published in

April 1939, did not hesitate to dedicate it to Reinhardt with "deep admiration and indebtedness." Wilder's view was not a product of reflection after the carnage; the second day into the play's doomed run, he wrote his attorney: "It's all been worth it. The things that I've learned about playwriting; the association with Reinhardt; the gradual improvement of the text of this play which in its revival (1948) will be a nifty." And five years later, in September 1943, from his post in Air Force Intelligence in North Africa, he wrote his sister regarding the ongoing interest in his farce: "I wish I were there to cut the play, and rebuild portions of it. Reviewing it in my memory. And started re-admiring Reinhardt so that I almost *signed up with him again*."

Wilder's prediction of *The Merchant*'s return to Broadway was off by seven years; in 1955, indeed, a very "nifty" revival did occur. But in fact he had to wait only a few months after the Broadway debacle for a good omen of what lay ahead; the play was published in April, and as soon as it was released to amateurs in October 1939, colleges and community groups began performing it around the country. This pattern of "constant demand" (a phrase in Wilder's business correspondence), augmented by serious feelers for translation and film rights to the play even before the end of World War II, made it clear to Wilder's managers that the question of a revival was never *whether* but *when*.

The actress and writer Ruth Gordon was responsible for the revival of *The Merchant*. Gordon was a Central Casting dream for a project she began agitating for in early 1951 with the determination, as Wilder put it in his journal, of a "resolute lioness," and the support and active help of her husband, playwright Garson Kanin. Wilder had, in fact, originally written the part of Dolly Levi with Gordon in mind, but apparently not wishing to be directed by Reinhardt, she had turned it down. Gordon's plan was canny: revive the play in London's West End, far from Broadway and any lingering memories of the earlier, ill-fated production. In addition, Gordon was well-known on the London stage for her 1936 triumph with Michael Redgrave in the Old Vic production of *The Country Wife*. Gordon's wish was a happy command for Wilder. To clear the way for the new production, anticipated as early as the fall of 1952, he had his agents withdraw all new performance rights for the bubbling *Merchant* as of February 22, 1952, until further notice. By May of that year, the distinguished Tyrone Guthrie, who had known Gordon well and worked with her previously, had signed on as the director. Inevitable delays occurred, but by the fall of 1953, Ruth Gordon's faith in *Merchant* was rewarded by the decision of the Edinburgh Festival to host its premiere in the summer of 1954, and of London's esteemed Tennent Productions, Ltd. to back it. Wilder's farce sailed into 1954 on a sea of high and happy hopes. By January 1954, *The Merchant of Yonkers* also had a new name. At first a change was thought unnecessary, but it appears that the issue was forced by lingering poor reviews from a 1952 North End London production that had just escaped the embargo on the play. In addition, Wilder was making a number of changes in the script. On November 28, 1953, he had written from Key West, Florida, to Gordon and Kanin:

> Dear Sweetnesses:
> For a Title: How about
> THE MATCHMAKER. There's a title-role for Ruthie. And a great help in Act II where the audience will see more clearly why she's telling lies for and about Cornelius.

If you don't like that, how about: THE GREEN
SHOOTS or JOIN HANDS. Oh, dear—I want one
that expresses the 'spring' out of bondage. The right
to enjoyment. Isn't title-hunting tormenting?

Readers will recognize that the playwright's second and
third title choices spring directly from his statement in the
preface to this volume that the play is about "the aspirations
of the young (and not only of the young) for a fuller, freer
participation in life."

It would be a mistake to say that the re-launching of *Mer-
chant/Matchmaker* was a cakewalk. Frayed nerves, tantrums,
long nights devoted to rewriting and pruning and cutting,
the fear of impending disaster are all part of *Merchant/
Matchmaker*'s story in 1954 in England. But Ruth Gordon's
instincts proved correct. The play Wilder called an "ugly
duckling" opened on August 16, 1954, in the Theatre Royal
in Newcastle-on-Tyne for a six-performance "provincial city"
tryout before its official debut at the Edinburgh Festival—
and came away a swan. "It is a long time since there was a
first night in Newcastle which pleased its audience to such a
degree," wrote a reviewer. The show, even in this large theater, was a sellout by the third performance.

The Matchmaker encountered a few harsh notices, typically from lordly big-city critics not fond of farce in the first
place, and a few admonitions about tempo, timing, length, or
the performance of a given actor. But starting in Newcastle,
and going on to sixteen performances in Edinburgh, then
to another ten weeks that fall in several additional provincial
cities—even a dash to participate in another festival in Berlin—the production achieved success on an ever-larger and
more glorious canvas. A sampling of praise gives the picture:

the play was called "glittering" and "glowing," "frisky" and "sparkling," "like planting a telephone pole, and seeing it burst into leaves and chestnut candles." The London opening on November 4, 1954, at the Theatre Royal Haymarket— "charming," "delicious and elegant," "abounding high spirits"—was all but an anticlimax for this now field-tested, finely tuned farce. And give or take the few requisite moments of fear, panic, and temper, the story repeated itself later in the United States where, after two more fine-tunings in Philadelphia and Boston, The Matchmaker commenced its "nifty" Broadway revival and run on December 5, 1955, with most of its original cast. Wilder was in Rome, but the telegram he received the next morning from his dramatic agent left no doubt about what had occurred at the Royale Theater on 45th Street: AUDIENCE RECEPTION WONDERFUL [stop] NOTICES WONDERFUL [stop] LINE AT BOX OFFICE BEST HAROLD

What are the differences between The Merchant and The Matchmaker? The major one was the directorial interpretation that extended to colorful and playful costumes and colorful and playful scenery (The Merchant had featured purples and period-piece furnishings). Guthrie's vision of the play and Gordon's interpretation of Dolly Levi stood in sharp contrast to Reinhardt's more classical vision of how to mount farce and Jane Cowl's "great lady" performance. "This malevolent pixie," wrote the redoubtable Kenneth Tynan of Ruth Gordon's performance at the time of the London opening, "flies at the part like a bat out of hell"— and he and audiences loved her for it.

Putting aside all questions of casting and rehearsal time, The Matchmaker was simply a different experience from The Merchant of Yonkers. The legendary stage publicist Richard

Maney, who had handled the 1938 production, put the issue this way in 1957: "As played by Cowl and directed by Reinhardt, *The Merchant of Yonkers* was a roguish lark. Guthrie and Miss Gordon reduced it to bawdy slapstick." "Reduced" has negative connotations, but what is clear is that slapstick "played" in 1954. The *New York Times* critic Brooks Atkinson, a Wilder champion, had been forced to write in 1938 about the play's "heavy feet." From London sixteen years later, he wrote enthusiastically about an event that "is broad and funny and seems a good deal more modern in spirit than machine-made goods like 'Anniversary Waltz' and 'The Tender Trap.'" Later, in New York, he would write admiringly of the play's "loud, vulgar, slapdash and uproarious" character. Did critics compare *The Matchmaker* to *The Merchant*? Often, but always by way of odious comparison. *Theatre Annual* phrased it this way: "[*The Matchmaker*] now careened where it once clattered and where it once sputtered, here exploded sky high."

What of the two scripts? In letters written to his dramatic agent and attorney in July 1954 from rehearsals in London, Wilder described *The Matchmaker* as "extensively rewritten." But only three months later he saw it differently. On October 7, 1954, with the play approaching its London opening, he wrote his agent, "The wastepaper baskets of Europe are full of my rewriting." He went on:

> Now here's the point of this letter—in all this rewriting what has happened is that the text has got back closer and closer to THE MERCHANT OF YONKERS. And that's natural: what I wrote in Arizona in 1938 was written when I had nothing else on my mind except THE MERCHANT. Now we change and change and finally it becomes clear that the orig-

inal form was best. So when it's finally published or released . . . it will be evident to all that The Matchmaker is merely a cut, trimmed, original, touched up YONKERS.

What were Wilder's own views of the Guthrie-Gordon revival? He was glad and he was grateful. The success of the play and of its film and musical progeny provided him and his family with a financial security they had never known. But the play was a learning experience for him, too. As rehearsals began in London, Wilder was at last temporarily thrown by watching his "happy little farce" subjected to a madcap interpretation. Shortly before the Newcastle opening, his sister wrote of his "agonizing experience" watching Guthrie "overdoing the play & losing it under a circus—the scenery & costumes belong in some other play. Miss G[ordon] is dashing around & screaming & waving her arms to suit herself." By the London opening Wilder realized that Gordon's performance was "glorious" and, as he told his publisher, "made it an entirely new play." He also believed that the times favored the play. The postwar world was still at sixes and sevens, but people were willing to—indeed, wanted to— laugh again. But it was a mark of Wilder's loyalty to where the play had come from that, as his last gesture to the work, he "again dedicated" it to Max Reinhardt.

How is our laughter quotient today? "If farce is a trivial untruth about life, our betters must be reprehended," Thornton Wilder wrote a Wellesley College theater company producing The Merchant after World War II. And however the play was directed, acted, and produced—for no play is ever produced the same way—Wilder remained proud to the end of his life for having contributed to an ancient and honorable theatrical tradition devoted to laughter. For this reason, no review of *Merchant/Matchmaker* could have pleased him more than Walter Kerr's in The *New York Herald Tribune* the morning after his farce's second coming on Broadway:

> Though he has nominally based his spectacular spree on a particular German comedy by Johann Nestroy, he has actually been busy taking a veritable inventory of the comic spirit, itemizing all the dives into cupboards, all the absurd uprushings of love, and even all the picture-postcard settings that have ever done duty in the cause of merriment.

THE SKIN OF OUR TEETH

Thornton Wilder began writing *The Skin of Our Teeth*, then titled "The Ends of the Worlds," on June 24, 1940, at the MacDowell Colony, the artists' and writers' retreat in Peterborough, New Hampshire that had played an influential role in the creation of *Our Town* three years earlier. Searching for a way to bear witness to a world increasingly at war, and inspired by the way James Joyce had presented "ancient man as an ever-present double to modern man" in *Finnegans Wake*, Wilder coupled this note in his journal entry of July 6, 1940 with these quasi-hopeful words: "During the last year subject after subject presented itself and crumbled away in my hands. Can this one hold out?" Hold out it did, although not without many dramatic moments not found in the script.

What Wilder started in New Hampshire, he did considerable work on in the fall of 1941 at the Chateâu Frontenac in Quebec, Canada, a still deeper retreat from places where people knew him, and in a country now officially at war. By November he had completed the first two acts. But two acts do not make a play. In the end, Act III, the war act, which he found the most difficult to write, was not ready until January 1, 1942, a year later. Many honorable distractions came between Wilder and his goal of finishing his drama, among them a three-month goodwill mission to Latin America for the Department of State, a summer term teaching a double course load at the University of Chicago, and an autumn trip to London as U.S. delegate to an international PEN conference. This last assignment played a significant role in the *Skin*'s history: The opportunity to view actual war damage and to talk with courageous civilians, soldiers, and fighter and bomber pilots in England and Scotland helped Wilder shape the third act he wanted—an act that would strike a hopeful note about the survival of the human race but that would not be "trite" or "evasive" (his words at the time). His search for the right language continued into the play's rehearsals when, as a last touch, he added George Antrobus's final speech. After the war Wilder recalled the act's creative challenge with these words to his friend Amy Wertheimer:

> I've always assumed a very slow curve of civilization.
> But I always affirm too that my toleration of humanity's failings is more affirmative than most "optimists."
> When I first wrote Skin of Our Teeth it lacked the motto-humanity-climbing-upward speeches of Mr. Antrobus at the end. I assumed that they were omnipresent in the play and didn't have to be stated. I assumed that they were self-evident—that's how highly I believed in mankind. But more and more of the early readers found the play "defeatist." So I wrote in the moral and crossed the t's and i's.

Wilder expected that Jed Harris, who had produced and

directed *Our Town*, would assume the same roles for *The Skin of Our Teeth*. Harris, however, turned him down. Wilder then offered the producer's role to Michael Myerberg, principally Leopold Stokowski's manager, but also an entertainment promoter whom Wilder had known casually for about five years. He made this unusual choice—Myerberg had almost no Broadway experience—because he had little faith that, with the exception of Harris, any experienced Broadway producer could do justice to a drama that, he predicted to his attorney, would "probably involve a complicated history." How right he was.

Myerberg, eager to make his mark on Broadway, orchestrated a production that included the exciting young director Elia Kazan and a galaxy of distinguished actors—Fredric March and Florence Eldridge as Mr. and Mrs. Antrobus, Montgomery Clift and Frances Heflin as Henry and Gladys, Florence Reed as the Fortune Teller, and the legendary Tallulah Bankhead as Sabina. But almost immediately Myerberg's unpredictable moods and management style combined with Bankhead's volatile temperament to make life unusually hellish for the cast and the author and his representatives, even by theater standards.

Backstage drama did not at first compromise the quality of the production. *Skin* played to mostly favorable press and many a sold-out house in its four-week, four-city tryout period in New Haven, Baltimore, Philadelphia, and Washington, D.C. Not that people necessarily understood a play that, according to an out-of-town *Variety* story, "bemuses and befuddles while it amuses." Had the reporter added the word "upset" to the list he would have scooped Wilder's own assessment, written to his family soon after rehearsals had begun: "I think it's a very good play, but it's so daringly written as to theatre-mood that it may well puzzle and upset instead of amuse and move." And upset it did; as long as there is Broadway lore it will likely include stories of taxis lining up early to snag the fares of people fleeing *Skin* at the end of Act I or II, some even jamming their fists through the play's posters along the way.

Out-of-town success is no guarantee of a Broadway hit, but in the case of *Skin*, which opened on November 18 at the Plymouth Theatre, it was. With few exceptions, reviews were strong, even raves: "A dramatic bombshell"—*Life*; "Theater-going became a rare and electrifying experience"—*New York Herald Tribune*; "Quite sure to prove the supreme novelty of the theater season"—*New York Daily News*. Two especially influential tastemakers praised the play this way: "One of the wisest and friskiest comedies written in a long time," critic Brooks Atkinson wrote in the *New York Times*; critic and commentator (and Wilder's friend) Alexander Woollcott called *The Skin of Our Teeth* "the nearest thing to a great play which the American theater has yet produced." To be sure, there were critics on the other side of the fence. As a general comment, they found tricks rather than substance. "[It] dolls up its theme rather than dramatizes it," said *Time*. "It is too overt, too garish, too sensational in the literal sense," wrote the *Commonweal* reviewer.

At the end of the day, the box office never lies. Through the first five months of the run, *The Skin of Our Teeth* rarely earned less than $20,000 a week in ticket sales, all but a sell-out. After falling off a bit to the $16,000 to $18,000 range in the normally slower months of March and April, sales jumped up again when the play was awarded the Pulitzer Prize for Drama in May.

Controversy is always good for box office. It did not hurt sales, therefore, when James Morton Robinson and Joseph Campbell, students of James Joyce, ignited a firestorm of public debate and comment when they accused Wilder in two articles published in *The Saturday Review of Literature* in December 1942 and January 1943 of writing "an Americanized re-creation, thinly disguised," of Joyce's *Finnegans Wake*. The accusers never used the word *plagiarism*, but they implied it, and the term appeared in the press. The charge, specious and malicious and dismissed with authority then and since, probably cost *Skin* the 1943 New York Drama Critics' Award, but not the Pulitzer Prize. At the time, Wilder chose not to respond publicly to the charges, other than to encourage those interested to embark on a daunting task: reading *Finnegans Wake* and deciding for themselves.

Wilder in fact was not in a position to give serious attention to his accusers even if he wanted to. Two months before the play went into rehearsal, he eagerly went on active duty with Army Air Force Intelligence, turning over the playwright's duties to his agent; his attorney; and his knowledgeable sister Isabel, a graduate of the Yale School of Drama. He saw the show only twice before leaving for overseas duty in North Africa in late May 1943.

Had the original cast held on, *Skin* might well have played far longer on Broadway than it did. But by June of 1943, backstage tensions had become so intolerable that March, Eldridge, and Bankhead, taking advantage of clauses in their contracts, left the show. Now playing to many empty seats, *Skin* limped through the always difficult summer months with new faces in key roles, especially in the part of Sabina. For better or for worse, it is clear that *Skin*'s success had come to depend on Tallulah Bankhead in this role.

In the more normal course of events, a work as famous—indeed, as infamous—as *The Skin of Our Teeth* could count on a successful post-Broadway national tour, and Myerberg planned one for the fall, starting with a two-week engagement in Boston. After the 359-performance Broadway run closed on Saturday, September 25, the play opened in Boston the following Monday, and closed after the first week. Gladys George, the new Sabina, was now out of the show, claiming throat problems. She was replaced by Lizabeth Scott. The box office was terrible. This "sudden eclipse," wrote a *Variety* reporter, "was no surprise to those who have followed the vagaries of the show."

A byproduct of *Skin*'s early demise was the earlier-than-anticipated release of the amateur and stock rights, and by 1944, the beginning of its enduring popularity with high school, college, and community drama groups. Nor has *Skin*, an expensive play to produce, faded from the professional stage. Since 1980, it has been produced some twenty times in stock and regional theaters around the country. Major productions since World War II have included a 1955 revival starring Mary Martin and Helen Hayes and a 1961 ANTA-American Repertory Company revival. Both these productions were sent abroad to at least twenty-four countries in Europe and Latin America as part of the State Department's cultural programming. In 1975, José Quintero directed a production with Elizabeth Ashley as Sabina that kicked off the American Bicentennial Theater season project at the John F. Kennedy Center for the Performing Arts. *Skin* had its last New York appearance in 1998, in a Central Park production directed by Irene Lewis, with Kristen Johnston as Sabina and John Goodman as Mr. Antrobus. To date, perhaps no British production is as famous as the 1945 *Skin* directed by Laurence Olivier and starring Vivian Leigh and Cecil Parker. And not to be forgotten are Wilder's own appearances as Mr. Antrobus on the stages of several notable summer theaters.

There have been several televised versions of *Skin*, of which San Diego's Globe Theatre's 1983 PBS "American

Playhouse" production is particularly well known, and available on videotape and DVD. Although *Skin* has attracted the interests of such talents as Leonard Bernstein, and the team of John Kander, Fred Ebb, and Joseph Stein, it has thus far resisted all attempts to be fashioned into film, opera, or musical.

The story of the play in translation is a different matter. Starting with a performance in German in Zürich's renowned Schauspielhaus in the spring of 1944, *The Skin of Our Teeth* has been produced in some twenty languages in more than forty countries. As Wilder notes in the preface to this volume, the play had a special resonance in Germany, where the first production occurred in the ruins of Darmstadt on March 31, 1946. By November 1949 it had been performed in both Eastern and Western zones more than 500 times by fifteen German companies playing in thirty cities. (By the late 1940s into the early 1960s, Wilder's works were banned in the Soviet Union and most Eastern bloc countries.) In short, *The Skin of Our Teeth*, so often thought of as especially American because of its eagerness, its high jinks, and its vision of human capability, is a well-established piece of world theater.

The experimental techniques Wilder employed in 1942—the play's anachronisms, its asides, its interruptions—are now familiar to a twenty-first-century audience raised on modern theater and television sitcoms. And contemporary critics have been known to squirm in their seats at Wilder's proclamations about patriotism and loyalty and what one admirer of the play in 1975 summarized as a perceived tendency toward "excessively abstract, dreamy allegory, populated by stock characters of popular cliché." Have the novelty of the play and its whimsy grown thin? Perhaps. But the record also shows that because of its theatricality and humor, and the sheer craziness of exploring and producing what is known in the business as a "theatrical bible," *The Skin of Our Teeth* also continues to attract and to hold the attention of actors, audiences, playwrights, and students today, more than sixty years after it opened.

And what of the play's larger message about the survival of the race and what Wilder later described as "the institution of the family understood as destiny and promise"? Listen again to the Fortune Teller at the end of Act II: "Think it over. . . ."

—Tappan Wilder
Chevy Chase, Maryland

Acknowledgments

—∿—

The back matter for this volume is constructed in large part from Thornton Wilder's words in unpublished material or publications not easy to come by. Those interested in additional information are referred to the separate editions of *Our Town* and *The Skin of Our Teeth*, published in 2003 by HarperCollins, to standard sources, and to the bibliography available at www.thorntonwildersociety.org.

Space permits me to extend thanks to only a few of the many people who have helped with this volume—Jackson Bryer, Robin Gibbs Wilder, and Barbara Whitepine; Robert Freedman and Selma Luttinger of the Robert A. Freedman Dramatic Agency; and Barbara Hogenson and Nicole Verity of the Barbara Hogenson Agency. Dr. Patricia Willis and the able staff of the Beinecke Library always deserve special applause, as does Penelope Niven, whose assistance, from start to finish, has been invaluable. A special bow also goes to John Guare, who has helped to make this new edition of a classic especially memorable and thoughtful. If there are errors in the back matter, I take responsibility for them, and welcome corrections.

UNPUBLISHED MATERIAL

Unless otherwise identified here, all unpublished materials are taken from one of two sources: the holdings in the Wilder Family Archives in the Yale Collection of American Literature at the Beinecke Rare Book and Manuscript Library, or the Wilder family's own holdings, including many of Thornton Wilder's legal and agency papers. Where deemed appropriate, minor corrections in spelling, punctuation, and format have been made silently. Wilder's correspondence with Alexander Woollcott is held at Harvard in the Houghton Library's Harvard Theater Collection; his letters to Dame Sibyl Colfax are housed in Special Collections, Fales Library at New York University; and his letters to Ruth Gordon are held by the Garson Kanin Estate. The Harvard Theater Collection is also the home of the original prompt script from which the Stage Manager's concluding lines are taken at the beginning of the *Our Town* Overview. The courtesies extended by these institutions and by Martha J. Wilson, for the Garson Kanin Estate, are gratefully acknowledged.

PUBLICATIONS

Tom Coley's "Our Town," a pamphlet dedicated to Isabel Wilder, was published privately in 1982. Wilder's "A Preface for Our Town," is reprinted in Donald Gallup, editor, *American Characteristics & Other Essays* (New York: Harper & Row, 1979; Authors Guild Backinprint edition, 2000), 100–103. The Reinhardt citation is from Huntly Carter's *The Theatre of Max Reinhardt* (New York: Mitchell Kennerley, 1914). Donald Haberman's view is from his *The Plays of Thornton Wilder: A Critical Study* (Middletown, CT: Wesleyan University Press, 1967), 23; and Richard Maney's from his memoir *Fanfare: The Confessions of a Press Agent* (New York: Harper & Row, 1957), 329. Wilder's foreword to the volume of Nestroy's plays is found in the Max Knight and Joseph Faby translation and edition of *Three Comedies by Johann Nestroy* (Frederick Ungar Publishing Company, 1967), v–x. Wilder's "Noting the Nature of Farce" is reprinted in *American Characteristics & Other Essays*, 112–114. Wilder's draft letter of December 17, 1942, was published as "A Footnote to *The Skin of Our Teeth*," *The Yale Review* 87:4 (October 1999), 68–70. All rights for unpublished and published work by Thornton Wilder are reserved.

AUTHOR PHOTO/ARTWORK

The Al Hirschfeld artwork on page 459 is reproduced by special arrangement with Hirschfeld's exclusive representative, the Margo Feiden Galleries Ltd., New York. This image was used by the MacDowell Colony for its invitation to the Centenary Celebration of Wilder's birth, held in New York City on April 15, 1997, at which Mr. Hirschfeld was present. As at least part of each of the three plays in this volume was written at the Colony, it seemed right and proper (and fun!) to employ this image once again for another special occasion.

© Al Hirschfeld

About the Author

In his quiet way, Thornton Niven Wilder was a revolutionary writer who experimented boldly with literary forms and themes, from the beginning to the end of his long career. "Every novel is different from the others," he wrote when he was seventy-five. "The theater (ditto). . . . The thing I'm writing now is again totally unlike anything that preceded it." Wilder's richly diverse settings, characters, and themes are at once specific and global. Deeply immersed in classical as well as contemporary literature, he often fused the traditional and the modern in his novels and plays, all the while exploring the cosmic in the commonplace. In a January 12, 1953, cover story, *Time* took note of Wilder's unique "interplanetary mind"—his ability to write from a vision that was at once American and universal.

A pivotal figure in the history of twentieth-century letters, Wilder was a novelist and playwright whose works continue to be widely read and produced in this new century. He is the only writer to have won the Pulitzer Prize for both Fiction and Drama. His second novel, *The Bridge of San Luis Rey*, received the Fiction award in 1928, and he won the prize twice in Drama, for *Our Town* in 1938 and *The Skin of Our Teeth* in 1943. His other novels are *The Cabala*, *The Woman of Andros*, *Heaven's My Destination*, *The Ides of March*, *The Eighth Day*, and *Theophilus North*. His other major dramas include *The Matchmaker*, which was adapted as the internationally acclaimed musical comedy *Hello, Dolly!*, and *The Alcestiad*. Among his innovative shorter plays are *The Happy Journey to Trenton and Camden* and *The Long Christmas Dinner*, and two uniquely conceived series, *The Seven Ages of Man* and *The Seven Deadly Sins*, frequently performed by amateurs.

Wilder and his work received many honors, highlighted by the three Pulitzer Prizes, the Gold Medal for Fiction from the American Academy of Arts and Letters, the Order of Merit (Peru), the Goethe-Plakette der Stadt (Germany, 1959), the Presidential Medal of Freedom (1963), the National Book Committee's first National Medal for Literature (1965), and the National Book Award for Fiction (1967).

He was born in Madison, Wisconsin, on April 17, 1897, to Amos Parker Wilder and Isabella Niven Wilder. The family later lived in China and in California, where Wilder was graduated from Berkeley High School. After two years at Oberlin College, he went on to Yale, where he received his undergraduate degree in 1920. A valuable part of his education took place during summers spent working hard on farms in California, Kentucky, Vermont, Connecticut, and Massachusetts. His father arranged these rigorous "shirt-sleeve" jobs for Wilder and his older brother, Amos, as part of their initiation into the American experience.

Thornton Wilder studied archaeology and Italian as a special student at the American Academy in Rome (1920–1921), and earned a master of arts degree in French literature at Princeton in 1926.

In addition to his talents as playwright and novelist, Wilder was an accomplished teacher, essayist, translator, scholar, lecturer, librettist, and screenwriter. In 1942, he teamed with Alfred Hitchcock to write the first draft of the screenplay for the classic thriller *Shadow of a Doubt*, receiving credit as principal writer and a special screen credit for his "contribution to the preparation" of the production. All but fluent in four languages, Wilder translated and adapted plays by such varied authors as Henrik Ibsen, Jean-Paul Sartre, and André Obey. As a scholar, he conducted significant research on James Joyce's *Finnegans Wake* and the plays of Spanish dramatist Lope de Vega.

Wilder's friends included a broad spectrum of figures on both sides of the Atlantic—Hemingway, Fitzgerald, Alexander Woollcott, Gene Tunney, Sigmund Freud, producer Max Reinhardt, Katharine Cornell, Ruth Gordon, and Garson Kanin. Beginning in the mid-1930s, Wilder was especially close to Gertrude Stein and became one of her most effective interpreters and champions. Many of Wilder's friendships are documented in his prolific correspondence. Wilder believed that great letters constitute a "great branch of literature." In a lecture entitled "On Reading the Great Letter Writers," he wrote that a letter can function as a "literary exercise," the "profile of a personality," and "news of the soul," apt descriptions of thousands of letters he wrote to his own friends and family.

Wilder enjoyed acting and played major roles in several of his own plays in summer theater productions. He also possessed a lifelong love of music; reading musical scores was a hobby, and he wrote the librettos for two operas based on his work: *The Long Christmas Dinner*, with composer Paul Hindemith, and *The Alcestiad*, with composer Louise Talma. Both works premiered in Germany.

Teaching was one of Wilder's deepest passions. He began his teaching career in 1921 as an instructor in French at Lawrenceville, a private secondary school in New Jersey. Financial independence after the publication of *The Bridge of San Luis Rey* permitted him to leave the classroom in 1928, but he returned to teaching in the 1930s at the University of Chicago. For six years, on a part-time basis, he taught courses there in classics in translation, comparative literature, and composition. In 1950–1951, he served as the Charles Eliot Norton Professor of Poetry at Harvard. Wilder's gifts for scholarship and teaching (he treated the classroom as all but a theater) made him a consummate, much-sought-after lecturer in his own country and abroad. After World War II, he held special standing, especially in Germany, as an interpreter of his own country's intellectual traditions and their influence on cultural expression.

During World War I, Wilder had served a three-month stint as an enlisted man in the Coast Artillery section of the army, stationed at Fort Adams, Rhode Island. He volunteered for service in World War II, advancing to the rank of lieutenant colonel in Army Air Force Intelligence. For his service in North Africa and Italy, he was awarded the Legion of Merit, the Bronze Star, the Chevalier Legion d'Honneur, and honorary officership in the Military Order of the British Empire (M.B.E.).

From royalties received from *The Bridge of San Luis Rey,* Wilder built a house for his family in 1930 in Hamden, Connecticut, just outside New Haven. But he typically spent as many as two hundred days a year away from Hamden, traveling to and settling in a variety of places that provided the stimulation and solitude he needed for his work. Sometimes his destination was the Arizona desert, the MacDowell Colony in New Hampshire, or Martha's Vineyard, Newport, Saratoga Springs, Vienna, or Baden-Baden. He wrote aboard ships, and often chose to stay in "spas in off-season." He needed a certain refuge when he was deeply immersed in writing a novel or play. Wilder explained his habit to a *New Yorker* journalist in 1959: "The walks, the quiet—all the elegance is present, everything is there but the people. That's it! A spa in off-season! I make a practice of it."

But Wilder always returned to "the house *The Bridge* built," as it is still known to this day. He died there of a heart attack on December 7, 1975.